Inclusion and Sexuality in Catholic Higher Education

Drawing on research conducted at 17 Catholic universities in the United States, making it the largest study of its kind, this volume explores effective practice in improving institutional policy relating to issues of sexuality.

The text calls attention to campus cultures of fear, shame, or denial around sexuality and highlights possible points of institutional resistance to changes in policy. Discussing topics such as sexual identity, sexuality education in the curriculum, Title IX, employee termination, and morality clauses, the book shows how staff and faculty are crucial in effecting change across Catholic campuses, providing valuable insight into the "unspoken rules" around sexuality within the shadow culture at Catholic institutions. Moreover, the text illustrates how institutions can maintain fidelity to Church teachings and even embrace notions of human dignity, solidarity, and the common good to achieve sexual inclusivity.

A unique study demonstrating how Catholic teaching can help support inclusive change around issues of sexuality and gender in higher education, it ultimately puts forward a practical framework for effecting change and improving student and staff support structures in Catholic institutions. It will thus appeal to researchers and academics working in the fields of Higher Education Management, Gender and Sexuality in Education, Religion, Gender and Sexuality, and the Sociology of Religion.

Mark A. Levand is an Associate Professor of the Practice and Director of Graduate Programs in the Center for Human Sexuality Studies at Widener University, USA. He is a Certified Sexuality Educator and Supervisor through the American Association of Sexuality Educators, Counselors, and Therapists (AASECT) and a Master Certified Health Education Specialist through the National Commission for Health Education Credentialing (NCHEC).

Routledge Research in Religion and Education
Series Editor Michael D. Waggoner, University of Northern Iowa, USA

17. **Curriculum Renewal for Islamic Education**
    Critical Perspectives on Teaching Islam in Primary and Secondary Schools
    Edited by Nadeem A. Memon, Mariam Alhashmi, and Mohamad Abdalla

18. **Islamic Religious Education in Europe**
    A Comparative Study
    Edited by Leni Franken and Bill Gent

19. **Teaching Religious Literacy to Combat Religious Bullying**
    Insights from North American Secondary Schools
    W. Y. Alice Chan

20. **Law, Education, and the Place of Religion in Public Schools**
    International Perspectives
    Edited by Charles J. Russo

21. **Engaging with Vocation on Campus**
    Supporting Students' Vocational Discernment through Curricular and Co-Curricular Approaches
    Edited by Karen Lovett and Stephen Wilhoit

22. **Equipping Educators to Teach Religious Literacy**
    Lessons from a Teacher Education Program in the American South
    Emile Lester and W. Y. Alice Chan

23. **Conceptualising Religion and Worldviews for the School**
    Opportunities, Challenges, and Complexities of a Transition from Religious Education in England and Beyond
    Kevin O'Grady

24. **Inclusion and Sexuality in Catholic Higher Education**
    Possibilities for Institutional Change
    Mark A. Levand

Inclusion and Sexuality in Catholic Higher Education

Possibilities for Institutional Change

Mark A. Levand

Routledge
Taylor & Francis Group
NEW YORK AND LONDON

First published 2023
by Routledge
605 Third Avenue, New York, NY 10158

and by Routledge
4 Park Square, Milton Park, Abingdon, Oxon, OX14 4RN

Routledge is an imprint of the Taylor & Francis Group, an informa business

© 2023 Mark A. Levand

The right of Mark A. Levand to be identified as author of this work has been asserted in accordance with sections 77 and 78 of the Copyright, Designs and Patents Act 1988.

All rights reserved. No part of this book may be reprinted or reproduced or utilised in any form or by any electronic, mechanical, or other means, now known or hereafter invented, including photocopying and recording, or in any information storage or retrieval system, without permission in writing from the publishers.

Trademark notice: Product or corporate names may be trademarks or registered trademarks, and are used only for identification and explanation without intent to infringe.

Library of Congress Cataloging-in-Publication Data
Names: Levand, Mark A., author.
Title: Inclusion and sexuality in Catholic higher education : possibilities for institutional change / Mark A. Levand.
Description: New York, NY : Routledge, 2023. | Series: Routledge research in religion and education | Includes bibliographical references and index.
Identifiers: LCCN 2022050875 (print) | LCCN 2022050876 (ebook) | ISBN 9781032110370 (hardback) | ISBN 9781032110394 (paperback) | ISBN 9781003218159 (ebook)
Subjects: LCSH: Catholic universities and colleges--Social aspects--United States. | Education, Higher--Religious aspects--Catholic Church. | Sexual minorities--Education (Higher)--United States. | Sex--Religious aspects--Catholic Church. | College environment--United States.
Classification: LCC LC501 .L48 2023 (print) | LCC LC501 (ebook) | DDC 378/.0712--dc23/eng/20230103
LC record available at https://lccn.loc.gov/2022050875
LC ebook record available at https://lccn.loc.gov/2022050876

ISBN: 978-1-032-11037-0 (hbk)
ISBN: 978-1-032-11039-4 (pbk)
ISBN: 978-1-003-21815-9 (ebk)

DOI: 10.4324/9781003218159

Typeset in Garamond
by SPi Technologies India Pvt Ltd (Straive)

Contents

Series Editor Foreword		vi
Acknowledgements		ix
Copyright Note		xi
1	Introduction and Setting the Stage	1
2	Getting to Know the Culture: Theories and History	13
3	General Themes: Catalysts in the Change Process	71
4	The Landscape for Change: Key Areas of Change and Reactions	90
5	Difficult or Easy? Themes in Supports and Challenges Faced by Changemakers	117
6	Over, Under, Around, or Through? How Changemakers Navigated the System	148
7	Voices of Change: Hopes for the Future and Suggestions for Improvement	167
8	A Framework for Change	181
9	The Future of Sexuality in Catholic Higher Education	192
	Appendix: Study Methods	214
	Index	229

Series Editor Foreword

The opening years of the 21st century brought increased attention to religion as an important dimension of culture and politics. The dramatic multi-pronged attacks of September 11, 2001, came as a jolting reminder of the potential for violent action that can have bases in religious motivations. Over the same period, we came to see an increase in religiously motivated activity in politics. In the United States, we see this in the evolution from the Moral Majority movement that emerged as a force in the late 1970s as the beginning of the New Religious Right. On further reflection, however, we can see the involvement of religion extending much further back as a fundamental part of our social organization rather than a new or emerging phenomenon. We need only recall the religious wars of early modern Europe through to the contentious development of US church and state relations as evidence of the longstanding role religion has played as a source of competing values and beliefs.

There has been a significant upturn in research and scholarship across many disciplines relative to the study of religion in recent decades. This is particularly the case in the area of the interplay of education and religion. While religious education—study *toward formation* in a particular faith tradition—has been with us for millennia, religion education—study *about* religion as an academic subject apart from theology is more recent.

Whereas theology departments proceeded from religious assumptions aiming to promulgate a faith tradition, the religious studies field emerged as a discipline that sought to bring a more objective social scientific approach to the study of religion. The origins of this approach date back to the European research centers that influenced US scholars beginning in the 18th century. The formalization of this trend, however, is a fairly recent phenomenon as illustrated by the 1949 formation of Society for the Scientific Study of Religion with its scholarly journal and the creation of religious studies departments across the United States in the wake of the US Supreme Court decision in 1963 that allowed, even encouraged, teaching *about* religion (rather than *for*) in public education institutions. That same year, the American Academy of Religion was born out of a group of scholars that had since 1909 been meeting under the various names related to biblical study.

It is out of this relatively recent increase in scholarly attention to religion and education that this book series arose. Routledge Publishers have long been an important presence in the respective fields of religion and of education. It seemed like a natural step to introduce a book series focused particularly on Research in Religion and Education. My appreciation extends to Max Novick for guiding this series into being in 2011 and now to Alice Salt and Sophie Ganesh for continuing Routledge's oversight.

In this 25th volume in this series, Mark Levand brings us *Inclusion and Sexuality in Catholic Higher Education: Possibilities for Institutional Change*. In the largest study of its kind, Levand examines the state of policy and practice regarding inclusion and sexuality in Catholic colleges and universities in the United States.

> The purpose of [this] study was to identify and describe the experience of employees attempting to introduce a systemic change around sexuality in Catholic colleges and universities. This study identifies themes and patterns associated with effecting change specific to meeting the needs of students in Catholic higher education. Concepts in Catholic social thought such as human dignity, solidarity, and the common good offer useful insight into how Catholic institutions can respond to issues of sexuality in ways that respect the dignity of others while being grounded in church tradition.
>
> (p. 7)

Working with 31 participants across 17 institutions, he used a qualitative research approach involving semi-structured in-depth interviews; these participants included faculty and staff from Residence life, Student and University life, Dean of Students, Campus Ministry, Health Services, and Title IX. A helpful appendix outlines his methodology and the bibliography is comprehensive.

Several themes surface from this work: general elements in the change process; specific areas of change and reactions encountered by changemakers; supportive factors in and barriers to the change process; changemaker communication strategies; learnings from changemakers that can inform future efforts. Case examples flesh out the intricacies of issues within unique institutional environments.

In any organizational context, issues emerging from sexuality are complex; they can encompass sexual assault, sexual trauma, comprehensive sexuality education, sexualization, intimacy and healthy relationships, contraceptive access, sexual behavior, and perhaps most fundamentally, sexual orientation, and gender identity. Add to this milieu millennia of religious dogma and practice and complexity can increase many fold. Levand contends, based upon his research, that Catholic colleges and universities are 15–20 years behind their secular counterparts in many, though not all, areas of sexuality issues.

In this volume Levand charts the challenging landscape for Catholic colleges and universities in dealing with sexuality issues in a comprehensive manner. He parses literature and research with nuance to note successes and to address areas where introducing change is needed and is most difficult. He argues that Catholic social thought can fruitfully address these issues while remaining grounded in church tradition.

Michael D. Waggoner
Book Series Editor
Research in Religion and Education

Acknowledgements

Doing research can be tough and isolating work. The creation, curation, and dissemination of those research findings, however, is rarely the product of a single person. This work has undergone various developments with a great deal of benevolent assistance and insights from others along the way. This work is the culmination of my doctoral dissertation research. The theology of interdependence is a common theme throughout this book and is most salient to me when I think about all of those who helped make this book possible.

I would like to thank the editorial team at Routledge that dedicated their time and energy to ensuring this book came together. Elsbeth Wright, AnnaMary Goodall, Alice Salt, Sophie Ganesh, and Charlene Price were instrumental in publishing this book in its final form. I also want to thank the *Routledge Research in Religion and Education* series editor Michael D. Waggoner for his commitment to this project through invaluable feedback. All of their work and dedication was helpful in forming this project into something digestible for a broader audience.

I extend my thanks to everyone who acted as sounding boards for my thoughts about this material, helping me to translate my thoughts and the data more clearly. My dissertation committee Don Dyson, Phil Rutter, and Meghan Pifer helped me hone the research questions early on in the process. I am eternally grateful for the dear friends and colleagues, including Eli Green, Bryan Massingale, Mina Beveney, Lorena Olvera, Karen Ross, Lisa Cunningham, and others who supported me throughout the process. Of particular mention would be Natale Vacalebre, who encouraged my pursuit of publication with insightful and enthusiastic mentorship. I am humbled by the support of my loving partner Sasha Canan who listened to me talk through chapter structures and theological applications for countless hours. Without this support, I would certainly never have completed this work.

I want to extend gratitude to the previous scholars on whose work this project is based. Thank you, Dennis Dailey and George Turner, for various reprint permissions. Without this framework for sexuality, our understanding of the concept may have been more difficult to communicate with a broader audience.

I am incredibly honored by the work of the participants of this study. Not only have they been working diligently within Catholic higher education to effect change, but they volunteered their time to participate in this study. Their dedication and passion for this work is inspiring and life-giving. I thank each and every one of the participants for the role they played in the dissemination of this information. Thank you for sharing your wisdom and insights in the work you do.

Copyright Note

The information contained in this book is based on a dissertation study; and at times may include content also appearing in the following publications:

Levand, M. A. (2018). *Effecting change around sexuality in Catholic higher education: A composite case-study analysis* (Publication No. 10812659) [Doctoral Dissertation, Widener University]. ProQuest Dissertations & Theses A&I.

Levand, M. A. (2021a). Communication strategies and responses to change around issues of sexuality in Catholic higher education. *Profesional de la Información*, 30(5), 1–14. https://doi.org/10.3145/epi.2021.sep.04

Levand, M. A. (2021b). Addressing the unaddressed: Changemakers' hopes for the future around issues of sexuality in Catholic higher education—theological insights. *Journal of Religion & Society*, 23, 1–16. http://moses.creighton.edu/JRS/toc/2021.html

Levand, M. A. (2022). Sexuality education as developmentally appropriate in the American Catholic higher education curriculum. *Sexuality, Gender, & Policy*, 5(2), 122–139. https://doi.org/10.1002/sgp2.12052

Levand, M. A., & Dyson, D. A. (2021). Areas of support and barriers to change around issues of sexuality in Catholic higher education. *Sexuality Research and Social Policy*, 18, 170–183. https://doi.org/10.1007/s13178-020-00447-9

Chapter 1

Introduction and Setting the Stage

What do we mean when we say sexuality? And what does sexuality in Catholic higher education look like? Why is it important to address matters of sexuality?

When educating parents and adults on puberty, I may ask them to think back to their own sexual development. When I ask, "Who remembers that being the least awkward time of their lives?" as one might expect, no one raises a hand. Similarly, when people are young adults, most people do not experience this as a time full of knowledge, with absolutely no questions at all about sexuality. Social development around sexuality can be a confusing time for many young adults, aged 18–24 (Bingaman, 2007; Erikson, 1963, 1968; Moreira et al., 2015). With little conversation around sexuality topics, concepts, or ethical decision-making, young adults may find themselves lost or without resources when making complex sexual decisions (Martino et al., 2008; Weinman et al., 2008). Many students in college and university life are met with the compounding difficulty of sexual navigation and new identity formation in a college atmosphere (Chickering & Reisser, 1993; Perry, 1970). Being away from parents and making their own decisions can be a formative process (Mullendore & Hatch, 2000). The higher education environment offers many avenues for exploration of young adult sexuality within peer interactions in classrooms, residence halls, or as a member of a sports team. These avenues, however, do not exist in a vacuum and are impacted by cultural and institutional forces such as values, symbols, language and metaphors, artifacts, rituals, and ceremonies (Schein, 1985). These forces create the conditions in which students navigate an understanding of sexuality in the world. In Catholic colleges and universities, these influencing factors can include the Catholic mission, church teachings and doctrine, or personal values of board members, trustees, and donors (Morey & Piderit, 2006). What you will read in this book will be an examination of faculty, staff, and administrators' lived experience of creating change around issues of sexuality in Catholic higher education.

The intersection of Catholicism and sexuality has a long history of being influenced by the doctors of the church in antiquity like Augustine of Hippo and St. Thomas Aquinas to more modern sexual theologians who are often also university professors (e.g., Augustine of Hippo, 1960; Bonner, 1962; Farley, 2006; Fox, 1995; Kosnik et al., 1977; Ruether, 1983; Torrell, 2005). Church teachings on sexuality from counsels and popes have, to varying degrees, impacted the way sexuality is presently discussed (e.g., Francis I, 2016; John Paul II, 1997; NCCB Committee on Marriage and Family, 1997; Paul VI, 1968; Pontifical Council for the Family, 1995; Sacred Congregation for the Doctrine of the Faith, 1975; United States Catholic Conference, 1991). With a mission to educate the whole person (John Paul II, 1990), the Catholic context can have a strong impact on the praxis of teaching and learning about sexuality. We will be getting more into those historical aspects in Chapter 2. In this chapter, we will focus on setting up the context: sexuality and Catholic higher education and why this study is so important today.

Sexuality

Matters of sexuality can be broadly understood to encompass many aspects of the human experience (Moglia, 1994). But what do we mean when we say *sexuality*? Some people may narrowly view the term "sexuality" to mean matters of a genital nature (genital sex/intercourse/coitus) or maybe include sexual orientation (Moglia, 1994; Myerson, 1992). We know from years of sexuality scholarship that *sexuality* addresses all of the aspects associated with being a sexual, gendered person—including biological, psychological, and social perspectives (Hedgepeth & Helmich, 1996). Theorists offer various models to enhance understanding of the breadth and complexity of human sexuality, such as a four-dimensional model (Greenberg et al., 1986), as being a ten-pointed star (Robinson et al., 2002), or as circles of sexuality (Advocates for Youth, 1995; Dailey, 1981, 2017). For this study, I used the popular educational tool the *Circles of Sexuality* to understand these many components (elaborated on further in Chapter 2). As sexuality is so broad and complex, there are many layers of sexuality found in higher education.

Sexuality in Higher Education

There are many facets of sexuality in higher education. At the institutional level, the college or university is impacted by its policies (e.g., whether or not orientation and gender identity is included in the school's non-discrimination policy) regarding sexuality for students, faculty, and staff and can be intimately tied to the school's mission (Morey & Piderit, 2006; Tierney, 1988). At the micro-level, the resources available (e.g., sexual health information, or support and social groups) to students, faculty, and staff can be influenced by these institutional regulations (Kezar, 2014). Other facets of sexuality can include the way sexuality is taught in a variety of departmental courses such as psychology, theology, or women and gender studies (Myerson, 1992; Stephens & Ott, 2020), sports and Title IX information such as gender equity and sexual harassment or discrimination (Francis, 2016; Lhamon, 2015; Rubin & Lough, 2015), gendered bathrooms (Greytak et al., 2009; Sausa, 2002), or the living arrangements of students (Buckner, 1981; Erlandson, 2014). *Sexuality* can also include student sexual activity or what the sex lives of students look like on campuses (McAnulty, 2012), the way a university views individuals with sexually and gender-diverse identities (Cramer, 2002), how sexual assault is addressed on campus (Ottens & Hotelling, 2001), where to find resources for sexual health information or counseling (Eisenberg, Lechner, et al., 2012b), and in some cases, morality clauses for employees which can terminate an employee from a job based on a poorly defined operation of acting "immorally" (Fleming et al., 2009). These are some of the many ways we see sexuality topics manifest in the higher education setting.

Higher Education's Management of Sexuality

Secular colleges manage the components of sexuality listed above in a number of ways. Examples include access to sexual health information (Eisenberg, Garcia, et al., 2012a) and focusing efforts on sexual assault training (Fouts & Knapp, 2001). Some Catholic colleges are also aware of the deficit of action around rape on campus and are overhauling the way they deal with sexual assault (Fletcher & Oxenden, 2015). The lack of knowledge and resources around sexual health and contraceptives on Catholic campuses means students are forced to find creative ways to access contraceptives or sexual health information (Winer, 2014). Regarding gender, secular colleges are required to make accommodations for students on gender identity (Lhamon, 2015). Catholic colleges and universities vary in the ways they deal with issues of gender identities—some are making changes for gender-neutral restrooms (Knap, 2016) and gender-inclusive housing (Snyder, 2016) while others are seeking exemptions from Title IX to slow down or prevent such accommodations (Bryk, 2015). Many universities may include sexuality in the curriculum in a variety of ways (Moglia, 1994; Myerson, 1992). When sexuality is included in curricula at Catholic institutions, it may go well or be a cause for concern (Editors, 1986; McCarty, 2014). Sexuality issues also occur in the realm of co-ed or gender-neutral living arrangements (Hobson, 2014; Willoughby et al., 2012) that may leave Catholic administrators in a difficult position with regard to current trends, tradition, and public perception (CNS Staff, 2015; Stimpson, 2011). The combination of Catholic and university culture plays a significant role in how institutions handle these decisions.

Catholic Higher Education as a Specific Context

In the case of Catholic institutions of higher education, the teachings of the Catholic Church strongly influence the rules and regulations of the college or university and, as a result, the resources available to students, faculty, and staff (Morey & Piderit, 2006). This influence can foster a lack of knowledge about sexuality at many different levels, often recounted in personal reflection (Anonymous, 2013). People who have gone to Catholic schools may be missing basic information about sexuality and sexual health before getting to college (Pagni, 2014). This interplay of church teaching and institutional regulation may leave many unaware of the ways sexuality exists in the world, influencing their understanding and interaction with others (McCarthy, 2015).

Institutions of Catholic higher education are often stereotyped as being oblivious to their students' sexual lives, as evidenced by bloggers (Anonymous, 2013; Pagni, 2014; Siebert, 2014) and supported by research (Riley, 1990). Student perception of administrators' lack of awareness about sexuality issues has been present in Catholic colleges and universities since the 1980s (Riley, 1990). There have been calls from those in academia and college life for Catholic colleges and universities to address the manifestation of issues of sexual assault and violence (Greiner, 2015), the culture of discrimination toward sexual minorities (Love, 1997), and restricted academic freedom (McCarty, 2014) around sexuality. These calls seem to target administrators and changemakers in hopes of enacting change efforts.

Some efforts for change are being made with varying degrees of success or failure. The University of San Francisco (2015) has successfully incorporated a sexual assault and harassment training policy that involves more progressive ideas around sexuality such as same-sex sexual advances. Alternatively, Love (1998) describes the factors impacting a support group for lesbian and gay students that ultimately led to the dissolution of the group (P. Love, personal communication, October 29, 2015). Other efforts to effect change are detailed in studies of the successful creation of LGB groups (Getz & Kirkley, 2006; McEntarfer, 2011) or the inclusion of orientation into non-discrimination policies (Archbold, 2012; Dionisopoulos, 2013; Nelson, 2012; Sheridan, 2010).

People in many of these settings are in the process of negotiating the Catholic identity of the institution and information about sexuality. Gaining a clearer picture of how this happens can contribute to the rich tradition of Catholicism and better serve members of these institutions.

Overview of the Book

The chapters in this book are broken down conceptually based on the groupings of themes that came from the qualitative data. Chapter 1 has been an introduction to the concepts and a broad overview of the study. Chapter 2 will have a great deal of theory, a little bit of history, and the recent research on the subject. This chapter will examine Catholic history and sexuality briefly to focus on the empirical research that informed this study. There will be more theological literature throughout the following chapters. Each of the following chapters will have a "theological insights" section that expounds on the theological literature related to the data. In other words, the following chapters will have a section about what insights theology has to offer to what we are seeing in the empirical data. What follows will not be in-depth theological analyses, but a look at theological complexities in relatively succinct ways for readers to see how these concepts apply to change in Catholic higher education.

Chapter 3 will be an overview of the broad emergent themes throughout the study. The later chapters will examine themes in specific areas of change (key topics, strategies for communication, etc.), but the broad emergent themes will be based on all of the interviews in total: *What was common throughout all of the interviews? What themes persisted across all of the institutions represented in the study?* I also examine some key aspects about sexual theology to explore how human sexuality is a Catholic theological good.

Chapters 4–7 will look at themes present in specific conceptual areas. In Chapter 4, we will take a look at the landscape for change, including the key concepts participants said need to be addressed in Catholic higher education as well as the reactions participants encountered in the process. These reactions will be important for contextualizing their methods of communication examined in Chapter 6. I also look at insights from theology about discrimination and communal repentance.

Chapter 5 will cover the themes in supports and barriers or challenges participants encountered in the change process. While the reactions addressed in Chapter 4 could act as barriers, Chapter 5 will address specific groups or behaviors that helped and obstacles that hindered change. These concepts are the reasons for the communication strategies discussed in the following chapter. I examine insights from theology about confronting fear, being in right relationship, and the Catholic social teaching (CST) principle of solidarity.

Chapter 6 will include the methods or communication strategies used by participants that assisted in effecting change. This chapter answers the broad question: *What effective strategies of communication did people use to effect change?* Gathering data, focusing on students, public trainings, and student protests and engaging the mission of the university, among others, were all ways these changemakers effected change. Building on the theological insights from solidarity, I further examine the concepts of the common good and addressing structural sin.

Chapter 7 will include voices for change. Participants shared with me their hopes for the future of Catholic higher education, and I collate some suggestions for improvements around these key issues. I examine the changes called for by the participants to make Catholic higher education more welcoming of conversations around sexuality. Changemakers suggested both theoretical and practical changes that Catholic higher education could make that address human sexuality more honestly. I include Catholic theological support for why these concepts are not only needed but are deeply rooted within the Catholic tradition addressing conscience and Catholic erotophobia.

In Chapter 8, I entertain the question "*How do I become a changemaker at my Catholic institution?*" and offer ideas and tools that employees at Catholic institutions can use to assist in the change process at their home institutions. I assess what each of these themes means for the state of sexuality in Catholic higher education and discuss future steps to take in research and in praxis, practically at one's own university. I describe a process I devised for assessing an institutional climate and addressing issues of sexuality in various types of Catholic universities or colleges. I conclude this chapter with insights from a theology of vocation.

Chapter 9 is a closing chapter bringing together what all this information means. I consider how changemaking around sexual orientation and gender identity is synonymous with LGBTQ ministry. I revisit some key theological concepts discussed throughout the book and name five general guidelines that Catholic higher education can follow for more inclusive change on matters of sexuality. I also offer specific suggestions with case study examples geared toward university administrators so they can be better equipped to address such matters. I conclude with directions for future research.

Why This Study?

Most of the studies that exist naming change around sexuality in Catholic higher education cover one, two, or three institutions at once (e.g., Coley, 2018; Getz & Kirkley, 2006; Hughes, 2018, 2020; Love, 1997, 1998; McEntarfer, 2011). In these studies, attention may be given to the institutional context, challenges therein, and the process of creating change, resulting in a failure to describe the structural components that encourage or discourage change but only at a small number of institutions. In the largest study of its kind, I will discuss all of these factors across 17 different Catholic colleges and universities in the United States.

The purpose of the current research study was to identify and describe the experience of employees attempting to introduce a systemic change around sexuality in Catholic colleges and universities. This study identifies themes and patterns associated with effecting change specific to meeting the sexuality needs of students in Catholic higher education. Concepts in Catholic social thought such as human dignity, solidarity, and the common good offer useful insight into how Catholic institutions can respond to issues of sexuality in ways that respect the human dignity of others while being grounded in church tradition. In this book, I will elaborate on the factors that emerged from this study, offering insights and theological evidence for inclusive change on matters of sexuality in Catholic higher education. Before we get to those, we will examine more of the history and literature relevant to the concepts in this book in Chapter 2.

References

Advocates for Youth. (1995). What is sexuality? In *Life planning education: A youth development program* (pp. 115–129). Author.

Anonymous. (2013). *What Catholic school teaches you about sex.* http://web.archive.org/web/20160325160045/http://vitaminw.co/society/what-catholic-school-teaches-you-about-sex

Archbold, M. (2012, September 27). Catholic college adds sexual identity to non-discrimination policy. *Catholic Education Daily.* http://web.archive.org/web/20131108193639/http://www.cardinalnewmansociety.org/CatholicEducationDaily/DetailsPage/tabid/102/ArticleID/1583/Catholic-College-Adds-Sexual-Identity-to-Non-Discrimination-Policy.aspx

Augustine of Hippo. (1960). *The confessions of st. Augustine* (J. K. Ryan, Trans.). Doubleday.

Bingaman, K. A. (2007). The postmodern life cycle and pastoral care and counseling. *Journal of Spirituality in Mental Health, 9*(1), 83–94. https://doi.org/10.1300/J515v09n01

Bonner, G. I. (1962). Libido and concupiscentia in St. Augustine. *Studia Patristica, 1*, 303–314.

Bryk, A. (2015). Title IX giveth and the religious exemption taketh away: How the religious exemption eviscerates the protection afforded transgender students under title IX. *Cardozo Law Review, 37*(2), 751–791.

Buckner, D. R. (1981). Developing coed residence hall programs for sex-role exploration. *Journal of College Student Personnel, 22*(1), 52–54.

Chickering, A. W., & Reisser, L. (1993). *Education and identity* (2nd ed.). Jossey-Bass.

CNS Staff. (2015). *Fordham changes restroom signs as part of 'gender inclusive' campaign.* http://www.cardinalnewmansociety.org/CatholicEducationDaily/DetailsPage/tabid/102/ArticleID/4512/Fordham-Changes-Restroom-Signs-as-Part-of-%E2%80%98Gender-Inclusive%E2%80%99-Campaign.aspx

Coley, J. S. (2018). *Gay on god's campus: Mobilizing for LGBT equality at Christian colleges and universities.* University of North Carolina Press.

Cramer, E. P. (Ed.). (2002). *Addressing homophobia and heterosexism on college campuses.* Huntington Park Press.

Dailey, D. M. (1981). Sexual expression and aging. In F. Berghorn & D. Schafer (Eds.), *The dynamics of ageing: Original essays on the processes and experiences of growing old* (pp. 311–330). Westview Press.

Dailey, D. M. (2017). Sexual expression and aging. *Quarterly Journal of the Life Planning Network, 4*(4), 34–52.

Dionisopoulos, T. (2013, October 9). Catholic college adds 'gender identity' and 'sexual orientation' to non-discrimination clause. *CampusReform.* http://www.campusreform.org/?ID=5144

Editors. (1986). Handle the Charles Curran case with care. *America*, 237–238. http://americamagazine.org/issue/100/charles-curran-case

Eisenberg, M., Garcia, C., Frerich, E., Lechner, K., & Lust, K. (2012a). Through the eyes of the student: What college students look for, find, and think about sexual health resources on campus. *Sexuality Research & Social Policy: Journal of NSRC, 9*(4), 306–316. https://doi.org/10.1007/s13178-012-0087-0

Eisenberg, M., Lechner, K., Frerich, E., Lust, K., & Garcia, C. (2012b). Characterizing sexual health resources on college campuses. *Journal of Community Health, 37*(5), 940–948. https://doi.org/10.1007/s10900-011-9536-6

Erikson, E. H. (1963). *Childhood and society.* W.W. Norton & Company.

Erikson, E. H. (1968). *Identity: Youth and crisis.* W. W. Norton & Company Inc.

Erlandson, K. (2014). Sexiled: Privacy acquisition strategies of college roommates. *Journal of College & University Student Housing, 40*(2), 12–29.

Farley, M. (2006). *Just love: A framework for Christian sexual ethics.* The Continuum International Publishing Group Inc.

Fleming, M. B., Cooley, A. H., & McFadden-Wade, G. (2009). Morals clauses for educators in secondary and postsecondary schools: Legal applications and constitutional concerns. *Brigham Young University Education & Law Journal, 2009*(1), 67–102. https://digitalcommons.law.byu.edu/elj/vol2009/iss1/4/

Fletcher, L., & Oxenden, M. (2015). Consenting to change. *U.S. Catholic, 9*, 18–21.

Fouts, B., & Knapp, J. (2001). A sexual assault education and risk reduction workshop for college freshmen. In A. J. Ottens & K. Hotelling (Eds.), *Sexual violence on campus: Politics, programs, and perspectives* (pp. 98–119). Springer.

Fox, T. C. (1995). *Sexuality and Catholicism*. George Braziller Inc.

Francis I. (2016). *Apostolic exhortation: Amoris laetitia*. https://w2.vatican.va/content/dam/francesco/pdf/apost_exhortations/documents/papa-francesco_esortazione-ap_20160319_amoris-laetitia_en.pdf

Francis, L. (2016). Title IX: An incomplete effort to achieve equality in sports. *Journal of the Philosophy of Sport, 43*(1), 83–99. https://doi.org/10.1080/00948705.2015.1112242

Getz, C., & Kirkley, E. (2006). Shaking up the status quo: Challenging intolerance of the lesbian, gay and bisexual community at a private Roman Catholic university. *College Student Journal, 40*(4), 857–869.

Greenberg, J. S., Bruess, C. E., & Sands, D. W. (1986). *Sexuality: Insights and issues*. Wm. C. Brown.

Greiner, K. A. (2015). *Who do we say that we are?: Changing the institutional culture around issues of sex and sexuality on Catholic campuses*. dailytheology.org. http://dailytheology.org/2015/09/13/who-do-we-say-that-we-are-changing-the-institutional-culture-around-issues-of-sex-and-sexuality-on-catholic-campuses/

Greytak, E. A., Kosciw, J. G., & Diaz, E. M. (2009). *Harsh realities: The experiences of transgender youth in our nation's schools*. GLSEN.

Hedgepeth, E., & Helmich, J. (1996). *Teaching about sexuality and HIV: Principles and methods for effective education*. New York University Press.

Hobson, A. (2014). Designing and implementing a successful gender-neutral housing community. *Journal of College and Character, 15*(1), 33–38. https://doi.org/10.1515/jcc-2014-0005

Hughes, B. E. (2018). Resilience of grassroots leaders involved in LGBT issues at a Catholic university. *Journal of Student Affairs Research and Practice, 55*(2), 123–136. https://doi.org/10.1080/19496591.2017.1366330

Hughes, B. E. (2020). "Put the Jesuit out front": How a Catholic, Jesuit university addresses LGBQ issues. *American Educational Research Journal, 57*(4), 1592–1624.

John Paul II. (1990). *Ex corde ecclesiae*. http://w2.vatican.va/content/john-paul-ii/en/apost_constitutions/documents/hf_jp-ii_apc_15081990_ex-corde-ecclesiae.html

John Paul II. (1997). *The theology of the body: Human love in the divine plan*. Pauline Books & Media.

Kezar, A. J. (2014). *How colleges change: Understanding, leading, and enacting change*. Routledge.

Knap, P. (2016). *Gender-neutral bathrooms have arrived at Catholic colleges*. http://www.ncregister.com/blog/pattyknap/gender-neutral-bathrooms-have-arrived-at-catholic-colleges

Kosnik, A., Carroll, W., Cunningham, A., Modras, R., & Schulte, J. (1977). *Human sexuality: New directions in American Catholic thought.* Paulist Press.

Lhamon, C. E. (2015). *Title IX resource guide.* https://www2.ed.gov/about/offices/list/ocr/docs/dcl-title-ix-coordinators-guide-201504.pdf

Love, P. G. (1997). Contradiction and paradox: Attempting to change the culture of sexual orientation at a small Catholic college. *Review of Higher Education, 20*(4), 381–398. https://muse.jhu.edu/article/30031

Love, P. G. (1998). Cultural barriers facing lesbian, gay and bisexual students at a Catholic college. *Journal of Higher Education, 69*(3), 298–323. https://doi.org/10.2307/2649190

Martino, S. C., Elliott, M. N., Corona, R., Kanouse, D. E., & Schuster, M. A. (2008). Beyond the 'big talk': The roles of breadth and repetition in parent-adolescent communication about sexual topics. *Pediatrics, 121*(3), 612–618.

McAnulty, R. D. (Ed.). (2012). *Sex in college: The things they don't write home about.* ABC-CLIO.

McCarthy, C. E. (2015). *Birth control, rape culture & Catholic higher education: Why aren't we even teaching what we already know?* dailytheology.org. http://dailytheology.org/2015/09/19/birth-control-rape-culture-catholic-higher-education-why-arent-we-even-teaching-what-we-already-know/

McCarty, R. W. (2014). Objects of the inquisition, or the trials of religion scholars at Catholic institutions who engage with sexuality studies. *Academe, 100*(1), 24–29. www.aaup.org

McEntarfer, H. K. (2011). "Not going away": Approaches used by students, faculty, and staff members to create gay–straight alliances at three religiously affiliated universities. *Journal of LGBT Youth, 8*(4), 309–331. https://doi.org/10.1080/19361653.2011.607623

Moglia, R. (1994). Sexuality education in higher education in the USA: Analysis and implications. *Sexual & Marital Therapy, 9*(2), 181–191. https://doi.org/10.1080/02674659408409580

Moreira, A. D., Halkitis, P. N., & Kapadia, F. (2015). Sexual identity development of a new generation of emerging adult men: The p18 cohort study. *Psychology of Sexual Orientation and Gender Diversity, 2*(2), 159–167. https://doi.org/10.1037/sgd0000099

Morey, M. M., & Piderit, J. J. (2006). *Catholic higher education: A culture in crisis.* Oxford University Press.

Mullendore, R. H., & Hatch, C. (2000). *Helping your first-year college student succeed: A guide for parents.* University of South Carolina, National Resource Center for the First-Year Experience and Students in Transition.

Myerson, M. (1992). Sex equity and sexuality in college-level sex education. In S. S. Klein (Ed.), *Sex equity and sexuality in education* (pp. 149–167). State University of New York Press.

NCCB Committee on Marriage and Family. (1997). *Always our children: A pastoral message to parents of homosexual children and suggestions for pastoral ministers.* United States Catholic Conference. http://www.usccb.org/issues-and-action/human-life-and-dignity/homosexuality/always-our-children.cfm

Introduction and Setting the Stage 11

Nelson, L. A. (2012, April 26). How Catholic? *Inside Higher Ed*. https://www.insidehighered.com/news/2012/04/26/tensions-over-social-issues-front-and-center-several-catholic-colleges

Ottens, A. J., & Hotelling, K. (Eds.). (2001). *Sexual violence on campus: Politics, programs, and perspectives*. Springer.

Pagni, C. (2014). *Catholic school sexual education leads to climactic revelations*. http://georgetownvoice.com/2014/01/30/catholic-school-sexual-education-leads-climactic-revelations/

Paul VI. (1968). *Humanae vitae*. http://w2.vatican.va/content/paul-vi/en/encyclicals/documents/hf_p-vi_enc_25071968_humanae-vitae.html

Perry, W. G. (1970). *Forms of intellectual and ethical development in the college years: A scheme*. Harcourt Brace Javanovich College.

Pontifical Council for the Family. (1995). *The truth and meaning of human sexuality: Guidelines for education within the family*. http://www.vatican.va/roman_curia/pontifical_councils/family/documents/rc_pc_family_doc_08121995_human-sexuality_en.html

Riley, D. M. (1990). ACCU student life questionnaire: A report. *Current Issues in Catholic Higher Education*, *10*(2), 6–10.

Robinson, B., Bockting, W. O., Rosser, B. R. S., Miner, M., & Coleman, E. (2002). The sexual health model: Application of a sexological approach to HIV prevention. *Health Education Research*, *17*(1), 43–57.

Rubin, L. M., & Lough, N. L. (2015). Perspectives of title IX pioneers: Equity, equality and need. *Journal of Intercollegiate Sport*, *8*(2), 109–130.

Ruether, R. R. (1983). *Sexism and god-talk: Toward a feminist theology*. Beacon Press.

Sacred Congregation for the Doctrine of the Faith. (1975). *Persona humana: Declaration on certain questions concerning sexual ethics*. http://www.vatican.va/roman_curia/congregations/cfaith/documents/rc_con_cfaith_doc_19751229_persona-humana_en.html

Sausa, L. A. (2002). Updating college and university campus policies: Meeting the needs of trans students, staff, and faculty. In E. P. Cramer (Ed.), *Addressing homophobia and heterosexism on college campuses* (pp. 43–55). Huntington Park Press.

Schein, E. H. (1985). *Organizational culture and leadership*. Jossey-Bass.

Sheridan, K. (2010, February 11). Students protest. *The Carroll News*. http://www.jcunews.com/2010/02/11/students-protest/

Siebert, E. (2014). *Sex, drugs and…Catholic colleges*. http://ncronline.org/blogs/ncr-today/sex-drugs-and-catholic-colleges

Snyder, S. (2016). *La Salle students want 'gender-neutral' housing*. http://articles.philly.com/2016-02-26/news/70943501_1_catholic-university-student-safety-colleges

Stephens, D. W., & Ott, K. M. (Eds.). (2020). *Teaching sexuality and religion in higher education: Embodied learning, trauma sensitive pedagogy, and perspective transformation*. Routledge. https://doi.org/10.4324/9780429327162

Stimpson, E. (2011). *Catholic universities see value of single-sex housing*. https://www.osv.com/OSVNewsweekly/Story/TabId/2672/ArtMID/13567/ArticleID/1834/Catholic-universities-see-value-of-singlesex-housing.aspx

Tierney, W. G. (1988). Organizational culture in higher education: Defining the essentials. *Journal of Higher Education*, *59*(1), 2–21.

Torrell, J. P. (2005). *Saint Thomas Aquinas: The person and his work* (R. Royal, Trans.; Revised ed., Vol. 1). Catholic University of American Press.

United States Catholic Conference. (1991). *Human sexuality: A Catholic perspective for education and lifelong learning*. United States Catholic Conference.

University of San Francisco. (2015). *Think about it*. https://myusf.usfca.edu/student-health-safety/think-about-it

Weinman, M., Small, E., Buzi, R., & Smith, P. (2008). Risk factors, parental communication, self and peers' beliefs as predictors of condom use among female adolescents attending family planning clinics. *Child & Adolescent Social Work Journal*, *25*(3), 157–170. https://doi.org/10.1007/s10560-008-0118-0

Willoughby, B. J., Larsen, J. K., & Carroll, J. S. (2012). The emergence of gender-neutral housing on American university campuses. *Journal of Adolescent Research*, *27*(6), 732–750. https://doi.org/10.1177/0743558412447852

Winer, C. (2014). *Student group challenges Fordham University condom, free speech policies*. http://college.usatoday.com/2014/10/05/students-challenge-fordham-university-condom-free-speech-policies/

Chapter 2

Getting to Know the Culture
Theories and History

> What concepts do I need to know to understand this study? Catholicism, sexuality, student development, and more.

In order to understand the impctus and grounding theories for this study, we will have to explore several facets of sexuality, Catholicism, and higher education. This chapter is full of theories on sexuality, evidence and studies in Catholic higher education, and a brief look at how the Catholic Church discusses sexuality.

The literature related to the experience of effecting change around sexuality on Catholic college and university campuses is scarce. Much of the information pointing to the need for this study comes from various areas of research involving attitudes around sexuality for students in high school (Maher & Sever, 2007) and college (Love, 1998), faculty and staff (McCarty, 2014), as well as academic writings (Freitas, 2008; Morey & Piderit, 2006; Riley, 1990) and theological writings (Farley, 2006; Lawler & Salzman, 2011; McCarthy, 2015). Let us first consider the guiding theories of research and sexuality used for this study. We will then explore the developmental nature of college-aged individuals between 18 and 24 years of age in regard to sexuality and religious/spiritual identity. This will help us contextualize the need for further research on addressing sexuality in higher education. Turning our attention toward higher education, we will then examine how colleges and universities address this development in students. To better understand the landscape of sexuality in Catholic higher education, we will briefly examine some key points in the relationship that Catholicism has with sexuality and what that means for how matters of sexuality play out in Catholic colleges and universities. Lastly, we will look at some of the calls for change people have made about the way Catholic higher education handles issues of sexuality. This should bring us up to speed with understanding the results of the study and some opportunities for how we can better address these issues in Catholic higher education.

DOI: 10.4324/9781003218159-2

Guiding Theories

This study was informed by an ecological psychological theory of study. The ecological psychological approach focuses on the relationship between the individual and their environment, seeing them as interconnected in determining an individual's perception and behavior (Jacob, 1987). To study change with regard to sexuality in Catholic higher education, components like clear definitions, developmental contexts, historical traditions, and present research are important to iterate because they clarify the environment in which this change is taking place.

In order to understand the importance of studying change around sexuality in Catholic higher education, it is important to define sexuality. With a variety of possible meanings, the broad spectrum of possible topics encompassed by the term "sexuality" will be identified and contextualized in the college setting. After contextualizing sexuality within the college setting, I explore several educational and developmental theories necessary to understand and support the appropriateness of dialogue about sexuality in the college setting. Not only does educational and developmental theory support this claim, but the Catholic context also encompasses a particular religious component often assisting in faith development—a necessary key factor in understanding the institutional culture around sexuality and the development of the whole person. How higher education manages these developmental changes will contribute to the context in which dialogue around sexuality takes place.

A discussion about issues of sexuality in higher education will be foundational to understanding how sexuality currently plays out in institutions of higher education generally. Covering sexuality from the Catholic lens will assist in a more in-depth look into how issues of sexuality currently exist in Catholic higher education today. The issues discussed about sexuality in higher education are then mirrored in how these same issues exist in Catholic colleges and universities. After a description of how issues of sexuality manifest in Catholic higher education, an examination of the calls for change from various members of the Catholic higher education culture will support the need for further study on the topic. This leads to a discussion on the most current research regarding changes around sexuality in Catholic higher education to inform me of the environment in which I conducted the present study.

Sexuality

Matters of sexuality can be broadly understood to encompass many aspects of the human experience (Moglia, 1994). Some people may view the term "sexuality" to mean matters of a genital nature (genital sex/intercourse/coitus) or maybe even include sexual orientation (Moglia, 1994; Myerson, 1992). Sexuality addresses all of the aspects associated with being a sexual, gendered person—including biological, psychological, and social perspectives (Hedgepeth & Helmich, 1996). Over the last few decades, there have been a few different models of sexuality that discuss the breadth and complexity of human sexuality. Let's examine a few here.

Greenberg, Bruess, and Sands (1986) described four aspects of what they call dimensions of total human sexuality: ethical, biological, psychological, and cultural. Ethical aspects of human sexuality include ideals, religious beliefs, moral opinions and actions, and values. If left unexamined, individuals may fail to see how these components might influence their interactions with others about matters of sexuality (Hedgepeth & Helmich, 1996). The authors explain biological components of sexuality to include reproduction, fertility, sexual arousal and response, growth and development, physiological cycles and changes, and physical appearance. The authors continued with psychological components of human sexuality including emotions, experiences, self-conceptions, motivation, expressiveness, and learned attitudes and behaviors. Finally, Greenberg et al. discuss cultural aspects of human sexuality to include family, neighbors, peers, houses of worship (religious components), school, dating, marriage, law, custom, media, and advertising.

Robinson et al. (2002) examined components of sexuality in relation to sexual health behavior, resulting in the broad conceptualization of sexuality as a ten-point star. Points include: talking about sex, culture and sexual identity, sexual anatomy functioning, sexual health care and safer sex, sexual challenges, body image, masturbation and fantasy, positive sexuality, intimacy and relationships, and spirituality. Some of the points may join seemingly unrelated or not mutually exclusive topics (i.e., culture and sexual identity). And while the purpose of this model is for sexological interventions, specifically with HIV prevention, it identifies more of the complexities of what is meant by the term "sexuality" as more than just a select few issues of sex and gender.

Dennis Dailey first described the *Circles of Sexuality* in the 1980s (1981). Having updated this concept in the 1990s and again in the 2010s, Dailey's *Circles of Sexuality* are an oft-used educational tool to describe the intersectional nature of sexuality within the human experience (Advocates for Youth, 1995; Dailey, 2017). Dailey's five circles include sensuality, intimacy, sexual identity, sexual health and reproduction, and sexualization.

Sensuality includes the comfort of one's own body as well as the physiological and psychological enjoyment of one's own body and the bodies of others. Concepts such as body image, skin hunger, sexual response, and fantasy are included in this category.

Dailey describes body image as the way people feel about their bodies and the way they function, heavily impacted by the media. He calls the need to touch and be touched "skin hunger" and includes it in this circle. For Dailey, sexual response includes arousal and orgasm while fantasy refers to the psychological pleasure from imagining sexual behaviors or experiences.

Intimacy refers to the experience of desiring closeness to another human being as well as reciprocation of such feelings. Concepts like sharing, caring, liking, loving, vulnerability, and risk-taking are all part of the experience of human sexuality. Emotional attachments or connections are components of this circle. The risk-taking in openness of feelings is seen as a crucial part of being close with others.

Dailey identifies *sexual identity* as a sense of who one is sexually. Sexual orientation is part of sexual identity, as well as gender identity and gender role. He uses sexual orientation to refer to the types of people to whom one is attracted (same gender, other gender, or both). Gender here is one's internal sense of being male or female. Dailey described gender role as these stereotyped social rules that guide what a man or woman can and cannot do.

The circle of *sexual health and reproduction* constitutes what most people may conceptualize when considering "sex education." Factual information about intercourse, physiology, reproduction, and organs are included in this circle. Dailey also includes feelings and attitudes about sexual relationships in this circle as well, indicating the importance of the subjective experience of sexual health information.

Understanding how bodies work and conception occurs is one main focus in this circle. Dailey recognized the wide range of feelings and attitudes that are associated with sexuality and sexual behaviors. Sexual intercourse as well as contraceptive information are also included in this circle for the prevention of unwanted pregnancies and various infections.

Finally, Dailey identifies *sexualization* as an important part of human sexuality. In this model, seduction is defined as using sex or sexuality to influence, manipulate, or control other people. Behaviors like flirting, seduction, sexual harassment, sexual abuse, and rape are included in this category.

The circle of sexualization is seen to have a wide range of behaviors from "harmlessly manipulative" to "sadistic and illegal." Sexuality can be used in ways such as flirtation and seduction to influence others' behavior. Dailey includes withholding sex from a partner to punish them as another such way sex can be used to influence. Sexual harassment in the form of demands or the exploitation of power, sexual abuse, and rape are all included for a holistic picture of sexuality.

Using Dailey's model of the *Circles of Sexuality* can be helpful in understanding some of the sexuality issues in higher education. Sensuality in higher education can include the impact of campuses' messages about healthy eating on body image, or the way students touch, hug, hold hands, or cuddle in various places on campus. Matters within the circle of intimacy that intersect with students' academic and social lives include intimacy between athletic friends, differing sexual orientations' expression of intimacy, or attempting to articulate a need for vulnerability but having few safe spaces.

Each of these circles with these many components exist as a model of sexuality within a specific socio-cultural context. Different socio-cultural contexts offer different values and/or ways of living out each of these topics of sexuality. Some scholars will also include a "values" circle in the middle of the model to identify that people have values associated with each area (Figure 2.1).

Issues within the circle of sexual identity in the collegiate atmosphere can include the formation of student organizations around orientation (e.g., Gay Straight Alliance (GSA), Lesbian, Gay, Bisexual, Transgender, Queer (LGBTQ) groups, etc.) to give a safe space for students experiencing oppression or bullying in various ways. Transgender students may fall through the cracks of the binary "Male-Female" structure with documentation forms in policy or with gendered restroom debates.

The circle of sexual health and reproduction on many campuses may include sexual health information and access. This can include pamphlets about safer sex, condoms, or various other resources about safer sex practices or STI statistics. However, discussions and programing about healthy relationships or the lack thereof may influence how students relate to each other and faculty/staff.

Within the circle of sexualization, the obvious issues of sexual assault on campuses or boundaries between students and faculty can impact campus life overtly or go underground with the potential to cause much more damage (Ziering & Dick, 2015). The movie *The Hunting Ground* (2015) depicts the ways in which reports of sexual assault can be ignored or mishandled by universities, permitting a culture of sexual assault on campus as the status quo for perpetrators of sexual assault has been to receive minimal to no consequence.

As an integral dimension of our personhood, sexuality inherently exists in many different ways in university life (Myerson, 1992). The *Circles of Sexuality* (Advocates for Youth, 1995; Dailey, 1981, 2017), along with the components of culture, ethics, and spirituality (Greenberg et al., 1986; Robinson et al., 2002), is a relatively comprehensive template for understanding sexuality as it pertains to college

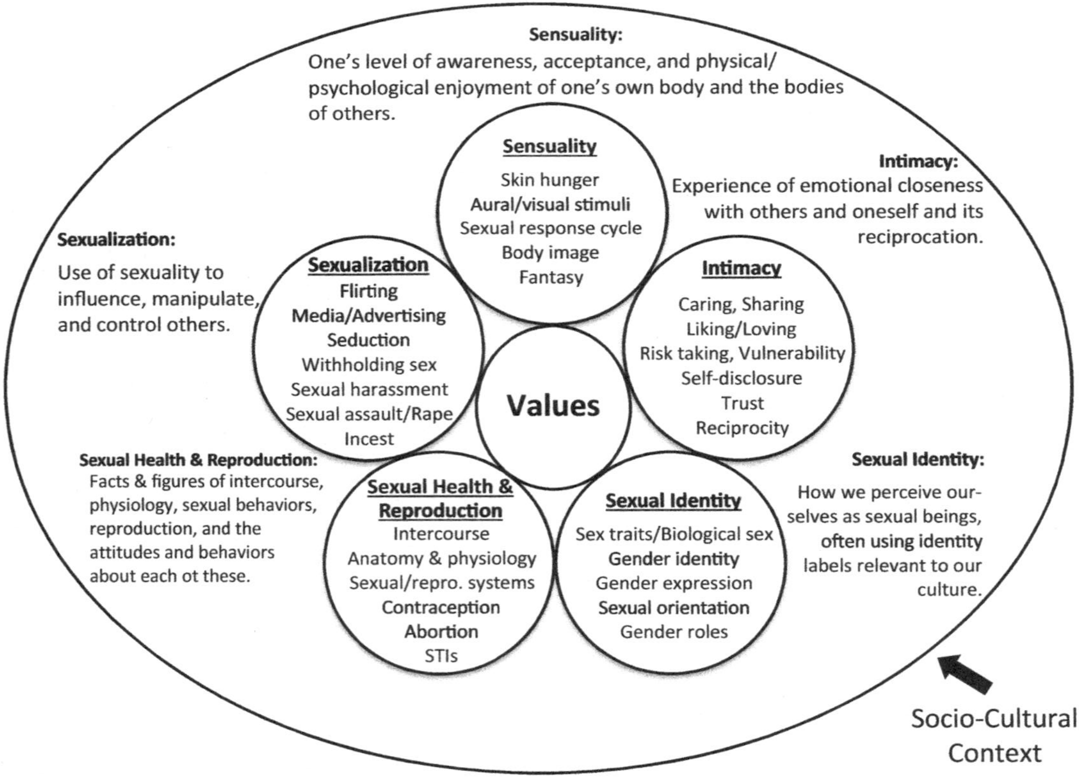

18 Getting to Know the Culture

Sensuality:
One's level of awareness, acceptance, and physical/psychological enjoyment of one's own body and the bodies of others.

Intimacy:
Experience of emotional closeness with others and oneself and its reciprocation.

Sexual Identity:
How we perceive ourselves as sexual beings, often using identity labels relevant to our culture.

Sexualization:
Use of sexuality to influence, manipulate, and control others.

Sexual Health & Reproduction:
Facts & figures of intercourse, physiology, sexual behaviors, reproduction, and the attitudes and behaviors about each ot these.

Sensuality
Skin hunger
Aural/visual stimuli
Sexual response cycle
Body image
Fantasy

Intimacy
Caring, Sharing
Liking/Loving
Risk taking, Vulnerability
Self-disclosure
Trust
Reciprocity

Sexual Identity
Sex traits/Biological sex
Gender identity
Gender expression
Sexual orientation
Gender roles

Sexualization
Flirting
Media/Advertising
Seduction
Withholding sex
Sexual harassment
Sexual assault/Rape
Incest

Sexual Health & Reproduction
Intercourse
Anatomy & physiology
Sexual/repro. systems
Contraception
Abortion
STIs

Values

Socio-Cultural Context

Figure 2.1 The Circles of Sexuality.

Adapted from Dailey, 2017 and Turner, 2020. Original *Circles of Sexuality* model authored by Dr. Dennis M. Dailey, PhD, Professor Emeritus, University of Kansas, Lawrence, Kansas.

and university life. When I interviewed participants for this study, the topics of discussion could have fallen within this broad range of the meanings of sexuality.

Late Adolescent and Young Adult Development

Considering the importance of individual development, many theorists discuss people in the college age range (18–24) as being in different developmental and life stages—a stage that Arnett (2000) identifies as *emerging adulthood*. Erikson (1963) describes the epigenetic principle of development that assumes the systematic emergence of each stage—meaning an individual may struggle moving onto further stages if a previous stage is not resolved. In Love's (2002) comparison of spiritual and cognitive developmental models, he describes how other theorists support this same claim. I will highlight key stages from developmental theorists pertinent to many individuals aged 18–24 years, followed by the impact of development on faith experience in regard to sexuality.

Theoretical Development

College-aged people find themselves in a particularly formative time in their lives as many of them have sexually matured to adulthood and are encountering many different psychosocial challenges that influence their college experience (Newman & Newman, 2012). Developmental and learning theorists contribute various stages or processes to our discussion of young adult sexuality. For the purpose of this study, this brief review of relevant theorists and stages will provide us with a theoretical grounding to better contextualize how students may relate to themselves and others sexually. Beginning with developmental theorists such as Freud (1920, 1963), Piaget (1952), Erikson (1963, 1968), Levinson (1978), and Levinson and Levinson (1996), I examine the psychosocial (or psychosexual) stages in which students may find themselves by naming the *Circles of Sexuality* with which they correspond. Subsequently, I will include some popular and relevant cognitive development processes used in much of the higher education literature for a more theoretical grounding of student sexual behavior.

One of the first 20th-century scholars to consider the sexual drive of adolescents is the psychologist Sigmund Freud (1920). He identified stages for psychosexual development based on the expression of the sexual drive. Freud (1920) was the first person to identify the sexual drive as a libido and suggest stages for its expression: oral, anal, phallic, latency, genital. For Freud (1963), many young adults are in the *genital* stage in which the libido is genitally focused. At this age, sexual interaction and gratification is sought through the genitals in partnered sexual expression. It is in this stage that any genital preoccupation college students may experience is seen as developmentally normal and appropriate. While many of Freud's theories are questioned today, the concept that young adult's sexual energy may be genitally focused is generally assumed to be true. Sexual behavior and internal motivations relate to Dailey's *Circles of Sexuality*. Not only does it relate to sexual behaviors within the circle of Sensuality, but also includes components of partnership in the circle of Intimacy involving trust and risk taking as well. Falling within the circle of Sensuality, sexual behavior involves sensations, sexual thoughts, and fantasies. Through sexual behavior, individuals may increase their understanding of how sexuality is used to influence power dynamics, encompassing the circle of sexualization as well.

The Swiss developmental psychologist Jean Piaget (1952) lends useful information to this discussion with stages of mental processing capabilities. Piaget's (1952) stages of cognitive development identify late adolescents to be capable of formal operational thought. This marks the ability to deal with hypothetical deductive reasoning and connecting larger thoughts and concepts. This developmental stage gives support for the pedagogical belief that students can comprehend and navigate the many facets that make up the complex nature of sexuality discussed above. Related to the *Circles of Sexuality*, formal operational thought provides individuals with the ability to understand complex ideas involved in gender identity. The intricacies of concepts in the circle of Sexual Identity such as orientation, gender identity, and gender roles all require higher-level thinking when incorporating them into one's identity. Also in the circle of Sensuality, messages about how the media affects body image require an understanding of society, cognitive processing, and the role of the media in consumer life (Slade, 1994).

The developmental psychologist Erik H. Erikson (1963, 1968) explained the psychosocial crisis that college-aged students may encounter in their time in higher education. A psychosocial crisis is the state of tension that results from the discord between a person's skill level at the beginning of a stage and what behaviors society expects from them (Erikson, 1963). For Erikson, many people in this age group are met with the psychosocial crisis of navigating identity. People in this age range experience the formation of an identity (ego-identity) as opposed to identity confusion. In this psychosocial crisis, Erikson believes individuals create their identity through their interactions with others. Supported by data from Marcia (1966), young adults are using this developmental time for exploration and synthesizing their experience of society and the subjective experience of self, searching for continuity within themselves.

Within the *Circles of Sexuality*, the circle of Sexual Identity is directly related to this psychosocial crisis. Placing oneself in the context of society is the exact struggle faced during this stage. Discovering different components of oneself—how one identifies their gender, if and to whom they are sexually attracted, what that means for people around them, etc.—incorporate a greater understanding of how one's sexual identity is also a part of their role in society.

Using data from the National Survey of Family Growth, a nationally representative survey of men and women aged 15–44 conducted by the National Center for Health Statistics, Finer and Philbin (2013) found that 61% of 18-year-olds and 71% of 19-year-olds are reported to have had sexual intercourse. Sex and sexuality are ample plains for students to navigate in-group–out-group dynamics and clearly navigate their own identity and behavior with others. Newer data suggests that as high as 85% of people aged 18–24 have engaged in sexual intercourse (Copen et al., 2016). This data indicates that the synthesizing of society and self is rife with peer knowledge and likely personal exposure to sexual interaction.

In the *Circles of Sexuality*, society can be seen to interact with several different circles. The above statistics indicate that a large number of students are sexually active. On a societal level, the circle of Sexual Health and Reproduction includes access to sexual health information—where people might acquire such information and how their knowledge of sexual health may affect those around them (i.e., pregnancy, STIs, etc.). Exposure to sexual interaction might also encompass the use of sex for money or withholding sex from partners to achieve a desired outcome, falling into the circle of Sexualization.

Daniel Levinson et al. (1978) discussed adult life stages in his book *Seasons of a Man's Life*, followed by a work with Judy Levinson and Levinson (1996), *Seasons of a Woman's Life*. These stages, based on Erikson's developmental stages, are focused on adulthood, relationships, and life milestones. And while the initial study with men can be used with women as well, Levinson and Levinson acknowledge that women have different resources and constraints (Pringle & McCulloch Dixon, 2003). For Levinson (1978), the early adulthood transition (ages 17–22) is seen as the time one makes the preliminary choices of one's adult life. College can be a time when people begin to express their autonomy being away from parental control (Mullendore & Hatch, 2000) and exercise that autonomy in daily choices. Navigating the way one behaves sexually (with self and others) is one of the many personal and relational realities faced in this transition to early adulthood.

The *Circles of Sexuality* have many components concerning choices of behavior in one's life. Within the circle of Sensuality, decisions are made about how one exhibits sexual behaviors, explores arousal, and identifies sensual pleasures. Concepts from other circles include which type of birth control, if any, to use (circle of Sexual Health and Reproduction), what they want dating to look like in their lives (circle of Intimacy), what types of people they will date or how they will express their gender identity (circle of Sexual Identity) and are all decided upon in this stage. Making these choices for oneself at this age will inform how they will continue to make these decisions moving forward.

Arnett (2000) built on the developmental models of Erikson and Levinson to discuss the age range of 18–25 as emerging adulthood. He described this stage as a common place for individuals to explore worldviews, types of work, intimate relationships, and sexuality in a way that lays a foundation for adult identity. For Arnett, this stage exists only in cultures that allow for a prolonged period of role exploration during the late teens and twenties (or college-age). This further exploration of sexuality and relationships lends itself to the synthesis of one's understanding of the world by gaining other viewpoints against which to compare and synthesize with one's own.

The foundational developmental theories listed above (largely put forth by psychologists) give a background on the life-stage position and cognitive tools at student's disposal. In the higher education literature, many different cognitive and student development theories have been proposed (Astin, 1984; Baxter Magolda, 1992; Belenky et al., 1986; Chickering & Reisser, 1993; King & Kitchener, 1994; Perry, 1970; Schlossberg et al., 1995), the majority of which build on the previous foundational developmental theorists. While expressing different processes, these theories all entail a path of growth that involves the emergence of an individual's own role as knower and authority. Each theory serves an important purpose for understanding students' experiences in university life. To contextualize student exploration of sexuality, I will focus on identity development, intellectual and epistemological stages, and the context of behavior in transition and involvement.

Chickering's (1969) and Chickering and Reisser (1993) student development theory has specific self-reflective components that are pertinent to the struggle college students may encounter regarding sexuality. His seven vectors, like many of the other theories, involve growth through integrating one's subjective experience with the world around them. Unlike the developmental theories above, however, this theory does not necessarily correspond with ages and are instead conceptualized as developmental vectors. Originally proposed in 1969, Chickering reworked the vectors in 1993 with the help of Linda Reisser. Chickering's (1969; Chickering & Reisser, 1993) seven vectors include developing competence, managing emotions, moving through autonomy toward interdependence, developing mature interpersonal relationships, establishing identity, developing purpose, and developing integrity.

Chickering and Reisser (1993) identified the first vector, *developing competence*, as involving the cultivation of the intellectual, interpersonal, and manual competence to manage interactions in college. This vector involves gaining skills necessary to comprehend, analyze, and synthesize their college experience. It is in student's reception of accurate feedback from others that their sense of competence increases, and they gain a stable sense of self-assurance.

The second vector, *managing emotions*, involves the recognition and healthy management of feelings such as anger, fear, anxiety, tension, depression, boredom, hurt, longing, desire, guilt, and shame (Chickering & Reisser, 1993). The theorists noted students must identify, regulate, and balance emotions in a way that they do not result in destructive tendencies (i.e., aggression, defense, etc.) but rather participatory tendencies.

Third, the *moving through autonomy toward interdependence* vector considers the process of gaining self-sufficiency and taking responsibility for pursuing one's own goals, followed by the recognition and acceptance of interdependence (Chickering & Reisser, 1993). For Chickering and Reisser, motivating oneself and solving problems in a self-directed way enables healthier forms of interdependence. They described this as a balance between being independent and longing for inclusion—respecting the autonomy of others, looking for ways to give and take.

Chickering and Reisser's (1993) fourth vector, *developing mature interpersonal relationships*, includes developing interpersonal and intercultural tolerance, and creating healthy intimate relationships. They described two major components of this vector: (1) the tolerance and appreciation of differences and (2) the capacity for intimacy. The authors identified that the capacity for healthy intimacy increases with a resulting shift in the quality of relationship with intimate partners and close friends.

The fifth vector, *establishing identity*, relies on the four previously mentioned vectors: competence, emotional maturity, autonomy, and positive relationships (Chickering & Reisser, 1993). This synthesis involves the emergence of an "I" who has a body that looks a certain way and feels a certain way about self, society, historical context, ethnicity, roles, and values. These are the components that make one distinct as the knower and authority acting in the world. This vector involves reflecting on one's historical and cultural connections and being able to contextualize oneself within them.

For Chickering and Reisser (1993), the sixth vector of *developing purpose* constitutes goals, commitments, and interests that emerge as important to oneself. The theorists pointed to vocation as paid or unpaid work (or both) that give a person meaning in their experience of society. They noted that clear values then help with the decision-making process often encountered during the many compromises one must make as an adult.

The last vector, *developing integrity*, like establishing identity, involves the synthesis of one's values with one's actions. Humanizing and personalizing values (or affirming core values) then allow an individual to make them congruent with one's social behavior. These sequential but overlapping stages described by the authors (humanizing of values, personalizing of values, and determining congruence) are the main components of this vector. Students are then able to understand the implications of a situation, clearly comprehend the consequences of alternative choices, and respond with conviction.

These seven vectors examine the human experience broadly and explicitly identify many ways in which a student can grow. Because most developmental theories pay little attention to emotions and relationships, Chickering and Reisser (1993) make it a point to include them as integral parts of this student development theory. In the *managing emotions* vector, they identify sexual desires as a major component of life and that learning to manage desires along with the accompanying emotions is a key part of student development. In the fifth vector, *establishing identity*, the theorists include things like body image, gender, and sexual orientation. Explicit mention of these aspects of personhood and interpersonal interaction—body image (circle of Sensuality), sexual orientation (circle of Sexual Identity), and healthy relationships (circle of Intimacy)—are what make these vectors stand apart from other student development theories. Chickering and Reisser (1993) identified these aspects of the student experience as important to the development of one's identity. Chickering (1969) observed that "independence and autonomy reveal shackles and barriers not recognized or felt before" (p. 40). The university setting can be a place where students are just learning about the various concepts in the *Circles of Sexuality* differently than in their adolescent years—a process that is developmentally appropriate and often in need of support.

Both epistemological stages (or ways of knowing) by Baxter Magolda (1992) and Belenky et al. (1986) include a transition from safety in universal truths to understanding subjective difference—certainty and safety in knowing truths from others through stages culminating in the integration or subjective knowledge, experience, and context. Similar to Perry's (1968, 1970, 1981) intellectual and ethical development, rather than seeing the world as dichotomous, a student's view is expanded to recognize subjectivity in the viewpoints of others. This growth culminates in an ongoing process of commitment to trusting that the viewpoints of others are right for them, together with a continuous reevaluation of these commitments. All three of these theories do not have general ages attached to each stage. This indicates that students in college may be growing through any one of these developmental stages while attempting to manage any component of sexuality. For example, the decision for a student to have sex for the first time, experiment with a new sexual behavior, or how to talk to friends about gender stereotypes may be more or less difficult depending on where they are developmentally, regardless of class (freshman, sophomore, junior, or senior). These examples in the circles of Sensuality and Sexual Identity are just a few of the many encounters students may have with sexuality in their college life.

Schlossberg's (1995) transition theory is important to the discussion of student sexual atmosphere as a model through which we understand the tools students have at their disposal when navigating challenging sexual situations or information. Schlossberg (1995) identified four major factors that influence a person's ability to cope in transition: situation, self, support, and strategy. Successes in coping with transition are influenced by the *situation*—what triggered it, timing in the student's life, previous experience in similar situations, etc. *Self* refers to the feelings and attitudes that one has toward the transition and the ability one possesses to deal with such transition. *Support* constitutes the types of social supports one has at their disposal. And *strategy* refers to the coping skills used in times of transition—action/inaction, reframing, and self-care. Mullendore and Hatch (2000) identify college as a time of great transition for students, including a change in parental supervision, freedom, and value judgements.

Students can experience transition within various *Circles of Sexuality*. Transition can happen around sexual orientation, gender identity or how to act or operate with people of the other gender (circle of Sexual Identity), how to make choices regarding a new sexual behavior (circles of Sensuality or Sexual Health and Reproduction), or how to terminate or have successful intimate relationships (circle of Intimacy). Confronting these transitions with a lack of language or skills in dealing with matters of sexuality can pose problems for successful navigation of transition.

Finally, Astin's (1984) involvement theory describes the role of student involvement in learning. Though Astin wrote specifically about student involvement in campus life with a strong emphasis on retention of students, it is also true for students' social behavior. For Astin (1984), growth and learning occur for students when they are engaged with their environments. Carl Roger's (1969) concept of student-centered learning reinforces this idea in an educational, cognitive, and social context. When students engage and learn when interacting with peers in classroom or social settings. Often in university life outside of the classroom, students will engage with matters of sexuality in many ways—navigating social norms involving sexual jokes (circle of Sexualization), how to engage in the dating culture (circles of Sensuality and Intimacy), or gauging the university climate for safe spaces to come out as non-heterosexual or not cisgender (circle of Sexual Identity). Student growth and learning about matters of sexuality are happening whether the school actively engages with these topics or not.

The purpose of introducing the above theories is to contextualize the developmental landscape in which many college students are navigating choices and realities involving sexuality. Numerous facets of the *Circles of Sexuality* such as choices of how to flirt, whom to engage with sexually, how to engage with people of the same or other genders, how to observe the institutional rules for each particular gender, how to make sexually healthy choices congruent with one's sense of self/values, and many other options are all present at this time in a student's life. This context for where students are developmentally lays a foundation for understanding how they may operate around matters of sexuality in higher education.

Of the students entering college, some choose to attend one over 226 Catholic institutions of higher education in the United States (Association of Catholic Colleges and Universities, 2022). Some students make intentional choices about having this next phase of their lives in a Catholic context. Focusing their education on liberal arts and the development of the whole person, exploring evolving ideas of spirituality, or participating in local and global community engagement are just a few reasons students may choose a Catholic college or university (Tarrant, 2016). Participating in social, volunteer, leadership, and community service activities can also be important parts of this spiritual or religious development (Love, 2001).

Importance of Faith Life and Development

Religiously affiliated colleges and universities have been a place from which many students seek education while maintaining a connection to their religious identity (Pascarella & Terenzini, 1991). Studies show that religious influence can have a positive impact on academic performance (Mooney, 2010; Sherkat, 2007). While academic performance is important, these religious institutions are also the context for the intersecting development of faith life or religion and sexuality.

Describing the complex relationship between religion, sexuality, and self, McCarty (2009) commented that "dialogue on religion and sexuality is difficult because these topics consist of deeply seated concepts of self, as well as one's relationship to other selves in the world" (p. 45). He continues to explain that people experience this difficulty "as they engage in self-exploration, whether by challenging boundaries, clinging to traditions, or exploring new avenues of being" (p. 45). This notion of self-exploration is consistent with the developmental theorists noted above. Recognizing this difficulty is important for further understanding the intersections of faith, sexuality, and student development.

This time period of developmental navigation (Arnett, 2000) involves not only sexuality, but synthesizing one's religious affiliation as well. (Callegher, 2010; Lee, 2002). In a study of 12 Canadian Catholic college students, Callegher (2010) found that students were open to negotiating the rigidity of Catholic morality in their own development and perceptions of the world—remaining Catholic while not completely condemning homosexuality. Similarly, through interviews on the college experience and how it relates to students' religion, Lee (2002) examined Catholic students' experience of their emerging identity and religious change in college. In Lee's study, both social and academic encounters on campus caused students to reevaluate their beliefs, but not to abandon their faith. Both studies identify the coexistence of identity development and faith negotiation around matters sexuality.

This negotiation of faith, morality, and development can look different in various settings. Donna Freitas (2008) in her book *Sex and the Soul* conducted qualitative surveys about the intersection of spirituality and sexuality with 534 students from seven different colleges and qualitative interviews with 111 randomly selected students. She noted many Catholic students exhibited a feeling of apathy or hostility toward their recollection of being taught about sexuality—highlighting words like shoved, pushed, and forced. She concluded that this hostility toward the force-feeding of faith they had experienced at home was relieved by the common notion on Catholic campuses that religion and faith are private experiences between an individual and their God.

These studies point to common experiences in negotiation of faith around matters of sexuality. One example of where this negotiation occurs most saliently is in the experience of sexual minority students.

The Experience of Sexual Minorities and Faith

When considering identity development and how to synthesize one's own convictions with their experience of the world, sexual orientation—one component of sexual identity—must be taken into account. A physician named Lars Ullerstam (1966) wrote a book called *The Erotic Minorities* in which he identified people with sexual affiliations apart from the mainstream as "sexual minorities." While this term was originally meant to include various types of what was called "deviant" sexual behavior, contemporary research uses the term with a more stringent definition in mind. In the research literature, "sexual minority" is a term often used to designate the orientation of study participants that are not heterosexual.

An oft-cited study on the religious conflicts experienced by lesbian, gay, and bisexual (LGB) individuals conducted by Schuck and Liddle (2001) found that approximately two-thirds of the 66 respondents had conflict between their sexual and religious identities. Factors such as denominational teachings, scripture, and congregational prejudice impacted this experience. This two-thirds number was also prevalent in a later study by Dahl and Galliher (2010) of 106 sexual minority young adults. The authors came to the conclusion that it was intolerance and perceived conflict that left respondents feeling frustrated, disillusioned, or alienated within religious organizations. They claimed that it was these factors that possibly lead to participants' disidentification with a religion.

Students with a sexual minority experience are also likely to experience discrimination on college campuses (Love, 1998). In the education setting, Francis et al. (2014) surveyed 271 secondary school students in the United Kingdom and found that students from Christian schools held more conservative sexual morality attitudes in general compared to their non-sectarian counterparts. The application of this study information is limited due to cultural context (the United Kingdom rather than the United States) and age group (13–15-year-olds rather than 18–24-year-olds). However, due to the global reach of Catholicism (Morey & Piderit, 2006) it can be considered that Catholic college and university students that come from Catholic secondary schools may also have more conservative sexual attitudes. With the fear of conservative university members, the coming out process can be perceived as quite difficult (Miceli, 2009).

Love (1998) explored cultural barriers facing LGB students at Catholic colleges. Data from interviews of 26 LGB individuals along with ally staff at a US Catholic college were coded for barriers to a positive experience at the university. Love found that students were likely to experience homophobia, heterosexism, discomfort with sexuality (erotophobia), invisibility, and stigma as a result of the Catholic culture on campus.

With the *Circles of Sexuality* as a framework for understanding sexuality in someone's life, combined with the developmental theories, and a look at how students make sense of their sexual and religious identities, we have a foundation for understanding that college is a highly developmental time around matters of sexuality. We can now look at higher education as a stage for these developmental changes, followed by a look at specific issues of sexuality in higher education.

Higher Education Management of Developmental Changes

Much of higher education addresses these developmental concerns with a focus on first-year college students' experience (Kidwell & Reising, 2005). Kidwell and Reising (2005) reflected on students who enter the college experience and encounter the world in a very different way than their middle and high school years. With an account of how students grow in methods of learning from dualistic (certainty about one or the other) to multiplicity (that there is more than what they "know"), the authors gave witness to the operationalization of the developmental and learning theories mentioned above. Many resources exist for parents, educators, and administrators (Ender & Newton, 2000; Mullendore & Hatch, 2000; Zuker, n.d.) in higher education that focus on applying these theories to the experience of first-year students.

These developmental and learning theories also sit within another context in higher education—the perceived intention of higher education. A lecture at the University of Cambridge by C. P. Snow (1959), a British novelist/scientist, in the mid-20th century sparked the discussion of education in industrialized societies. He described two different academic cultures: literary intellectuals on one end and (physical) scientists on the other. Snow observed that on a societal level, in the workplace and education, these fields seem to be at odds—not communicating—describing what he experienced as a social and political self-differentiation by each group. Snow described this split as a "mutual incomprehension ... hostility, dislike, but most of all, lack of understanding" (p. 4). In this apparent feud, literary intellectuals viewed scientists as brash, boastful, and unaware of the human condition, while scientists saw non-scientists as lacking foresight, unconcerned with society, and anti-intellectual.

Mediating this hostility, Snow spoke against polarizing these fields claiming that science "has got to be assimilated along with [art], and as part and parcel of, the whole of our mental experience, and used as naturally as the rest" (Snow, 1959, p. 18). The bifurcation that Snow lamented still exists in some ways in education today. More recently, Buller (2014) articulated this dichotomy in terms of the purpose of higher education: liberal arts education versus job preparation. Buller spoke specifically from the lens of academic freedom and administrators being driven toward STEM education, minimizing funding for the humanities.

Job preparation versus liberal arts education stands as a backdrop for the current higher education climate. Scholars are still echoing Snow's sentiment of having science and the arts work together (Bevins, 2011). While there is no consensus in general higher education today (Benson & Boyd, 2015; Shapiro, 2005), Catholic colleges and universities generally espouse a liberal arts education that often focuses specifically on whole person development (Morey & Piderit, 2006). This close tie of Catholic institutional use of liberal arts education should not be mistaken for a "religion versus science" dichotomy—a claim that is apparently popular enough to require mention. In a column dedicated to updating Snow's historic essay, Krauss (2009) wrote to those who polarize this dichotomy as religion versus the sciences. Krauss said Snow was not railing against religion, but ignorance—likely focusing on what Snow calls the intellectual loss. A loss that, according to a number of educational institutions, seems to be resolving with a growing belief that STEM and liberal arts work hand-in-hand (Klebnikov, 2015).

Although the debate still continues today in higher education at large, the Catholic liberal arts focus on how to make students more well-rounded, socially conscious people has been a notion supported by the American Council on Education (1937, 1949) prior to the 1960s. Specific to this study, Catholic colleges and universities have had a standing tradition of focusing on the totality and meaning of the human person—for moral implications and the development of the whole person (John Paul II, 1990).

Issues of Sexuality in Higher Education

As noted above, because of the ubiquity of sexuality in the human experience, its presence permeates many facets of university life. Largely grouped into sexuality within oneself and interactions with others, higher education has had a history of addressing and resolving these issues in many different ways. Brief examples of areas of sexuality in higher education include the way sexuality is taught in a variety of departmental courses (Galbreath, 2012; Moglia, 1994; Myerson, 1992; Stephens & Ott, 2020), sports and Title IX information (Francis, 2016; Office for Civil Rights, 2021; Rubin & Lough, 2015), gendered bathrooms (Greytak et al., 2009; Sausa, 2002), living arrangements of students (Buckner, 1981; Erlandson, 2014), student sexual activity (McAnulty, 2012), the way a university views individuals with minority sexual identities (Cramer, 2002), how sexual assault is addressed on campus (Ottens & Hotelling, 2001), where to find resources for sexual health information or counseling (Eisenberg, Lechner et al., 2012b), and in some cases morality clauses for employees (Fleming et al., 2009).

On the topic of sexual activity on college campuses, McAnulty (2012) compiled a book about sex in college life. By describing possible issues in sexuality present on college campuses, this text identified several categories. Possible components of sexuality in college life include sex, intimacy and dating (Perlman & Sprecher, 2012), love (Regan, 2012), infidelity (McAnulty & McAnulty, 2012), sexual orientation (Kauth & Bradford, 2012), sexual risk taking (Gil-Rivas, 2012), and even sexual problems and dysfunctions (Kleinplatz, 2012). All of these components encompass at least one (if not more) circle of sexuality that college students may (and administrators will!) encounter.

Curriculum

Sexuality has been addressed in university curricula through a variety of departments—biology, social science, and health fields as described by Myerson (1992). Supported by other scholars, sexuality has also been called for to be addressed academically in departments of psychology, theology (Stephens & Ott, 2020), anthropology, cultural and developmental studies (Moglia, 1994), and women and gender studies (Galbreath, 2012). This reality of interdisciplinary ubiquity was described by the philosopher-psychologist John Money (1982) when he claimed that the study of sexuality is multivariate and not just one of these areas by itself. Such courses have been shown to reduce levels of homophobia (Rogers et al., 2009; Wright & Cullen, 2001) and even enhance interpersonal relationships (Henry, 2013).

Sports and Title IX

Another way that higher education deals with issues of sexuality is in athletics and gender discrimination. Title IX of the Education Amendment Act of 1972 prohibits discrimination based on sex in education programs and activities in federally funded schools (Office for Civil Rights, 2021). Claiming to protect from all forms of sex discrimination (Office for Civil Rights, 2021), Title IX has been, for many years, the basis for requiring sports teams for women (Rubin & Lough, 2015). While Title IX may have originally focused on gender equity as experienced by athletic departments, it also protects against sexual violence, coercion, assault, and gender discrimination including gender- or sex-based harassment (Office for Civil Rights, 2021). This movement within higher education resulted in attempted sports team equity (Francis, 2016; Rubin & Lough, 2015), sexual harassment policies, and sexual assault prevention programs (Ottens & Hotelling, 2001).

Gendered Bathrooms

Related to Title IX's claim to protect from discrimination based on gender identity (Office for Civil Rights, 2021) is the growing issue of gendered bathrooms (Greytak et al., 2009; Sausa, 2002). In writing about updating higher education policies to meet the needs of transgender students, Sausa (2002) identified safety in bathrooms and locker rooms as one of the key issues facing transgender students today. In a report on the experience of transgender youth in US schools, Greytak et al. (2009) recount that there are policies and practices that enforce gender segregation in these areas, making it a difficult and potentially dangerous situation for many transgender students. Pertinent to the present study, concerns are being raised about the protection of transgender students under Title IX in schools who may claim a religious exemption in order to avoid accommodations (Bryk, 2015). Encompassed by the circle of sexuality having to do with gender identity, discussing topics of transgender students' safety and university policy are another facet of sexuality in higher education.

Living Arrangements

Another example of an area in higher education in which issues of sexuality may arise is in student living arrangements such as residence halls and dormitories. Living environments have been a topic of discussion in higher education in recent years, spanning coed and gender-inclusive living environments (Hobson, 2014; Willoughby et al., 2012) and sexual privacy (Erlandson, 2014). Buckner (1981) discussed coed living arrangements as a positive way for students to begin challenging ideas of stereotypes and continuing constructive conversations about sex differences outside of the classroom. He proposed programs of this type may be beneficial in helping students explore sex role differences. This claim is supported by the growing body of literature about institutional implementation of gender-neutral housing (Hobson, 2014; Willoughby et al., 2012).

Focusing on Ohio University and gender inclusivity, Hobson (2014) documented the need for and implementation of gender-neutral housing policies. She concluded with a call for more universities to do the same—a call that Willoughby et al. (2012) pre-empted in examining over 140 universities' discussions of gender-neutral housing policy. Willoughby and colleagues found that policies were developing on the west and east coasts as well as in the Midwest for gender inclusion, and will in the future likely include heterosexual romantic couples.

Whether it is exploring sex roles or sexual activity, residence halls are rife with potential issues of sexuality. Erlandson (2014) studied how college students navigate privacy for sexual activity. Of the 164 participants, an overwhelming majority (82%) have dealt with some form of request for privacy from their roommates for sexual activity—a term the author identifies colloquially as *sexiled* (Erlandson, 2014). Whether it is sexual privacy or gendered housing, living arrangements will likely include aspects related to sexuality.

Minority Sexual Identities

Another aspect of sexuality encountered in higher education is policy around those with sexual minority identities. In an edited book on addressing homophobia and heterosexism, Cramer (2002) addressed the need for colleges and universities to take a closer look at the way sexual minority individuals were being treated. Citing several studies about LGBT students' likelihood of experiencing harassment, discrimination, and intimidation (Bochenek & Brown, 2001; D'Augelli, 1992; Franklin, 1998; Herek, 1993; Westefeld et al., 2001), Cramer compiled a review of the literature and recommendations for a variety of practices in higher education. From safe space and ally training (Draughn et al., 2002) to recommendations for policy adjustment concerning transgender students (Sausa, 2002), and classroom environmental and educational practices to raise awareness of discrimination against sexual minority students (Bennett, 2002; Yep, 2002; Zavalkoff, 2002), this compilation of essays described the adjustment of practices and policies in higher education stemming from a difference in sexual orientation and identity.

Sexual Assault

Sexual assault is an increasing concern on college and university campuses in the United States (Ottens & Hotelling, 2001; White House Task Force to Protect Students From Sexual Assault, 2014). The conversation on sexual assault in college and university life has expanded from a discussion of exclusively heterosexual female-focused acquaintance rape (Lonsway, 1996) and date rape (Muehlenhard & Linton, 1987) to begin including LGBTQ individuals (National Coalition of Anti-Violence Programs, 2012; Tuel, 2001) and men as well (Bullock & Beckson, 2011). Male sexual assault in college is becoming more of a topic discussed in the media while resources for men may seem limited (Kassie, 2015).

Issues of sexuality are not only present in the fact that sexual assault is about sexual behaviors, but issues of gender and relationship are also key factors in rape prevention education (Fouts & Knapp, 2001). An older study of mixed and single sex educational formats showed that only the all-male cohort displayed any reduction in rape-related attitudes and myths (Berkowitz, 1994). Concerning education with men on college campuses, participant perceptions of masculinity and gender norms have been shown to be key factors in effective education (Rich et al., 2010).

Sexual Health Information

Another issue of sexuality that may arise on college campuses is the access to sexual health information, counseling, or resources. Historically, the most prevalent aspects of resources availability in the research literature have been condom distribution programs (Blake et al., 2003; Kirby et al., 1999; Schuster et al., 1998) and LGBT resources (Eisenberg, 2002; Fine, 2012). Eisenberg, Lechner, et al. (2012a) assessed sexual resource availability at 28 colleges in one US state. Although the availability of resources seemed directly tied to the presence of a health center on campus, the researchers suggest providing links and referrals to sexual health resources in the community (clinics/websites) which could assist in addressing the sexual health needs of students (Eisenberg, Lechner, et al., 2012a). Making these resources available can influence the students' perceptions of resource accessibility, their own comfort, or resource usefulness (Eisenberg, Garcia, et al., 2012b). Discussing students' interest in and comfort with sexual health information and resource availability is another aspect of sexuality in the higher education setting.

Morality Clauses

The conversation about sexuality does not only affect students. At times, the reach of sexuality in higher education can impact employees' positions as well. Some religious colleges and universities will require faculty and staff members to sign morality clauses, using "immoral behavior" as grounds for termination (Fleming et al., 2009). Whether describing illegal or criminal behavior, or more unclear connection of employee sexual relations in their personal life, Fleming et al. (2009) describe the complexities that morality clauses encounter in the courts, such as specific institutional regulations and the lack of clear language at some universities. Employees may face difficult or challenging choices in life that could threaten their jobs under such clauses (DeBernardo & Shine, 2021).

The above examples of sexuality in higher education, whether in courses, extracurricular activities, discrimination laws, gendered bathrooms, sexual minorities, sexual assault, sexual health information, or morality clauses play a part in the sexual lives of people in the university setting. These realities are present in higher education public and private, religious and non-sectarian schools alike. The specific context for the present study is Catholic higher education—a contextual difference to consider more in-depth first by a brief look at sexuality and Catholicism, and then at the cultural context of how that plays out in Catholic higher education.

Sexuality and Catholicism

This study was placed within the context of Catholicism and higher education. To better understand sexuality in Catholic higher education, let's look briefly at some important aspects of Catholicism and sexuality that influence the present-day intersection of these two concepts.

Catholicism has a long history with sexuality (Salzman & Lawler, 2008). Being a faith tradition within Christianity, one of the largest religions in the world (Pew Research Center, 2012), the Catholic Church has encountered sexuality as part of the human existence for centuries (e.g., sexual desires, marriage, conception, etc.) (Kosnik et al., 1977). While it would be quite extensive and beyond the scope of this work to detail this historical journey, let's briefly address some important aspects of sexuality in the history of the Catholic Church that may be impacting the current beliefs and attitudes toward sexuality in Catholic institutions of higher education. After addressing key historical points, we can identify some of the more recent church documents that likely influence some contemporary Catholics' views on issues of sexuality.

Points in Catholic History

Augustine

Throughout the history of the Christian Church, likely the largest influence on sexuality in church doctrine is Augustine of Hippo (354–430 C.E.) (Fox, 1995). As the Bishop of Hippo (396–430), Augustine contributed many lasting works to Christian theology, including the concepts of Grace, the unity of the church in love, the cross and resurrection of Christ, and the Trinity (Levering, 2013). Augustine also influenced church history with theology on human nature, specifically the Doctrine of Original Sin which was partly accepted by the Church Council of Orange in 529 C.E. (Bokenkotter, 2004). In the early parts of his life, Augustine had been influenced by Manicheism—as a heresy of the time that focused on the dualistic nature of the body (evil) and spirit (good) (Augustine of Hippo, 1960). In his theology of humanity, he saw sexual drives as sinful and full of shame (Bourke, 1958). And while some scholars insist that a correct understanding of Augustine's views on sexuality must be considered within the context of his doctrine of the lust for power (Bonner, 1962) and writings of his earlier years (Hunter, 1994), his view of sexuality is still critiqued as being particularly pessimistic (Farley, 2006; Genovesi, 1996; Kosnik et al., 1977).

Augustine saw any sexual pleasure, even for procreation within marriage, as being somewhat sinful (Augustine of Hippo, 1887; Hunter, n.d.). In one of his most influential works, *The Confessions*, Augustine's attitudes toward the power of sexual desire frequently reflect its sinful disposition: "Clouds arose from the slimy desires of the flesh ... swept my feeble youth over the crags of desire and plunged me into a whirlpool of shameful deeds" (Augustine of Hippo, 1960, p. 65). In a review of sexuality and Catholicism, Fox (1995) observed that the story of human sexuality has been strewn with ignorance, fear, corruption, and abusive power—identifying Augustine as having a lasting pessimism on sexuality in the Catholic Church.

Aquinas

The writings of Thomas Aquinas took the next logical step. As a medieval scholastic, Aquinas attempted to understand these theological truths through reason and disciplined philosophical methods (Fox, 1995). Following the logical progression of Augustinian thought, Aquinas fleshed out natural law and how sexuality's main goal is procreation (Sigmund, 1988). Bridging the discourse between Augustine and the Greek philosopher Aristotle, Aquinas departed from Augustine's suspicion of sexual pleasure—sexual pleasure can be seen as good and not immoral, but as long as procreation is the end goal, and not the pleasure itself (Fox, 1995; Kosnik et al., 1977).

Jansenism

Another possible source of lasting impact on sexuality in US Catholic culture is Jansenism and its strictness of adherence, specifically around sexuality (Messenger, 1993). Jansenism was a Catholic theological movement originating from the posthumously published work of the Dutch theologian Cornelius Jansen, who died in 1638 (Bokenkotter, 2004). Originating in France, this movement emphasized original sin, human depravity, the necessity of divine grace, and predestination (Scheper-Hughes, 1983; Sedgwick, 1990). When the French clerics migrated to Ireland (because they were exiled due to this strict interpretation of human depravity), the Irish respect for clerical power was an ideal setting for the repression of all bodily realities, specifically sexuality (Scheper-Hughes, 1983). Reaching its zenith in the 1930s, Jansenist influence led to notions of bodily suffering and punishment as giving glory to God (Messenger, 1993).

This focus on bodily suffering has impacted Irish culture for several centuries, as evidenced in a recent study by Kitchin and Lysaght (2004). In an ethnographic study, the authors discussed sexuality with inhabitants of rural Ireland. The researchers identified correlations of the taboo nature of sexuality with historical influences of Jansenism. After reviewing historical documents, they observed the closeness of the church and the state in Ireland resulted in an intertwining of secular civility and Catholic morality—beliefs within a church setting (Catholic/Jansenist) became cultural and societal norms for all citizens. This is an attitude about sexuality that some link to Irish-American Catholicism and that is presumed to have had an impact on American culture (Messenger, 1993).

Sex Abuse Scandal

Examining sexuality through a contemporary Catholic lens cannot be done without considering the sex abuse scandal that became public knowledge through the 1980s and 1990s (Maher et al., 2006). Knowledge of sexual abuse by priests grew until stories of sexual assault by priests were reported in a story in the Boston Globe in 2002 (Steinfels, 2002). The stories of abuse led to questions which yielded the bishops' constant movement of offending priests into different parishes, which many see as the primary scandal (Ammicht-Quinn et al., 2004; Plante, 2004; Rimassa, 2002; The Investigative Staff of the Boston Globe, 2002). The aftermath of this investigation resulted in responses by the Catholic Church in many forms: constructing committees (Dempsey et al., 1992), the creation of training programs to train church employees to be aware of predatory behaviors (The National Catholic Risk Retention Group, 1999), charters that commissioned studies (Terry et al., 2011), and the awareness of similar scandals occurring in various countries such as Ireland, which resulted in an encyclical from Pope Benedict XVI (2010) condemning such abuse of children and power. Scholars discussed clergy's fear of the topic of sexuality (Rimassa, 2002) and their suffering from prejudice as a result of the scandal (Nines, 2006). It is clear that this sexual abuse scandal has made a lasting impression on the American Catholic Church and how sexuality is discussed in the Catholic context (Morey & Piderit, 2006). If changes around sexuality are happening in Catholic higher education, there might be sensitivity to the abuse of power and potential harmful outcomes of sex in light of this scandal.

Contemporary Church Documents

In understanding present-day applications of theological past, another component to consider is the teaching of the Catholic Church. The mission of Catholicism, laid out in the document *Dei Verbum* (Dogmatic Constitution on Divine Revelation), is derived from three main sources: tradition, scripture, and the magisterium (or teaching office) of the church (Flannery, 1996). These are the three channels from which the church draws its wisdom. Along with the historical traditions and the bible, the church also promulgates documents on important matters as official church teaching.

One such important matter in the work of the Catholic Church is about theological anthropology. Concerning the nature of humanity (or human nature), theological anthropology is ultimately a discourse on how humans exist in relationship to God and others (Cortez, 2010). Sexuality is an inescapable reality that has a strong impact on religion (Schwarz, 2013). The Catholic theological anthropology, described in proclamations on human nature, is often where teachings about sexuality reside. There have been various writings throughout history concerning a Catholic theological anthropology. Below are some of the more recent church documents that address the nature of sexuality. A brief look at these documents will make clearer the relationship of Catholic identity to sexuality within institutions of higher education.

Humanae Vitae

An encyclical written by Pope Paul VI (1968), *Humanae Vitae* (Of Human Life), focused heavily on methods of birth control. It is a tradition in church documents to reaffirm the teachings of previous documents. In this document, Paul VI reaffirmed the meaning of sex and sexuality (unitive and procreative), marital love (the context for having sex), and parental responsibility in educating children about sexuality. New to this document was the focus on methods of birth control and contraception used by the general public. Within a Catholic theological anthropology, this call for a prohibition of artificial contraceptives (e.g., barrier methods, hormonal birth control, etc.) is rooted in natural law—that a prevention of pregnancy through these means is against the natural order (which is the joining of the male and female gametes causing fertilization). The letter does advocate for methods of natural family planning, as a couple is then open to the possibility of new life in sexual activity.

This document relates most explicitly to the *Circles of Sexuality* model in the circle of Sexual Health and Reproduction. In Catholic institutions, issues of sexuality will be impacted by these teachings. Issues of sexual behavior, access to contraceptives, and living arrangements are just a few matters impacted by this teaching. More on how this plays out in Catholic higher education below.

Persona Humana

A document put out by a special teaching office of the church called the Sacred Congregation for the Doctrine of the Faith (CDF) (1975) is called *Persona Humana* (On the Human Person) or the *Declaration on Certain Questions Concerning Sexual Ethics*. This document was written as a reaction concerning the pervasiveness of sexuality in books, reviews, magazines, and other means of social communication. The guiding concern was the corruption of morals, the most serious indication of which was the "unbridled exaltation of sex" (para.1). Major topics addressed in this document included masturbation, homosexuality, chastity, and the meaning of sex. With new trends in the world of sexuality in both social (e.g., sexual revolution) and scientific (e.g., homosexuality being removed from the DSM in 1973) communities, the CDF found it important to "repeat the Church's doctrine on certain particular points, in view of the urgent need to oppose serious errors and widespread aberrant modes of behavior" (para.6). For the church, it was important to reassert the Catholic stance on issues of morality—masturbation and homosexuality were disordered, chastity (or mediation of the sexual appetite) should be practiced, and the meaning of sexual intercourse was still unitive and procreative within the matrimonial bond. This document brought the church teachings on homosexuality and premarital sex to the forefront of the Catholic sexual morality discussion.

Within the *Circles of Sexuality*, issues of sexual behavior and sexual identity are heavily impacted by this teaching. Issues of sexual health often involve various behaviors contrary to this teaching, possibly leaving areas of development unaddressed. The treatment of sexual minorities often draws on this teaching as a justification for discrimination. How this plays out in Catholic institutions of higher education is addressed below.

Theology of the Body

Another important occurrence in the realm of Catholic sexual theology was a series of 129 lectures given by Pope John Paul II from 1979–1984 on the nature of the human person (Hogan, 2003; John Paul

II, 1979–1984) called *Theology of the Body* (TOB) and later compiled into book form (John Paul II, 1997). These talks focused on a variety of components of the human person such as the nature of being a man or a woman in relation to God, celibacy, virginity, marriage, and contraception. George Weigel, a biographer of John Paul II, called Theology of the Body a "theological time bomb" to have a tremendous effect reshaping Catholic thought on embodiment (West, 2003, p. xv). The work has inspired an entire institute dedicated to teaching the messages found in these lectures (tobinstitute.org, 2020).

In this theological anthropology, Pope John Paul II described the creation of one's man-ness or woman-ness as directly related to one's genital nature. One's sex determines who one is—a constituent part, rather than just an attribute, of a person that determines their original meaning (TOB, 10.1–10.2). He describes celibacy and virginity as a call to holiness in continence (sexual abstinence) and an ideal sexual state for the Kingdom of God (heaven) (TOB, 74). John Paul II links the scriptural reference to eunuchs—intersex individuals, or those whose genitals were mutilated by self or others and are unable to procreate—to people who are called to a life of abstinence for the sake of the Kingdom of God.

John Paul II reiterated and described marriage as the proper place for sexual activity (often referred to as the "conjugal" or "marital" act) (TOB, 125.2). He reflected on the human condition and the nuptial meaning of the body—that is, the body's design for a marital relationship (TOB, 14). Contraception then is contrary to procreativity, one of the two main purposes of sexual intercourse (and by extension, marriage), robbing it of its interior truth and thus ceases to be an act of love (TOB, 119).

Theology of the Body has had a wide reach, as each lecture has been designed to stand on its own for a general audience (Hogan, 2003). This influential theology has been accused of being particularly conservative (Goodstein, 2005) and has undergone Catholic criticism as well (Curran, 2006). Charles Curran, a Catholic moral theologian, critiqued the theological claims of John Paul II naming that they may not be appropriate for all bodies—specifically the elderly and unmarried (e.g., homosexual, single, widowed)—as the "nuptial meaning" of sexuality cannot apply to those in a non-nuptial state (Curran, 2006).

Other Documents

A series of other church documents comment on sexuality in various capacities. To further contextualize Catholic views on sexuality, various documents mention sexuality as something profoundly human and an integral part of our identities (United States Conference of Catholic

Bishops, 1991), deem parents as the first and foremost educators of children (Pontifical Council for the Family, 1995), and claim that acting on "homosexual inclinations" is morally wrong (Congregation for the Doctrine of the Faith, 1986) and that homosexuality is a pastoral concern deserving of love and respect (NCCB Committee on Marriage and Family, 1997). These documents are considered important to this study because an institution of Catholic higher education will be historically and traditionally bound to the Catholic church in its identity and how sexuality is described in university policy (John Paul II, 1990).

Doctrine Operationalized in Catholic Higher Education

Ex Corde Ecclesiae (From the Heart of the Church) (John Paul II, 1990) is a document written to describe the role of Catholic universities in the mission of the church. It focuses on the function of Catholic higher education as a hub for community and cultural transmission while also addressing more specific aspects that constitute a university (academic freedom, faculty faith affiliation, etc.). In this document, Pope John Paul II (1990) repeatedly stated that the goal of Catholic higher education is to educate the whole person. The holistic view of education is a position that Rausch (2010) recounted to be a tradition since the mid-16th century. *Humanitas* is translated from the Greek *paideia*—an ideology for educating a person into an adult capable of realizing their role in society so that they could take part in the community (Rausch, 2010). Educating the whole person is a notion commonly seen in the mission statements of many Catholic colleges and universities (Morey & Piderit, 2006). Sexuality then—one aspect of the whole person—is addressed (or not addressed) in many different ways in colleges and universities. Some methods of addressing matters of sexuality consider this crucial holistic aspect of education, while others do not. Let's examine a few brief examples of how issues of sexuality have been recently addressed in Catholic higher education.

Curriculum

In Catholic institutions today, many faculty and staff members are subject to suppressed academic freedom because of matters pertaining to sexuality in the curriculum (McCarty, 2014). In a recent article, religious studies professor Rich McCarty (2014) discussed how dangerous the church hierarchy can be to academic freedom as laid out in the document *Ex Corde Ecclesiae* (From the Heart of the Church) written by Pope John Paul II (1990). John Paul II identified that universities guarantee academic freedom "so long as the rights of the individual person and of the community are preserved within the confines of the truth and the common good" (John Paul II, 1990, para. 12). McCarty (2014) draws attention to the ambiguity of the terms "truth" and "common good" with concern about who gets to define these terms—a concern that, ultimately, it is the church and not the university that gets to define such terms.

When faculty members engage in academic dialogue on matters of sexuality, there might be risks of condemnation, intimidation, or silencing that interferes with academic freedom (McCarty, 2014). McCarty (2014) recounted bishops' condemnation of books on sexuality from Catholic theologians like Salzman and Lawler's (2008) book, *The Sexual Person*, on a renewed Catholic anthropology and Farley's (2006) book, *Just Love*, on justice and sexual love. McCarty noted that these books get condemned when their contents, even though engaging in honest academic dialogue, are viewed by the bishops as contrary to church teachings. He continued to describe the tension between the practice of academia and the US bishops—disagreement in academia is an opportunity for dialogue, though the bishops view this as dissent from the church.

Another point of curricular tension was the case of moral theologian Charles Curran's position being threatened at the Catholic University of America. Curran was called into question of dissent from church authority because of positions he held that varied from the church's authoritative teaching on matters including homosexuality, masturbation, premarital sex, and abortion (Editors, 1986). Because Curran taught Catholic theology as well as other moral viewpoints, his clerical status as a priest gave rise to the discussion of whether this was dissent from church teaching versus academic freedom (Editors, 1986). He maintained the position that this perceived dissent was a critical ethical evaluation of church teachings and was supported by past presidents of the Catholic Theological Society of America in a signed statement which addressed academic integrity by noting that "enemies of the Catholic Church in the United States have argued that Catholic colleges and universities are not independent academic institutions" (Editors, 1986, p. 237). They went on to note that "if Father Curran were removed from his position as a professor of theology at the Catholic University of America, it would be far more difficult to rebut this charge"—calling upon readers of the statement to consider the degree to which academic freedom applies at Catholic institutions (Editors, 1986, p. 237). The D.C. superior court noted the struggle of academic freedom and Catholic universities had been going on for many years prior (D.C. Superior Court, 1989).

Not all of the curricular engagement around sexuality on Catholic campuses is discouraged. Instructors from several religiously affiliated universities—a couple Catholic—discussed pedagogy of engaging sexuality and religious studies (Ott & Stephens, 2017). This collaboration culminated into a book on teaching sexuality and religion in higher education (Stephens & Ott, 2020). It seems to stand, however, that it is a cultural norm that at Catholic institutions, scholars likely feel threatened when engaging with sexuality topics in the classroom (Freitas, 2017; Levand & Dyson, 2021).

Sports and Title IX

Because as Title IX is a federal law, any school that accepts money from the federal government is bound to the non-discrimination policies described therein (Office for Civil Rights, 2021). At Catholic institutions, federal financial assistance usually comes in the form of research grants or federal financial aid for students (Theriot, 2011). While Catholic institutions are bound to Title IX, the Cardinal Newman Society—a Catholic college alumni group who organized to purportedly promote Catholic education in accordance with *Ex Corde Ecclesiae*—has been advocating for Catholic universities to seek religious exemptions for accommodations based on gender identity (Cassandra, 2016b; Scharfenberger, 2016; Theriot, 2011). While the religious exemptions originally focused on sports (Cassandra, 2016b), faculty were also involved in this debate. Faculty at Marquette are reported to have made the argument that Title IX infringes on their academic freedom by expanding what constitutes a hostile environment, making it unable for them to teach Catholic theology (Scharfenberger, 2016; Smith, 2016).

While there are federal laws about gender protection for cisgender women, the Catholic context of a campus may affect the climate of gender dynamics. In an article on gender in the culture of Catholic colleges, Lafleur (2015) discussed the role of Catholic culture in fostering a hegemonic (or oppressive), heteronormative masculinity. Through a study on a Catholic college's men's beauty pageant, Lafleur described the function of the pageant as encouraging conformity and discouraging differences of gender and sexuality on campus—a practice she describes as upholding the marginalization of women and gay students. The author notes that the reinforcing of this dominant masculinity is exclusive and—though policies of the church endorse and perpetuate sexism, homophobia, and patriarchal norms—it goes against a "care for all persons" teaching of the church. This operationalization of hegemonic masculinity has been talked about from a feminist theological perspective for decades as having stemmed from a patriarchal anthropology rather than an egalitarian one (Ruether, 1983).

Gendered Bathrooms

Gender-neutral bathrooms are often seen in higher education as an issue of safety and inclusivity (Greytak et al., 2009; Sausa, 2002). More liberal Catholic campuses are also adopting gender-neutral restrooms, often as a student-led initiative (Gallina, 2015). More conservative Catholic media outlets have discussed this progress as unfortunate, often framing the stories alongside Catholic voices condemning modern gender theory (CNS Staff, 2015; Donlon, 2016; Knap, 2016). For example, in an article titled "Gender Theory Madness: 9 Catholic Universities Fall for 'Gender-Neutral' Bathrooms" by a student faction of an American Society for the Defense of Tradition, Family, and Property, the author framed gender theory as going against God and the church (Donlon, 2016). He concluded the article with a panicked call to oppose the "Jennerization" of Catholic campuses—a reference to the popular Olympic gold medalist who came out as transgender in 2015 (Donlon, 2016). And while there is an apparent moral panic and fear of binary sex category erasure, Catholic universities are still moving forward with instituting gender-inclusive restrooms (CNS Staff, 2015).

Living Arrangements

Coed living arrangements, meaning men and women in the same building (whether separated by wing, hall, or floor), is seen as a national norm for colleges and universities in the United States (Melton, 2014; Peterson, 2014). In a Catholic news article on the mixed-gender housing trend, the Catholic University of America (CUA) has been seen as going the opposite direction by reinstituting single-sex residence halls (Stimpson, 2011). Other Catholic institutions, like Franciscan University of Steubenville, include residence hall visitation rules such as prescribed hours on when the other sex can visit or students needing to keep the room door open at all times (Stimpson, 2011). The hope in making residence halls single-sex was that students would be having less sex and engage in less binge drinking (Levine, 2011; Peterson, 2014; Stimpson, 2011). When that policy was reviewed in a D.C.-based magazine years later, however, it became evident that students found creative ways around these regulations (Peterson, 2014).

Gender-neutral housing is also a topic of discussion in Catholic higher education (Cassandra, 2016a; CNS Staff, 2015). Students at Catholic universities like La Salle in Philadelphia have indicated in preliminary surveys that they are open to gender-neutral housing (Cassandra, 2016a; Snyder, 2016). The University of San Francisco, keeping up with the secular universities, even implemented gender-inclusive housing for the 2015–16 academic year (CNS Staff, 2015).

The concern expressed by Catholic administrators about students who are fertile and of different sexes living in the same room likely stems from the long-held Catholic belief that cohabitation implies consummation—that living together means people will be having sex—expressed in church law (Beal et al., 2000, Can. 1061, para. 2).

Minority Sexual Identities

Minority sexual identities were discussed above as an example of sexuality in higher education requiring the protection of students facing discrimination (Cramer, 2002). Over the last several years, Catholic colleges and universities have been incorporating sexual orientation into their non-discrimination policies—a debate often documented in university newspapers (Archbold, 2012; Dionisopoulos, 2013; Nelson, 2012). Because of the religious status of the universities, this was often a choice of the administrators and the board of trustees. There had been some cases of the administration opting not to include sexual orientation in the non-discrimination clauses, which caused students to protest until protection of students, faculty, and staff was ensured by its inclusion (Sheridan, 2010). This concern for discrimination was rekindled after the approval of Title IX exemptions for religious institutions, possibly opening doors to new avenues of discrimination (Stack, 2015). This reinforces the notion that within Catholic higher education, the policies around sexuality will both influence and be influenced by the student experience (Morey & Piderit, 2006). In a comparative analysis of Catholic and non-Catholic institutions, Miceli (2009) found a significant difference in the *perceived limitation* of programs and services targeted toward LGB individuals at Catholic institutions—that programs and resources for LGB students were perceived as less available to Catholic students.

Sexual Assault

The way Catholic universities handle sexual assault is not particularly different than how secular colleges and universities handle such crimes. The level of corruption and misinformation about how a college should handle sexual assault cases has been a phenomenon present in higher education for decades. According to one report put out by the U.S. Department of Justice, about 80% of rape and sexual assault would go unreported by students (Sinozich & Langton, 2014).

James Keenan (2015), an ethicist and moral theologian at Boston College, identified the way sexual assault is dealt with as a scandal within Catholic colleges and universities as part and parcel of the American university culture. Catholic colleges and universities are by no means exempt from becoming some of the biggest perpetrators of mishandling sexual assault cases on campus. In Indiana, St. Mary's college and the University of Notre Dame, for example, infamously mishandled the sexual assault case of a student that ended up in various media articles (Parrott, 2012) and documentaries (Ziering & Dick, 2015).

Some Catholic colleges and universities have been changing their policies in an attempt to better address sexual assault. In an article on adopting policies of sexual assault prevention, Fletcher and Oxenden (2015) said that Marquette University underwent such a change after overhauling policies due to mishandled cases in 2011. This change, as Fletcher pointed out, resulted from shifting standards in the conviction process from the "clear and convincing evidence" model often used in courtrooms to the "preponderance of evidence" model recommended by Title IX—or equally weighted evidence showing a "more likely than not" base of assault (National Association of College and University Attorneys, 2011).

Sexual Health Information

Another issue of sexuality in higher education is access to sexual health information (Eisenberg, Garcia, et al., 2012b). Due to the Catholic view about the purpose of sexuality as described in the church documents above, gaining access to sexual health information on Catholic campuses can be, at times, somewhat difficult. Trying to address this issue in the public eye, McCarthy (2015) identified the difficulty in gaining access to sexual health material on Catholic campuses. The author recounts that information such as pamphlets may not be disseminated uniformly. Many Catholic colleges may simply refer students to off campus facilities for such information, a practice that particularly conservative groups such as the Cardinal Newman Society (2011, 2015) call a "scandalous relationship." While information may be scarce, access to contraceptives is often absent. Peer condom distribution, for example, has been met at one Catholic college with threats of disciplinary action (Landergan, 2013). Despite these threats from administration, policies preventing the distribution of contraceptives did not go unchallenged by Catholic university students (Peterson, 2014; Winer, 2014).

Morality Clauses

McCarty (2014) also points to the reality that not only writings on sexuality can affect employment, but so can one's own sexual personhood. He cited stories of sociology professor Jodi O'Brien and Laine

Tadlock. O'Brien had a job offer rescinded from Marquette University once they saw her writings on marriage, family, and gender contrary to Catholic teaching—a decision that the president was very clear was not about her sexual orientation at all. Tadlock, director of an education program at Benedictine University, lost her position after publishing a wedding announcement in the State's Journal Register—something that was condemned as public disregard for fundamental Catholic beliefs. Events similar to those involving the sexuality-based decisions of jobs including O'Brien and Tadlock in the Roman Catholic hierarchy created what McCarty (2014) calls a silence-inducing culture of fear, citing the church's own moral and theological anxieties as the source. New Ways Ministry, a Catholic organization in support of LGBTQ+ rights and dignity keep a list of instances of this identity-based termination (DeBernardo & Shine, 2021).

To review the argument thus far, after considering developmental changes as they apply to students and their faith development, we looked at the management of issues in sexuality in general higher education. After considering that some students choose to spend that developmental time period in a Catholic setting, we looked at sexuality within a specific Catholic context by reviewing important contributing factors to church teachings on sexuality. We just finished taking a look at examples of how institutions of Catholic higher education have recently addressed issues of sexuality. Given that many Catholic institutions contribute to a silence-inducing culture of fear around sexuality (McCarty, 2014), let's look at some of the calls for change in the way Catholic schools deal with issues of sexuality.

Calls for Change

As we saw above, Catholic history plays an important role in how current Catholic colleges and universities deal with issues of sexuality. Many of the tensions in how sexuality is managed in Catholic higher education have led to calls for change throughout the years and across disciplines.

Institutional Change

Religious institutions have been identified by scholars to be sources of learning about sexuality (Shapiro, 1980). In a review of the resources available for adolescent sexual development, among home, school, community and peer networks, Shapiro (1980) identified religious institutions as important sources of information. This sentiment has been echoed by leading sexuality professionals as well (Sexuality Information and Education Council of the United States [SIECUS], 2004;

WHO Regional Office for Europe and BZgA, 2010). This call recognizes the multifaceted nature of human development, seeing religious affiliation as integral to the identities of youth and a place for sexual information. Specific to the Catholic context, a survey of Catholic colleges and universities put out by the Association of Catholic Colleges and Universities assessed academic programs that focused on values development, including programs addressing issues of human sexuality. The study found that issues of human sexuality were rated as not effective and the least addressed topic by the administration (Riley, 1990). The author of the study calls for a more focused effort towards addressing human sexuality at Catholic colleges and universities—a need that still seems to continue today (Franz, 2016). There are many voices who encourage discussion of gender on Catholic campuses such as the president of the Association of Catholic Colleges and Universities who notes this dialogue should happen with the mantra: "Kindness first, foremost and always" (Holtschneider, 2022, para. 47).

Curricular Change

In the curriculum, both Estanek (2008) and Moglia (1994) identified areas for improvement (collaboration and expansive analysis) and recommended avenues for change. In a compilation of sources about appropriate student development and its role in transformational learning, Estanek (2008) focuses her efforts on whole person development. She recognized the developmental complexities faced by students today and called for increased communication across leadership roles to expand discussions of how student learning and development takes place on campus. This collaboration of leadership among campus ministers, faculty, and student affairs professionals is—for Estanek—essential in addressing students' cognitive, psychosocial, and spiritual development.

Moglia (1994) called for a specifically curricular change in regard to sexuality in higher education. He recognized the interdisciplinary reality of sexuality claiming that "the breadth of scholarly concern is indicative of the importance of the subject" (p. 190). Moglia focused on addressing sexuality across disciplines, including theology. He called for an expanded analysis of sexuality in academic departments, noting that the view of the psychologist will be just as important as the view of the theologian (Moglia, 1994).

Sexual Assault Management

A number of Catholic writers have taken to the blogosphere also calling for a change in the way colleges and universities address sexuality.

On the matter of sexual assault, many Catholic writers have taken to blogs to call for change (Cuddeback, 2015; DeCostanza, 2015; Greiner, 2015; O'Brien, 2015). Cuddeback (2015) writes about the overwhelming issue of sexual assault on college campuses hoping for a culture of resistance to sexual assault. Greiner (2015) builds on this call for addressing sexual assault by saying that Catholicism should not only be leading the dialogue denouncing sexual assault but should also be a leader in promoting integrative and healthy sexual attitudes. For Greiner, it is the Catholic mission and identity that compels these institutions to include all aspects of the human experience in the education process, including sexuality. Galarneau and O'Neill (2015) discussed Catholicism as a compelling source for action and Catholic colleges as having a unique opportunity to address sexual assault with Catholic social teaching to create a violence free community.

DeCostanza (2015) focused on care for survivors of sexual assault. He called for Catholic universities to address the needs of those who have experienced trauma by enacting evidenced-based trainings on sexual violence, thereby making the community a safer place for trauma survivors. DeCostanza calls for more comprehensive trainings for ministers, including the multitude of ways people experience embodiment (i.e., after a sexual assault), paying particular attention to not taking a voice away from the survivors who need it. O'Brien (2015) echoed this sentiment, saying Catholic places need to be safer spaces for sexual assault survivors, especially amidst the culture of shame fostered in many Catholic circles around premarital sex regardless of whether it is consensual or not. Scholars and activists are still advocating for change around this topic, feeling little has changed in the last decade (Selak, 2021).

Some Catholic colleges and universities are participating in the calls for change in sexual assault prevention by creating training programs that are inclusive of many different aspects of sexuality. The University of San Francisco (2015), for example, created a seemingly effective program for sexual assault prevention on campuses called *Think About It* that alludes to same-sex partners, thinking through sexual choices, and is relatively progressive in matters of sexuality from a Catholic university (Siebert, 2014). The program gained enough momentum, as of the fall of 2014, 170 schools had instituted this Jesuit-university-born training (Novak, 2014).

Maher (2003) observed that church responses to sexuality can take either a more exclusive ecclesial approach which or a more inclusive pastoral approach attending to the needs of the people. In Cuddeback's (2015) plea for a culture against sexual assault, she calls for religious leaders to admit pastoral mistakes—specifically around sexuality. The Bishop of Springfield, Massachusetts, Mitchell Rozanski, is an example of a Catholic leader doing this well. Bishop Rozanski published a letter on Ash Wednesday of 2016—a holy day that marks repentance for Catholics—asking the general public's forgiveness for those hurt by the church's hurtful language or actions regarding sexuality (Rozanski, 2016). In this apology, Rozanski also acknowledged that the church often fails in recognizing the hurt it has caused—an important step in opening the dialogue about how the church can help support and advocate for those who experience sexual trauma, even (or especially) by members of the church. And while this mentality can lead to more inclusive and comprehensive responses to sexual assault, as is the case of University of San Francisco's (2015), as well as with other Catholic universities in California due to state mandates (Desmond, 2014), there is still much work to be done.

Access to Contraceptives

Access to birth control is another area focused on by Catholic advocates for sexual information. In a reflective piece about birth control on Catholic college campuses, McCarthy (2015) sheds light on the lack of dissemination of contraceptive material on Catholic campuses. Even information on the matters of birth control permissible by the Catholic church (i.e., natural family planning) are difficult to come by unless a couple is engaged to be married in the Catholic church. She posed the question to universities: "Why are we, in an institution of higher learning, effectively and actually prohibiting other adults—because most undergraduates are really, legally adults—from learning something, period?" Citing church teaching of dignity for the human person, McCarthy identified that the lack of adequate sexual health information, in fact, runs counter to the Catholic mission, as care for the human person is central to its identity.

Academic Freedom

In McCarty's (2014) article on academic freedom discussed above, he identified some instances of the Catholic Church silencing scholars for their work or condemning texts engaged in sexual ethics, such as Farley (2006) and Salzman and Lawler (2008). Regarding the particular issue of academic freedom around sexual ethics and academic dialogue, he called for administrative support of faculty involved with topics that may cause tense or arduous relations with church officials. A call that he hopes to find answered in the work of Pope Francis. A year later, McCarty (2015) looked to Pope Francis' (2014) apostolic exhortation *Evangelii Gaudium* as a source of support. In *Evangelii Gaudium* (The Joy of the Gospel), Francis looks to encourage evangelization within the Catholic Church, specifically promoting the idea of dialogue—in regard to academia, this involves dialogue across academic disciplines, including those that do not agree with the Catholic Church. McCarty points to resources for this freedom for scholars involved in sexual ethics as well as LGBT individuals within the apostolic exhortation. The document, McCarty stated, stands as an owning of academic language of sexuality scholars and is less focused on the harmful moral language used in the prior church rhetoric.

Ethical Leadership

Leaders of Catholic universities often lack the practice and expertise in managing issues pertaining to sexuality (Riley, 1990). Minimal leadership formation might contribute to the mishandling of matters of sexuality in the institutional setting. Focusing on institutional forces of the administrators and faculty members, Schuttloffel (2013) called for the intentional formation of Catholic school leaders to require the skills, knowledge, and disposition necessary for successful leadership. This study was a survey of Catholic higher education leaders in England, the Netherlands, and Australia. Data from the study suggested three common themes in contemplative Catholic school leaders' decision-making: the impact of their personal life stories, the view of their leadership as a vocation, and priority given to relationships (Schuttloffel, 2013). The author called for the intentional faith formation of school leaders as they will be an integral part of the formation of both the institution and its community members. This notion of leaders lacking a sound faith formation is also empirically supported by Morey and Piderit (2006) in their book on Catholic higher education. In line with this call for well-rounded leadership, Catholic moral theologian James Keenan's (2015) called for teaching ethics to administrators. He observed that while Catholic universities teach about ethics, administrators are often not formally trained in professional university ethics at all. This concern is summed up by Keenan, "the American university teaches how others are to be ethical, but it does not teach itself to be ethical" (Keenan, 2015, p. 18).

Previous Research

The literature about the experience of effecting change around sexuality on Catholic college and university campuses is scarce (Getz & Kirkley, 2006; Love, 1997, 1998). A few studies have considered the struggles and successes with incorporating a student alliance centered on orientation (Gay, Lesbian, Bisexual Alliance, GSA, etc.) into university life (Love, 1998; McEntarfer, 2011), about the general experience of being a sexual minority on college campuses with regard to administrative support or hindrance (Getz & Kirkley, 2006; Miceli, 2009), perceptions of leaders in a Catholic high school (Maher & Sever, 2007), or about primary or secondary sex educator experiences (Eisenberg, Madsen, et al., 2012c; Landry et al., 2000).

Barriers to Sexuality Education

Barriers are likely to arise when incorporating sexuality into any educational setting due to its sensitive nature (Hedgepeth & Helmich, 1996). In the general field of sexuality education, two studies have focused on the experiences of sexuality educators in the public realm and areas that they feel a lack of support (Eisenberg, Madsen, et al., 2012c; Landry et al., 2000). In a qualitative study of 5th and 6th grade sexuality education teachers, researchers found that teachers identified administrators, policies, parental responses, time, and students' maturity levels as challenges to teaching about sexuality (Landry et al., 2000). Some educators reported difficulty in teaching certain topics (birth control or sexual orientation) due to pressure or the fear of pressure from administrators, parents, or community members (Landry et al., 2000). Given that these realities (in conjunction with others, such as church officials) exist in Catholic higher education (Morey & Piderit, 2006), these same concerns might also be present.

A decade later, Eisenberg, Madsen, et al. (2012c) conducted a focus group with 31 teachers and 10 community-based educators and found barriers of sexuality education to include parents, administrators, time, financial resources, diversity of the student body, and district, school, or state policies preventing such education. The researchers noted specifically that some policies supporting teachers would mitigate some of the structural barriers to teaching about sexual health, as this seemed to be the largest concern. While the Landry et al. (2000) and Eisenberg, Madsen, et al. (2012c) studies do not consider the Catholic or university context, the perceived barriers described by sexuality educators help supply nuance to the incorporation sexuality into an educational institution and its sensitive nature, raising awareness to barriers possibly consistent with the population of the current study.

Catholic Context

In a qualitative study on the perceived barriers of seven teachers in a Catholic high school who were addressing the topic of homosexuality, researchers found that perceived barriers included at varying degrees: the Catholic identity of the school, the fear of community reaction, and the lack of support from faculty and administration within the school (Maher & Sever, 2007). Researchers found that while Catholic identity was listed as a barrier, it was not listed as a strong barrier, with many teachers working either around it or within the Catholic tradition. Participants reported that the strongest barrier was the fear of community reaction—concerns linked to funding/donors, fear of parental reaction, being known as the "gay" school, or being labeled as gay for wanting to help gay students (Maher & Sever, 2007). This fear of community reaction also kept the administration from supporting changes in the way education of homosexuality was conducted in the school (Maher & Sever, 2007). This ties back to the concerns of morality clauses regarding a culture of fear around sexuality in the Catholic context identified by McCarty (2014).

Catholic University Context

In the Catholic university context, one study by Getz and Kirkley (2006) qualitatively assessed the experience of individuals on a campus LGB awareness program as well as any transformative effects it had on the campus community. The program, called Rainbow Educators, was a group of students, faculty, staff, and administrators devoted to expanding visibility and acceptance of LGB individuals. The researchers noted the emergence of three major themes: an increased awareness of social identity (their own and others), a demonstrated improved confidence to serve as allies to the LGB community, and a perceived overall positive impact the program had on the campus community (Getz & Kirkley, 2006). This study noted the positive effects of a resource and awareness program on campus but does not detail the experience of those who worked to bring about the program and the various challenges and successes involved.

McEntarfer (2011) examined the creation of GSAs at three religiously affiliated institutions, two of which were Catholic, one mainstream Protestant. Of the three universities, all of them had LGBTQ student organizations (Rainbow Alliance, Spectrum, and PRIDE) with varying degrees of difficulty working with the administration. The author coded these methods of navigation as collaborative, conciliatory, assertive, and underground/subversive—seemingly on a spectrum from most to least cooperative. In collaborative navigation, the organizations were able to work with the administration, going through the proper channels to meet the needs of the group. Through conciliatory navigation, groups needed to concede to university limitations, such as where or how a group can advertise its name. Assertive techniques often involved publicly confronting the limitations such as rallies, sit-ins, protests, or petitions. The underground or subversive techniques involved resisting limitations in a less public way—identified by the author as potentially risking the existence of the GSA—through such means as secret groups or meetings (McEntarfer, 2011).

McEntarfer (2011) framed the study using Social Movement Theory (SMT), specific to large, disruptive advocacy movements (Embry & Grossman, 2006). In this case, she was looking for similarities on the smaller, institutional level of advocacy for GSAs on religious campuses. The author situated the GSA movements in SMT by recognizing the students working through the political process, garnering resources for themselves through university or extra-university means, and properly framing themselves in relation to the administration which lent itself to understanding the barriers and the best avenues for operation. All of the barriers listed in this article are related to university policy because any routes of communication students or faculty could use are governed by institutional policy.

In his book *Gay on God's* Campus, Jonathan Coley (2018) reports of studying LGBT student groups at four different Christian institutions of higher education (two Protestant and two Catholic). He discussed tactics for communication used by these student groups to effect change, not unlike McEntarfer. Coley addressed this communication in the context of LGBT activism and how they effect change within their universities and within activist group participants. I address these tactics more in-depth in the chapter on communication strategies, but Coley offered a useful comparison between the Catholic and Protestant context that I do not address within the 17 universities represented in this book.

Bryce Hughes (2015) conducted a dissertation case study on LGBTQ issues in a Jesuit university that yielded a few academic publications (Hughes, 2018; Hughes, 2019; Hughes, 2020). Hughes examined grassroots leadership in the institution pertaining to LGBT issues and organizational change. His study yielded much useful information about communication strategies, motivations, and sources of resilience for students, faculty, and staff in their efforts to make campus life more accepting of LGBT individuals. I will address his study in more detail in each of the following chapters about these components.

Love (1997) conducted 41 qualitative interviews (N = 26) to discover and attempt to change the culture around sexual orientation at a small Catholic college. Participants included LGB students, ally administrators, faculty, and the academic dean. In the cultural atmosphere, the author coded data into categories of contradictions and paradoxes. One of the paradoxes listed included barriers to the institutional leaders, resulting in them not being able to lead. These barriers consisted of the fear of parents, board of trustees, alumni, priests, parishes, and potential funding sources (Love, 1997). Any successful aspects of this study seemed to be more about successful components in the change movement than actual successful outcomes—that support was found in unlikely places like campus ministry or that many of the strong advocates were LGB Catholics who felt called to work on these issues. Love (1997) did note as one of these paradoxes that less overt homophobia is more dangerous—as one cannot avoid what one cannot see. In part, the purpose of the present study was to help gain clarity of some of the less visible barriers in order to better address them.

Finally, Love (1998) also wrote about cultural barriers specifically from the experience of LGB students. On the institutional level, the author identified three cultural barriers: perceptions of Catholicism (i.e., that homophobia is in line with Catholic ideals), fear of external and peripheral constituencies (local ordinaries, the church hierarchy, donors, board of trustees, alumni, parents of current and prospective students), and lack of appropriate ways to discuss orientation. These barriers also echo attitudes of fear and lack of resources that have appeared throughout this chapter (i.e., McCarthy, 2015; McCarty, 2014).

Chapter Summary

Let's look at the topical journey we took to get here. The term "sexuality" is a broad category encompassing many aspects of the human experience. Late adolescents and young adults aged 18–24 encounter many important developmental changes that intersect with their sexuality. Higher education is an important developmental environment. Faith life can also play in important role in shaping the higher education experience. There are many topics of sexuality in higher education, including developments in the curriculum, sports and Title IX information, gendered bathrooms, living arrangements of students, student sexual activity, the way a university views individuals with minority sexual identities, how sexual assault is addressed on campus, where to find resources for sexual health information or counseling, and morality clauses for employees.

Throughout history, sexuality has been part of the Catholic dialogue through various scholars and church documents likely impacting the present dialogue on sexuality in Catholic higher education. There have been calls for change around how Catholic colleges and universities have addressed or ignored issues of sexuality. Previous research, though scarce, has yielded methods of navigation, contradictions and paradoxes in change efforts, and institutional-level barriers.

What's to Come?

All of these components lead us to the study in this book. This chapter has been a general foundation for a more detailed understanding of change efforts in Catholic higher education. The study that I conducted involved hearing from 31 employees at 17 different Catholic colleges and universities in the United States. These participants shared with me their efforts in effecting change around sexuality in Catholic higher education (for more information about the methods of the study, see the Methods Appendix). In the next several chapters, I will explain what I observed from these interviews, what these findings mean, what we can learn from them, and discuss how the Catholic context can be a place to foster inclusive change.

References

Advocates for Youth. (1995). What is sexuality? In *Life planning education: A youth development program* (pp. 115–129). Author.

American Council on Education. (1937). *The student personnel point of view*. American Council on Education Studies, Issue 3.

American Council on Education. (1949). *The student personnel point of view*. American Council on Education Studies, Issue 13.

Ammicht-Quinn, R., Haker, H., & Junker-Kenny, M. (2004). Introduction. In R. Ammicht-Quinn, H. Haker, & M. Junker-Kenny (Eds.), *The structural betrayal of trust: Concilium 2004/3* (pp. 7–12). SMC Press.

Archbold, M. (2012, September 27). Catholic college adds sexual identity to non-discrimination policy. *Catholic Education Daily*. http://web.archive.org/web/20131108193639/http://www.cardinalnewmansociety.org/CatholicEducationDaily/DetailsPage/tabid/102/ArticleID/1583/Catholic-College-Adds-Sexual-Identity-to-Non-Discrimination-Policy.aspx

Arnett, J. J. (2000). Emerging adulthood: A theory of development from the late teens through the twenties. *American Psychologist, 55*(5), 469–480. https://doi.org/10.1037/0003-066X.55.5.469

Association of Catholic Colleges and Universities. (2022). *Catholic higher education faqs*. http://www.accunet.org/Catholic-Higher-Ed-FAQs

Astin, A. W. (1984). Student involvement: A developmental theory for higher education. *Journal of College Student Personnel, 25*(4), 297–308.

Augustine of Hippo. (1887). *Of the good of marriage* (C. L. Cornish, Trans.; Vol. 3). Christian Literature Publishing Company. http://www.newadvent.org/fathers/1309.htm

Augustine of Hippo. (1960). *The confessions of st. Augustine* (J. K. Ryan, Trans.). Doubleday.

Baxter Magolda, M. B. (1992). *Knowing and reasoning in college: Gender-related patterns in students' intellectual development*. Jossey-Bass.

Beal, J. P., Coriden, J. A., & Green, T. J. (Eds.). (2000). *New commentary on the code of canon law*. Paulist Press.

Belenky, M. F., Clinchy, B. M., Goldberger, N. R., & Tarule, J. M. (1986). *Women's ways of knowing: The development of self, voice, and mind*. Basic Books.

Bennett, S. (2002). Addressing homophobia and heterosexism in the mental health classroom: An intersubjective frame for learning. In E. P. Cramer (Ed.),

Addressing homophobia and heterosexism on college campuses (pp. 133–143). Huntington Park Press.
Benson, M. T., & Boyd, H. R. (2015). The "public" university: Recalling higher education's democratic purpose. *Thought & Action, 31*, 69–84.
Berkowitz, A. D. (1994, January 1). A model acquaintance rape prevention program for men. *New Directions for Student Services, 65*, 35–42.
Bevins, S. (2011). Stem: Moving the liberal arts education into the 21st century. *Technology & Engineering Teacher, 71*(4), 10–13.
Blake, S. M., Ledsky, R., Goodenow, C., Sawyer, R., Lohrmann, D., & Windsor, R. (2003). Condom availability programs in massachusetts high schools: Relationships with condom use and sexual behavior. *American Journal of Public Health, 93*(6), 955–962. https://doi.org/10.2105/AJPH.93.6.955
Bochenek, M., & Brown, A. W. (2001). *Hatred in the hallways: Violence and discrimination against lesbian, gay, bisexual, and transgender students in U.S. Schools.* Human Rights Watch.
Bokenkotter, T. (2004). *A concise history of the Catholic church.* Doubleday.
Bonner, G. I. (1962). Libido and concupiscentia in St. Augustine. *Studia Patristica, 1*, 303–314.
Bourke, V. J. (Ed.). (1958). *Saint Augustine: The city of god* (G. G. Walsh, D. B. Zema, G. Monahan, & D. J. Honan, Trans.). Doubleday.
Bryk, A. (2015). Title IX giveth and the religious exemption taketh away: How the religious exemption eviscerates the protection afforded transgender students under title IX. *Cardozo Law Review, 37*(2), 751–791.
Buckner, D. R. (1981). Developing coed residence hall programs for sex-role exploration. *Journal of College Student Personnel, 22*(1), 52–54.
Buller, J. L. (2014). The two cultures of higher education in the twenty-first century and their impact on academic freedom. *AAUP Journal of Academic Freedom, 5*, 1–8.
Bullock, C. M., & Beckson, M. (2011). Male victims of sexual assault: Phenomenology psychology, physiology. *Journal of the American Academy of Psychiatry and the Law, 39*(2), 197–205.
Callegher, J. D. (2010). Attitudes toward homosexuality among Catholic-educated university graduates. *Catholic Education: A Journal of Inquiry & Practice, 13*(3), 306–328. https://doi.org/10.15365/joce.1303032013
Cassandra, A. (2016a). *La Salle univ. Students approve of gender-neutral housing in online ballot.* http://www.cardinalnewmansociety.org/CatholicEducationDaily/DetailsPage/tabid/102/ArticleID/4681/La-Salle-Univ-Students-Approve-of-Gender-Neutral-Housing-in-Online-Ballot.aspx
Cassandra, A. (2016b). *NCAA won't punish Catholic colleges for title IX gender identity exemptions.* http://www.cardinalnewmansociety.org/CatholicEducationDaily/DetailsPage/tabid/102/ArticleID/4795/NCAA-Won%E2%80%99t-Punish-Catholic-Colleges-for-Title-IX-Gender-Identity-Exemptions.aspx
Chickering, A. W. (1969). *Education and identity.* Jossey-Bass.
Chickering, A. W., & Reisser, L. (1993). *Education and identity* (2nd ed.). Jossey-Bass.

CNS Staff. (2015). *Fordham changes restroom signs as part of 'gender inclusive' campaign*. http://www.cardinalnewmansociety.org/CatholicEducationDaily/DetailsPage/tabid/102/ArticleID/4512/Fordham-Changes-Restroom-Signs-as-Part-of-%E2%80%98Gender-Inclusive%E2%80%99-Campaign.aspx

Coley, J. S. (2018). *Gay on god's campus: Mobilizing for LGBT equality at Christian colleges and universities*. University of North Carolina Press.

Congregation for the Doctrine of the Faith. (1986). *Letter to the bishops of the Catholic church on the pastoral care of homosexual persons*. http://www.vatican.va/roman_curia/congregations/cfaith/documents/rc_con_cfaith_doc_19861001_homosexual-persons_en.html

Copen, C. E., Chandra, A., & Febo-Vazquez, I. (2016). Sexual behavior, sexual attraction, and sexual orientation among adults aged 18–44 in the United States: Data from the 2011–2013 national survey of family growth. *National Health Statistics Reports (NHSR), 88*, 1–13.

Cortez, M. (2010). *Theological anthropology: A guide for the perplexed*. T&T Clark International.

Cramer, E. P. (Ed.). (2002). *Addressing homophobia and heterosexism on college campuses*. Huntington Park Press.

Cuddeback, L. (2015). *The fragility of hope: Resisting a culture of sexual violence*. dailytheology.org. http://dailytheology.org/2015/09/18/the-fragility-of-hope-resisting-a-culture-of-sexual-violence/

Curran, C. E. (2006). *The moral theology of pope John Paul II*. Georgetown University Press.

D.C. Superior Court. (1989). Universities: Teaching eligibility. *Daily Washington Law Reporter, 117*(62), 653–662. http://counsel.cua.edu/res/docs/Curran.pdf

D'Augelli, A. R. (1992). Lesbian and gay male undergraduates' experiences of harassment and fear on campus. *Journal of Interpersonal Violence, 7*(3), 383–395.

Dahl, A., & Galliher, R. (2010). Sexual minority young adult religiosity, sexual orientation conflict, self-esteem and depressive symptoms. *Journal of Gay & Lesbian Mental Health, 14*(4), 271–290. https://doi.org/10.1080/19359705.2010.507413

Dailey, D. M. (1981). Sexual expression and aging. In F. Berghorn & D. Schafer (Eds.), *The dynamics of ageing: Original essays on the processes and experiences of growing old* (pp. 311–330). Westview Press.

Dailey, D. M. (2017). Sexual expression and aging. *Quarterly Journal of the Life Planning Network, 4*(4), 34–52.

DeBernardo, F., & Shine, R. (2021). *Employees of Catholic institutions who have been fired, forced to resign, had offers rescinded, or had their jobs threatened because of LGBT issues*. https://www.newwaysministry.org/issues/employment/employment-disputes/

DeCostanza, J. (2015). *Accompanying survivors: Holding trauma and doing it well*. dailytheology.org. http://dailytheology.org/2015/09/17/accompanying-survivors-holding-trauma-and-doing-it-well/

Dempsey, J. Q., Gorman, J. R., Madden, J. P., & Spilly, A. P. (1992). *The cardinal's commission on clerical sexual misconduct with minors*. Archdiocese of Chicago.

Desmond, J. F. (2014). *How Catholic universities address sexual-assault issues.* http://www.ncregister.com/daily-news/how-catholic-universities-address-sexual-assault-issues/

Dionisopoulos, T. (2013, October 9). Catholic college adds 'gender identity' and 'sexual orientation' to non-discrimination clause. *CampusReform.* http://www.campusreform.org/?ID=5144

Donlon, J. (2016). *Gender theory madness: 9 Catholic universities fall for 'gender-neutral' bathrooms.* http://www.tfpstudentaction.org/get-involved/online-petitions/gender-theory-madness-9-catholic-universities-fall-for-gender-neutral-bathrooms.html#footnotes_702

Draughn, T., Elkins, B., & Roy, R. (2002). Allies in the struggle: Eradicating homophobia and heterosexism on campus. In E. P. Cramer (Ed.), *Addressing homophobia and heterosexism on college campuses* (pp. 9–20). Huntington Park Press.

Editors. (1986). Handle the Charles Curran case with care. *America,* 237–238. http://americamagazine.org/issue/100/charles-curran-case

Eisenberg, M. E. (2002) The association of campus resources for gay, lesbian, and bisexual students with college students' condom use. *Journal of American College Health, 51*(3), 109–116.

Eisenberg, M., Garcia, C., Frerich, E., Lechner, K., & Lust, K. (2012b). Through the eyes of the student: What college students look for, find, and think about sexual health resources on campus. *Sexuality Research & Social Policy: Journal of NSRC, 9*(4), 306–316. https://doi.org/10.1007/s13178-012-0087-0

Eisenberg, M., Lechner, K., Frerich, E., Lust, K., & Garcia, C. (2012a). Characterizing sexual health resources on college campuses. *Journal of Community Health, 37*(5), 940–948. https://doi.org/10.1007/s10900-011-9536-6

Eisenberg, M. E., Madsen, N., Oliphant, J. A., & Resnick, M. (2012c). Policies, principals and parents: Multilevel challenges and supports in teaching sexuality education. *Sex Education, 12*(3), 317–329. https://doi.org/10.1080/14681811.2011.615614

Embry, R. A., & Grossman, F. D. (2006). The Los Angeles county response to child abuse and deafness: A social movement theory analysis. *American Annals of the Deaf, 151*(5), 488–498.

Ender, S. C., & Newton, F. B. (2000). *Students helping students: A guide for peer educators on college campuses.* Jossey-Bass.

Erikson, E. H. (1963). *Childhood and society.* W.W. Norton & Company.

Erikson, E. H. (1968). *Identity: Youth and crisis.* W. W. Norton & Company Inc.

Erlandson, K. (2014). Sexiled: Privacy acquisition strategies of college roommates. *Journal of College & University Student Housing, 40*(2), 12–29.

Estanek, S. M. (2008). Transformational learning and student life. *Journal of Catholic Higher Education, 27*(2), 223–237.

Farley, M. (2006). *Just love: A framework for Christian sexual ethics.* The Continuum International Publishing Group Inc.

Fine, L. E. (2012). The context of creating space: Assessing the likelihood of college LGBT center presence. *Journal of College Student Development, 53*(2), 285–299. https://doi.org/10.1353/csd.2012.0017

Finer, L. B., & Philbin, J. M. (2013). Sexual initiation, contraceptive use, and pregnancy among young adolescents. *Pediatrics, 131*(5), 886–891. https://doi.org/10.1542/peds.2012-3495

Flannery, A. (Ed.). (1996). *Vatican council II: The basic sixteen documents.* Costello.

Fleming, M. B., Cooley, A. H., & McFadden-Wade, G. (2009). Morals clauses for educators in secondary and postsecondary schools: Legal applications and constitutional concerns. *Brigham Young University Education & Law Journal, 2009*(1), 67–102.

Fletcher, L., & Oxenden, M. (2015). Consenting to change. *U.S Catholic, 9,* 18–21.

Fouts, B., & Knapp, J. (2001). A sexual assault education and risk reduction workshop for college freshmen. In A. J. Ottens & K. Hotelling (Eds.), *Sexual violence on campus: Politics, programs, and perspectives* (pp. 98–119). Springer.

Fox, T. C. (1995). *Sexuality and Catholicism.* George Braziller Inc.

Francis I. (2014). *Apostolic exhortation: Evangelii gaudium.* http://w2.vatican.va/content/francesco/en/apost_exhortations/documents/papa-francesco_esortazione-ap_20131124_evangelii-gaudium.html

Francis, L. (2016). Title IX: An incomplete effort to achieve equality in sports. *Journal of the Philosophy of Sport, 43*(1), 83–99. https://doi.org/10.1080/00948705.2015.1112242

Francis, L. J., ap Siôn, T., & Village, A. (2014). Measuring the contribution of independent Christian secondary schools to students' religious, personal, and social values. *Journal of Research on Christian Education, 23*(1), 29–55.

Franklin, K. (1998). *Psychosocial motivations of hate crimes perpetrators: Implications for educational intervention.* Paper presented at the Annual Convention of the American Psychological Association, San Francisco, CA.

Franz, M. (2016). Sex, milk, and cookies: Tackling sexual health promotion on a Catholic college campus. *All College Thesis Program, 2016–2019, 13.* https://digitalcommons.csbsju.edu/honors_thesis/13

Freitas, D. (2008). *Sex and the soul: Juggling sexuality, spirituality, romance, and religion on America's college campuses.* Oxford University Press.

Freitas, D. (2017). A response to Elisabeth T. Vasko: The risk and reward of teaching about sexual assault for the theologian on a Catholic campus. *Teaching Theology & Religion, 20*(2), 171–174. https://doi.org/10.1111/teth.12384

Freud, S. (1920). *A general introduction to psychoanalysis.* Boni and Liveright Publishers.

Freud, S. (1963). *The sexual enlightenment of children.* Collier Books.

Galarneau, J., & O'Neill, S. (2015). Educating for justice: Creating a mission-driven model of bystander intervention to address sexual violence at U.S. Catholic colleges and universities. *Journal of Catholic Higher Education, 34*(2), 257–279.

Galbreath, B. L. (2012). An argument for teaching a human sexuality course within the context of a women and gender studies program. *American Journal of Sexuality Education, 7*(1), 62–77. https://doi.org/10.1080/15546128.2012.651002

Gallina, A. (2015). *Gender neutral bathrooms in progress.* http://www.fordhamobserver.com/gender-neutral-bathrooms-in-progress/

Genovesi, V. J. (1996). *In pursuit of love: Catholic morality and human sexuality* (2nd ed.). The Liturgical Press.

Getz, C., & Kirkley, E. (2006). Shaking up the status quo: Challenging intolerance of the lesbain, gay and bisexual community at a private Roman Catholic university. *College Student Journal, 40*(4), 857–869.

Gil-Rivas, V. (2012). Sexual risk taking among college students: Correlates and consequences. In R. D. McAnulty (Ed.), *Sex in college: The things they don't write home about* (pp. 211–220). ABC-CLIO.

Goodstein, L. (2005). Young Catholics seek to restore old values on sex. *The New York Times.* http://www.nytimes.com/2005/04/14/world/worldspecial2/young-catholics-seek-to-restore-old-values-on-sex.html?_r=0

Greenberg, J. S., Bruess, C. E., & Sands, D. W. (1986). *Sexuality: Insights and issues.* Wm. C. Brown.

Greiner, K. A. (2015). *Who do we say that we are?: Changing the institutional culture around issues of sex and sexuality on Catholic campuses.* dailytheology.org. http://dailytheology.org/2015/09/13/who-do-we-say-that-we-are-changing-the-institutional-culture-around-issues-of-sex-and-sexuality-on-catholic-campuses/

Greytak, E. A., Kosciw, J. G., & Diaz, E. M. (2009). *Harsh realities: The experiences of transgender youth in our nation's schools.* GLSEN.

Hedgepeth, E., & Helmich, J. (1996). *Teaching about sexuality and HIV: Principles and methods for effective education.* New York University Press.

Henry, D. S. (2013). Couple reports of the perceived influences of a college human sexuality course: An exploratory study. *Sex Education, 13*(5), 509–521. https://doi.org/10.1080/14681811.2013.767195

Herek, G. M. (1993). Documenting prejudice against lesbians and gay men on campus: The Yale sexual orientation survey. *Journal of Homosexuality, 25*(4), 15–30.

Hobson, A. (2014). Designing and implementing a successful gender-neutral housing community. *Journal of College and Character, 15*(1), 33–38. https://doi.org/10.1515/jcc-2014-0005

Hogan, R. M. (2003). *An introduction to John Paul II's theology of the body.* http://www.nfpoutreach.org/Hogan_Theology_%20Body1.htm

Holtschneider, D. (2022). *Catholic universities should welcome discussion of gender issues.* https://outreach.faith/2022/05/catholic-universities-should-welcome-discussion-of-gender-issues/

Hughes, B. E. (2015). *"Who am I to judge?": How a Jesuit university addresses LGBT issues on campus* (Publication No. 3706207) [Doctoral Dissertation, University of California, Los Angeles]. ProQuest Dissertations & Theses A&I.

Hughes, B. E. (2018). Resilience of grassroots leaders involved in LGBT issues at a Catholic university. *Journal of Student Affairs Research and Practice, 55*(2), 123–136. https://doi.org/10.1080/19496591.2017.1366330

Hughes, B. E. (2019). "You're not like everyone else": Sexual orientation microaggressions at a Catholic university. *Journal of Catholic Education, 22*(3), 14–35. https://doi.org/10.15365/joce.2203022019

Hughes, B. E. (2020). "Put the Jesuit out front": How a Catholic, Jesuit university addresses LGBQ issues. *American Educational Research Journal, 57*(4), 1592–1624.

Hunter, D. G. (1994). Augustinian pessimism? A new look at Augustine's teaching on sex, marriage and celibacy. *Augustinian Studies, 25,* 153–177.

Hunter, D. G. (n.d.). *Sex, sin and salvation: What Augustine really said.* http://www.jknirp.com/aug3.htm

Jacob, E. (1987). Qualitative research traditions: A review. *Review of Educational Research, 57*(1), 1–50. https://doi.org/10.3102/00346543057001001

John Paul II. (1979–1984). *General audiences: John Paul II's theology of the body.* https://www.ewtn.com/catholicism/library/general-audiences-john-paul-iis-theology-of-the-body-8565

John Paul II. (1990). *Ex corde ecclesiae.* http://w2.vatican.va/content/john-paul-ii/en/apost_constitutions/documents/hf_jp-ii_apc_15081990_ex-corde-ecclesiae.html

John Paul II. (1997). *The theology of the body: Human love in the divine plan.* Pauline Books & Media.

Kassie, E. (2015). *Male victims of campus sexual assault speak out 'we're up against a system that's not designed to help us'.* http://www.huffingtonpost.com/2015/01/27/male-victims-sexual-assault_n_6535730.html

Kauth, M. R., & Bradford, A. (2012). Sexual orientation and college students. In R. D. McAnulty (Ed.), *Sex in college: The things they don't write home about* (pp. 169–188). ABC-CLIO.

Keenan, J. (2015). Practice what you teach. *U.S. Catholic, 80*(2), 17–20.

Kidwell, K. S., & Reising, B. (2005). Understanding the college first-year experience. *Clearing House, 78*(6), 253–255.

King, P. M., & Kitchener, K. S. (1994). *Developing reflective judgment.* Jossey-Bass. http://www.umich.edu/~refjudg/reflectivejudgmentmodel.html

Kirby, D., Brener, N. D., Brown, N. L., Peterfreund, N., Hillard, P., & Harrist, R. (1999). The impact of condom distribution in seattle schools on sexual behavior and condom use. *American Journal of Public Health, 89*(2), 182–187.

Kitchin, R., & Lysaght, K. (2004). Sexual citizenship in Belfast, Northern Ireland. *Gender, Place & Culture: A Journal of Feminist Geography, 11*(1), 83–103. https://doi.org/10.1080/0966369042000188567

Klebnikov, S. (2015). Liberal arts vs. Stem: The right degrees, the wrong debate. *Forbes.com.* http://www.forbes.com/sites/sergeiklebnikov/2015/06/19/liberal-arts-vs-stem-the-right-degrees-the-wrong-debate/#2a1c39fe41ec

Kleinplatz, P. J. (2012). Sexual problems and dysfunctions among college students. In R. D. McAnulty (Ed.), *Sex in college: The things they don't write home about* (pp. 243–261). ABC-CLIO.

Knap, P. (2016). *Gender-neutral bathrooms have arrived at Catholic colleges.* http://www.ncregister.com/blog/pattyknap/gender-neutral-bathrooms-have-arrived-at-catholic-colleges

Kosnik, A., Carroll, W., Cunningham, A., Modras, R., & Schulte, J. (1977). *Human sexuality: New directions in American Catholic thought.* Paulist Press.

Krauss, L. M. (2009). C. P. Snow in New York. *Scientific American, 301*(3), 32–32. http://www.scientificamerican.com/article/an-update-on-cp-snows-two-cultures/

Lafleur, S. (2015). Where else could that ever happen? The reproduction of heteronormative masculinity on a Catholic college campus. *Humanity & Society, 39*(3), 274–293. https://doi.org/10.1177/0160597614555980

Landergan, K. (2013). *BC tells students to stop dispensing condoms.* https://www.bostonglobe.com/metro/2013/03/26/boston-college-threatens-discipline-against-students-who-are-distributing-condoms/VgAEfWbvEXMCtz6UPLllNI/story.html

Landry, D. J., Singh, S., & Darroch, J. E. (2000). Sexuality education in fifth and sixth grades in U.S. Public schools, 1999. *Family Planning Perspectives, 32*(5), 212–219.

Lawler, M. G., & Salzman, T. A. (2011). The mystery of sexuality: Catholic reflections. *Theology & Sexuality, 17*(2), 161–180.

Lee, J. J. (2002). Changing worlds, changing selves: The experience of the religious self among Catholic collegians. *Journal of College Student Development, 43*(3), 341–356.

Levand, M. A., & Dyson, D. A. (2021). Areas of support and barriers to change around issues of sexuality in Catholic higher education. *Sexuality Research and Social Policy, 18,* 170–183. https://doi.org/10.1007/s13178-020-00447-9

Levering, M. (2013). *The theology of Augustine: An introductory guide to his most important works.* Baker Academic.

Levine, S. (2011). *Finding your way in gender-neutral housing.* http://college.usatoday.com/2011/11/10/finding-your-way-in-gender-neutral-housing/

Levinson, D. J., Darrow, C. N., Klein, E. B., Levinson, M. H., & McKee, B. (1978). *The seasons of a man's life.* Alfred A. Knopf, Inc.

Levinson, D. J., & Levinson, J. D. (1996). *The seasons of a woman's life.* Knopf.

Lonsway, K. A. (1996). Preventing acquaintance rape through education. *Psychology of Women Quarterly, 20*(2), 229–265.

Love, P. G. (1997). Contradiction and paradox: Attempting to change the culture of sexual orientation at a small Catholic college. *Review of Higher Education, 20*(4), 381–398. https://muse.jhu.edu/article/30031

Love, P. G. (1998). Cultural barriers facing lesbian, gay and bisexual students at a Catholic college. *Journal of Higher Education, 69*(3), 298–323. https://doi.org/10.2307/2649190

Love, P. G. (2001). Spirituality and student development: Theoretical connections. *New Directions for Student Services, 95*(7), 7–16.

Love, P. G. (2002). Comparing spiritual development and cognitive development. *Journal of College Student Development, 43*(3), 357–373.

Maher, M. J. (2003). Some background on addressing the topic of homosexuality in Catholic education. *Catholic Education: A Journal of Inquiry & Practice, 6*(4), 498–515.

Maher, M. J., & Sever, L. M. (2007). What educators in Catholic schools might expect when addressing gay and lesbian issues: A study of needs and barriers. *Journal of Gay & Lesbian Issues In Education, 4*(3), 79–111.

Maher, M. J., Sever, L. M., & Pichler, S. (2006). The priest sex scandal and its effects on trust and respect: How Catholic college students think about Catholic leadership. *Journal of Religion & Abuse, 8*(3), 35–62. https://doi.org/10.1300/J154v08n03_03

Marcia, J. E. (1966). Development and validation of egoidentity status. *Journal of Personality & Social Psychology, 3*(5), 551–558.

McAnulty, R. D. (Ed.). (2012). *Sex in college: The things they don't write home about*. ABC-CLIO.

McAnulty, R. D., & McAnulty, D. P. (2012). Infidelity in college dating relationships. In R. D. McAnulty (Ed.), *Sex in college: The things they don't write home about* (pp. 143–168). ABC-CLIO.

McCarthy, C. E. (2015). *Birth control, rape culture & Catholic higher education: Why aren't we even teaching what we already know?* dailytheology.org. http://dailytheology.org/2015/09/19/birth-control-rape-culture-catholic-higher-education-why-arent-we-even-teaching-what-we-already-know/

McCarty, R. W. (2009). Facilitating dialogue on religion and sexuality using a descriptive approach. *New Directions for Student Services, 125*, 39–46.

McCarty, R. W. (2014). Objects of the inquisition, or the trials of religion scholars at Catholic institutions who engage with sexuality studies. *Academe, 100*(1), 24–29. www.aaup.org

McCarty, R. W. (2015). A new hope? Pope Francis, the academy, and LGBT scholars and scholarship. *AAUP Journal of Academic Freedom, 6*, 1–12.

McEntarfer, H. K. (2011). "Not going away": Approaches used by students, faculty, and staff members to create gay–straight alliances at three religiously affiliated universities. *Journal of LGBT Youth, 8*(4), 309–331. https://doi.org/10.1080/19361653.2011.607623

Melton, A. C. (2014). *Coed campus housing a national norm*. http://bismarcktribune.com/lifestyles/faith-and-values/coed-campus-housing-a-national-norm/article_cf60ba5a-7bdb-11e4-830e-0380d654ec38.html

Messenger, J. C. (1993). Sex and repression in an Irish folk community. In D. N. Suggs & A. W. Miracle (Eds.), *Culture and human sexuality: A reader* (pp. 3–37). Brooks/Cole Pub.

Miceli, M. J. (2009). *Coming-out at Catholic and non-Catholic colleges and universities* (Publication No. 3355077) [Doctoral Dissertation, Johnson & Wales University]. ProQuest Dissertations & Theses A&I.

Moglia, R. (1994). Sexuality education in higher education in the USA: Analysis and implications. *Sexual & Marital Therapy, 9*(2), 181–191. https://doi.org/10.1080/02674659408409580

Money, J. (1982). Sexosophy: A new concept. *Journal of Sex Research, 18*(4), 364–366. https://doi.org/10.1080/00224498209551162

Mooney, M. (2010). Religion, college grades, and satisfaction among students at elite colleges and universities*. *Sociology of Religion, 71*(2), 197–215. https://doi.org/10.1093/socrel/srq035

Morey, M. M., & Piderit, J. J. (2006). *Catholic higher education: A culture in crisis*. Oxford University Press.

Muehlenhard, C. L., & Linton, M. A. (1987). Date rape and sexual aggression in dating situations: Incidence and risk factors. *Journal of Counseling Psychology, 34*(2), 186–196.

Mullendore, R. H., & Hatch, C. (2000). *Helping your first-year college student succeed: A guide for parents*. University of South Carolina, National Resource Center for the First-Year Experience and Students in Transition.

Myerson, M. (1992). Sex equity and sexuality in college-level sex education. In S. S. Klein (Ed.), *Sex equity and sexuality in education* (pp. 149–167). State University of New York Press.

National Association of College and University Attorneys. (2011). *Nine questions likely to arise in your sexual assault policy review*. Author. http://www.nacua.org/securedocuments/outline/docs/x_discrimination/x-12-02-11_attachment1.pdf

National Coalition of Anti-Violence Programs. (2012). *Hate violence against lesbian, gay, bisexual, transgender, queer, and HIV-affected communities in the United States in 2011*. http://www.avp.org/storage/documents/Reports/2012_NCAVP_2011_HV_Report.pdf

NCCB Committee on Marriage and Family. (1997). *Always our children: A pastoral message to parents of homosexual children and suggestions for pastoral ministers*. United States Catholic Conference. http://www.usccb.org/issues-and-action/human-life-and-dignity/homosexuality/always-our-children.cfm

Nelson, L. A. (2012, April 26). How Catholic? *Inside Higher Ed*. https://www.insidehighered.com/news/2012/04/26/tensions-over-social-issues-front-and-center-several-catholic-colleges

Newman, B. M., & Newman, P. R. (2012). *Development through life: A psychological approach* (11 ed.). Cengage Learning.

Nines, J. L. (2006). *Sexuality attitudes and the priesthood* (Publication No. 304920338) [Doctoral Dissertation, Widener University]. ProQuest Dissertations & Theses A&I.

Novak, P. (2014). *USF devises program to create culture of campus safety*. http://www.sfgate.com/news/article/Insight0824-novak-5704548.php

O'Brien, B. (2015). *The casings of our heart: Talking honestly and angrily about campus sexual assault*. dailytheology.org. http://dailytheology.org/2015/09/13/the-casings-of-our-hearts-talking-honestly-and-angrily-about-campus-sexual-assault/

Office for Civil Rights. (2021). *Title IX and sex discrimination*. https://www2.ed.gov/about/offices/list/ocr/docs/tix_dis.html

Ott, K., & Stephens, D. W. (2017). Embodied learning: Teaching sexuality and religion to a changing student body. *Teaching Theology & Religion, 20*(2), 106–116. https://doi.org/10.1111/teth.12373

Ottens, A. J., & Hotelling, K. (Eds.). (2001). *Sexual violence on campus: Politics, programs, and perspectives*. Springer.

Parrott, J. (2012). Getting through? How Catholic campuses are responding to sexual assault. *USCatholic.org, 77*(1), 12–17. https://uscatholic.org/articles/201112/getting-through-how-catholic-colleges-are-responding-to-sexual-assault/

Pascarella, E. T., & Terenzini, P. T. (1991). *How college affects students: Findings and insights from twenty years of research*. Jossey-Bass.

Paul VI. (1968). *Humanae vitae*. http://w2.vatican.va/content/paul-vi/en/encyclicals/documents/hf_p-vi_enc_25071968_humanae-vitae.html

Perlman, D., & Sprecher, S. (2012). Sex, intimacy, and dating in college. In R. D. McAnulty (Ed.), *Sex in college: The things they don't write home about* (pp. 91–117). ABC-CLIO.

Perry, W. G. (1968). *Patterns of development in thought and values of students in a liberal arts college: A validation of a scheme. Final report*. U.S. Department of Health, Education, and Welfare.

Perry, W. G. (1970). *Forms of intellectual and ethical development in the college years: A scheme.* Harcourt Brace Javanovich College.

Perry, W. G. (1981). Cognitive and ethical growth: The making of meaning. In A. W. Chickering (Ed.), *The modern American college* (pp. 76–116). Jossey-Bass.

Peterson, B. (2014). *The unintended consequences of Catholic university's sex experiment.* http://www.washingtonian.com/2014/11/04/the-unintended-consequences-of-catholic-universitys-sex-experiment/

Pew Research Center. (2012). *The global religious landscape: A report on the size and distribution of the world's major religious groups as of 2010.* https://assets.pewresearch.org/wp-content/uploads/sites/11/2014/01/global-religion-full.pdf

Piaget, J. (1952). *Origins of Intelligence in children* (M. Cook, Trans.). International Universities Press, Inc.

Plante, T. G. (Ed.). (2004). *Sin against the innocents: Sexual abuse by priests and the role of the Catholic church.* Praeger.

Pontifical Council for the Family. (1995). *The truth and meaning of human sexuality: Guidelines for education within the family.* http://www.vatican.va/roman_curia/pontifical_councils/family/documents/rc_pc_family_doc_08121995_human-sexuality_en.html

Pope Benedict XVI. (2010). *Pastoral letter of the holy father Pope Benedict XVI to the Catholics of Ireland.* http://w2.vatican.va/content/benedict-xvi/en/letters/2010/documents/hf_ben-xvi_let_20100319_church-ireland.html

Pringle, J. K., & McCulloch Dixon, K. (2003). Re-incarnating life in the careers of women. *Career Development International, 8*(6), 291–300.

Rausch, T. P. (2010). *Educating for faith and justice: Catholic higher education today.* Liturgical Press.

Regan, P. C. (2012). Love, college style. In R. D. McAnulty (Ed.), *Sex in college: The things they don't write home about* (pp. 119–142). ABC-CLIO.

Rich, M. D., Utley, E. A., Janke, K., & Moldoveanu, M. (2010, Fall). "I'd rather be doing something else:" Male resistance to rape prevention programs. *Journal of Men's Studies, 18*(3), 268–290. https://doi.org/10.3149/jms.1803.268

Riley, D. M. (1990). ACCU student life questionnaire: A report. *Current Issues in Catholic Higher Education, 10*(2), 6–10.

Rimassa, P. S. (2002). *A descriptive study of 15 Roman Catholic priests, church doctrine on human sexuality and contemporary human sexuality information* (Publication No. AAI3073049) [Doctoral Dissertation, University of Pennsylvania]. ProQuest Dissertations & Theses A&I. Philadelphia, PA. http://repository.upenn.edu/dissertations/AAI3073049

Robinson, B., Bockting, W. O., Rosser, B. R. S., Miner, M., & Coleman, E. (2002). The sexual health model: Application of a sexological approach to HIV prevention. *Health Education Research, 17*(1), 43–57.

Rogers, A., McRee, N., & Arntz, D. L. (2009). Using a college human sexuality course to combat homophobia. *Sex Education: Sexuality, Society and Learning, 9*(3), 211–225.

Rogers, C. R. (1969). *Freedom to learn.* Merrill.

Rozanski, M. T. (2016). *The wideness of god's mercy: A pastoral letter reflecting on evangelization.* http://diospringfield.org/pastoralletter/PastoralLetterEnglish.pdf

Rubin, L. M., & Lough, N. L. (2015). Perspectives of title IX pioneers: Equity, equality and need. *Journal of Intercollegiate Sport, 8*(2), 109–130.

Ruether, R. R. (1983). *Sexism and god-talk: Toward a feminist theology.* Beacon Press.

Sacred Congregation for the Doctrine of the Faith. (1975). *Persona humana: Declaration on certain questions concerning sexual ethics.* http://www.vatican.va/roman_curia/congregations/cfaith/documents/rc_con_cfaith_doc_19751229_persona-humana_en.html

Salzman, T. A., & Lawler, M. G. (2008). *The sexual person: Toward a renewed Catholic anthropology.* Georgetown University Press.

Sausa, L. A. (2002). Updating college and university campus policies: Meeting the needs of trans students, staff, and faculty. In E. P. Cramer (Ed.), *Addressing homophobia and heterosexism on college campuses* (pp. 43–55). Huntington Park Press.

Scharfenberger, K. (2016). *Catholic colleges should claim Title IX exemptions, says Newman Society president.* http://www.cardinalnewmansociety.org/CatholicEducationDaily/DetailsPage/tabid/102/ArticleID/4645/Catholic-Colleges-Should-Claim-Title-IX-Exemptions-Says-Newman-Society-President.aspx

Scheper-Hughes, N. (1983). From anxiety to analysis: Rethinking Irish sexuality and sex roles. *Women's Studies, 10*(2), 147–160.

Schlossberg, N. K., Waters, E. B., & Goodman, J. (1995). *Counseling adults in transition: Linking practice with theory.* Springer.

Schuck, K. D., & Liddle, B. J. (2001). Religious conflicts experienced by lesbian, gay and bisexual individuals. *Journal of Gay & Lesbian Psychotherapy, 5*(2), 63–82.

Schuster, M. A., Bell, R. M., Berry, S. H., & Kanouse, D. E. (1998). Impact of a high school condom availability program on sexual attitudes and behaviors. *Family Planning Perspectives, 30*(2), 67–88.

Schuttloffel, M. M. J. (2013). Contemplative leadership practice: The influences of character on Catholic school leadership. *Catholic Education: A Journal of Inquiry & Practice, 17*(1), 81–103.

Schwarz, H. (2013). *The human being: A theological anthropology.* William B. Eerdmans Publishing Company.

Sedgwick, A. (1990). Jansen and the Jansenists. *History Today, 40*(7), 36–42.

Selak, A. (2021). How Catholic colleges can address the epidemic of sexual violence on campuses. *National Catholic Reporter.* https://www.ncronline.org/news/accountability/how-catholic-colleges-can-address-epidemic-sexual-violence-campuses

Sexuality Information and Education Council of the United States [SIECUS]. (2004). *Guidelines for comprehensive sexuality education: Kindergarten through 12th grade* (3rd ed.). National Guidelines Task Force. http://sexedu.org.tw/guideline.pdf

Shapiro, C. H. (1980). Sexual learning: The short changed adolescent male. *Social Work, 25*(6), 489–493.

Shapiro, H. T. (2005). *A larger sense of purpose: Higher education and society.* Princeton University Press.

Sheridan, K. (2010, February 11). Students protest. *The Carroll News.* http://www.jcunews.com/2010/02/11/students-protest/

Sherkat, D. E. (2007). *Religion and higher education: The good, the bad, and the ugly.* Social Science Research Council Online Forum. http://religion.ssrc.org/reforum/Sherkat.pdf

Siebert, E. (2014). *Sex, drugs and...Catholic colleges.* http://ncronline.org/blogs/ncr-today/sex-drugs-and-catholic-colleges

Sigmund, P. E., Ed. & Trans. (1988). *St. Thomas Aquinas on politics and ethics.* W. W. Norton & Company.

Sinozich, S., & Langton, L. (2014). *Rape and sexual assault among college-age females, 1995–2013.* http://www.bjs.gov/index.cfm?ty=pbdetail&iid=5176

Slade, P. D. (1994). What is body image? *Behaviour Research and Therapy, 32*(5), 497–502. https://doi.org/10.1016/0005-7967(94)90136-8

Smith, P. J. (2016). *Gender identity vs. Catholic identity face-off after title IX expansions.* National Catholic Register. http://www.ncregister.com/daily-news/gender-identity-vs.-catholic-identity-face-off-after-title-xi-expansions/

Snow, C. P. (1959). *Two cultures and the scientific revolution.* Cambridge University Press.

Snyder, S. (2016). *La Salle students want 'gender-neutral' housing.* http://articles.philly.com/2016-02-26/news/70943501_1_catholic-university-student-safety-colleges

Stack, L. (2015, December 10). Religious colleges obtain waivers to law that protects transgender students. *New York Times.* http://www.nytimes.com/2015/12/11/us/religious-colleges-obtain-waivers-to-anti-discrimination-law.html

Steinfels, P. (2002). *Abused by the media.* http://archive.thetablet.co.uk/article/14th-september-2002/9/abused-by-the-media

Stephens, D. W., & Ott, K. M. (Eds.). (2020). *Teaching sexuality and religion in higher education: Embodied learning, trauma sensitive pedagogy, and perspective transformation.* Routledge. https://doi.org/10.4324/9780429327162

Stimpson, E. (2011). *Catholic universities see value of single-sex housing.* https://www.osv.com/OSVNewsweekly/Story/TabId/2672/ArtMID/13567/ArticleID/1834/Catholic-universities-see-value-of-singlesex-housing.aspx

Tarrant, A. (2016). *Choosing a Catholic college.* http://www.collegexpress.com/interests/catholic/articles/find-catholic-college/choosing-catholic-college/

Terry, K. J., Smith, M. L., Schuth, K., Kelly, J. R., Vollman, B., & Massey, C. (2011). *The causes and context of sexual abuse of minors by Catholic priests in the United States, 1950–2010: A report presented to the United States conference of Catholic bishops by the John Jay college research team.* United States Conference of Catholic Bishops. https://www.usccb.org/sites/default/files/issues-and-action/child-and-youth-protection/upload/The-Causes-and-Context-of-Sexual-Abuse-of-Minors-by-Catholic-Priests-in-the-United-States-1950-2010.pdf

The Cardinal Newman Society. (2011). *A scandalous relationship: Catholic colleges and planned parenthood.* https://newmansociety.org/wp-content/uploads/Web-A-Scandalous-Relationship-Catholic-Colleges-and-Planned-Parenthood-April-2011.pdf

The Cardinal Newman Society. (2015). *A more scandalous relationship: Catholic colleges and planned parenthood.* http://newmansociety.org/wp-content/uploads/A-More-Scandalous-Relationship-Final1.pdf

The Investigative Staff of the Boston Globe. (2002). *Betrayal: The crisis in the Catholic church*. Little, Brown and Company.

The National Catholic Risk Retention Group. (1999). Taking bigger and bigger steps. *Communicare*, *1*(1), 1–4. https://www.virtusonline.org/virtus/newsletters/VIRTUS_26.pdf

Theriot, K. (2011). *Protecting Catholic colleges from external threats to their religious liberty*. The Center for the Advancement of Catholic Higher Education. http://www.cardinalnewmansociety.org/Portals/0/CENTER/Theriot.pdf

tobinstitute.org. (2020). *Theology of the body institute*. http://tobinstitute.org/

Tuel, B. D. (2001). Sexual assault: When victims are gay, lesbian, or bisexual students. In A. J. Ottens & K. Hotelling (Eds.), *Sexual violence on campus: Politics, programs, and perspectives* (pp. 190–217). Springer.

Turner, G. W. (2020). The circles of sexuality: Promoting a strengths-based model within social work that provides a holistic framework for client sexual well-being. In A. N. Mendenhall & M. Mohr Carney (Eds.), *Rooted in strengths: Celebrating the strengths perspective in social work* (pp. 305–325). University of Kansas Libraries.

Ullerstam, L. (1966). *The erotic minorities: A Swedish view*. Grove Press.

United States Conference of Catholic Bishops. (1991). *Human sexuality: A Catholic perspective for education and lifelong learning*. United States Catholic Conference.

University of San Francisco. (2015). *Think about it*. https://myusf.usfca.edu/student-health-safety/think-about-it

West, C. (2003). *Theology of the body explained: A commentary on John Paul II's "gospel of the body"*. Gracewing Publishing.

Westefeld, J. S., Maples, M. R., Buford, B., & Taylor, S. (2001). Gay, lesbian, and bisexual college students the relationship between sexual orientation and depression, loneliness, and suicide. *Journal of College Student Psychotherapy*, *15*(3), 71–82.

White House Task Force to Protect Students From Sexual Assault. (2014). *Not alone: The first report of the white house task force to protect students from sexual assault*. https://obamawhitehouse.archives.gov/sites/default/files/docs/report_0.pdf

WHO Regional Office for Europe and BZgA. (2010). *Standards for sexuality education in europe: A framework for policy makers, educational and health authorities and specialists*. Federal Center for Health Education, BZgA. https://www.bzga-whocc.de/fileadmin/user_upload/WHO_BZgA_Standards_English.pdf

Willoughby, B. J., Larsen, J. K., & Carroll, J. S. (2012). The emergence of gender-neutral housing on American university campuses. *Journal of Adolescent Research*, *27*(6), 732–750. https://doi.org/10.1177/0743558412447852

Winer, C. (2014). *Student group challenges fordham university condom, free speech policies*. http://college.usatoday.com/2014/10/05/students-challenge-fordham-university-condom-free-speech-policies/

Wright, L. W., & Cullen, J. M. (2001). Reducing college students' homophobia, erotophobia, and conservatism levels through a human sexuality course. *Journal of Sex Education & Therapy*, *26*(4), 328–333.

Yep, G. A. (2002). From homophobia and heterosexism to heteronormativity: Toward the development of a model of queer interventions in the university classroom. In E. P. Cramer (Ed.), *Addressing homophobia and heterosexism on college campuses* (pp. 163–176). Huntington Park Press.

Zavalkoff, A. (2002). Teaching the teachers: Confronting homophobia and heterosexism in teacher education programs. In E. P. Cramer (Ed.), *Addressing homophobia and heterosexism on college campuses* (pp. 243–253). Huntington Park Press.

Ziering, A. (Producer), & Dick, K. (Director). (2015). *The hunting ground* [Motion Picture]. A. Ziering; Chain Camera Pictures. http://www.thehuntinggroundfilm.com/

Zuker, R. F. (n.d.). *Ten stages in the transition from high school to college.* Unpublished.

Material from this chapter may also appear in the following source:

Levand, M. A. (2022). Sexuality education as developmentally appropriate in the American Catholic higher education curriculum. *Sexuality, Gender, & Policy, 5*(2), 122–139. https://doi.org/10.1002/sgp2.12052

Chapter 3

General Themes
Catalysts in the Change Process

> What were some factors apparent across all of the interviews? What components make up the specific intersection of issues of sexuality in Catholic higher education?

After completing the interviews, I compared all of the cases to each other to see what themes emerged as present across all cases. Sexuality topics exist in all of higher education. Catholicism has much to say around topics of sexuality outside of higher education. But what specifically about the intersection of all three of these components: sexuality, Catholicism, and higher education? Paying particular attention to environmental factors, several themes arose from the experience of change around issues of sexuality that help expand the landscape of sexuality in Catholic higher education. I have termed these 17 themes as "Catalyst Themes" that appeared to have thematic importance enough for participants to mention them consistently. These 17 themes include bishop proximity, closeness to student experience, representation/visibility, out faculty/staff, respect/trust, "politeness," external atmosphere, negative public or media attention, sexual shame, legality, hostile environment/safety, lack of resources, pushing the envelope/persistence, Catholic identity navigation, the institutionalization of change, curiosity about other schools, and sexual/religious identity dichotomy. In this chapter, I will briefly describe each of these themes and consider what they mean for the rest of the study. Table 3.1 lists these themes in brief detail.

Catalyst Themes

Bishop Proximity

How much or how little the bishop was involved affected how much fear a community had around being reprimanded by him. Often, though not always, the more involved the bishop was (and these

Table 3.1 Overarching themes in Catholic higher education affecting the change process around issues of sexuality

Theme	Definition	Example
Bishop Proximity	How much or how little the bishop was involved in the change.	A bishop hearing about a change and asking the president of the university to prevent it from happening; a bishop supporting a change happening at a university.
Closeness to Student Experience	Less direct student contact often correlated with resistance to change.	A faculty/staff person who hears from students about an issue often while an administrator who does not interact with students fails to see why a change is necessary.
Representation & Visibility	Public visibility or representation of sexually and gender diverse peoples, content, or messaging.	An institutional statement of support for sexual or gender minorities; drag or pride advertisements; language that recognizes diverse identities in institutional policy.
Out Faculty, Staff, & Administrators	Having out sexually and gender diverse people in leadership roles at the university.	An openly bisexual or transgender dean, professor, or director on campus.
Respect & Trust	How much the employees respected and trusted institutional operation and leadership and how much respect employees felt they received from their university.	A dean respecting the institutional culture/communication to effect a change; a faculty member or student feeling disrespected from an institutional policy or practice.
"Politeness"	The expectation—often from administration—that requests for change should be communicated in a specific, culturally bound manner viewed as desirable by the holder of power (e.g., cordial, non-confrontational).	An administrator honoring one change because they felt it was communicated more politely than other requests for change.

(Continued)

Table 3.1 (Continued)

Theme	Definition	Example
External Atmosphere	Socio-historical contexts of the university, including geo-political environment, broader cultural events, and/or societal circumstances.	The federal legalization of gay marriage in the United States; the murder of Matthew Shepard.
Negative Public or Media Attention	The release of news or targeting of a university by media or public discourse centering on university operations or decisions in a negative light.	A university is at the center of a social media campaign for how poorly they managed sexual assault cases; a university avoids making a change for fear of possible negative attention.
Sexual Shame	The concept of sexuality topics being shameful, dirty, bad, wrong, or otherwise deserving of guilt; shaming the sexual lives or behavior of others.	University leaders avoiding topics of sexuality in university life due to personal feelings of shame or avoidance; cultural messaging that someone should be ashamed for having sex.
Legality	Changes influenced or required by local, state, or federal law.	Providing same-sex partner benefits for employees because of state mandates.
Hostile Environment/ Safety	The presence of an unsafe environment for sexually and gender diverse people as a reason to enact a change.	Students using slurs to refer to sexually and gender diverse peers, resulting in a training on tolerance and inclusivity.
Lack of Resources	Absence of time, money, space, employee-power, and resources for matters pertaining to sexuality.	Leadership relying on an over-burdened queer student group to enact change with no employee support; no funding for sexual health programming.
Pushing the Envelope	Persistence of a changemaker when working toward a change.	Despite frequent miscommunication in the office of student affairs, an employee continues working toward bringing a drag show to campus.

(Continued)

Table 3.1 (Continued)

Theme	Definition	Example
Catholic Identity Navigation	Working within the Catholic identity of the institution to move change forward, or viewing Catholic identity as a nuisance, obstacle, or something to work around.	Dialoging with Catholic teaching on solidarity to organize a pride march; viewing the Catholic identity as disconnected from lived experience and should be disregarded.
Institutionalization of Change	How embedded in the institutional structure and culture a given change was. The more institutionalized a change, the more likely it was to last.	Funding for an LGBTQ+ Center Director ensures its continuation; a single employee responsible for the Transgender Day of Visibility prayer service which ceased once that employee left the school.
Curiosity About Other Schools	Many employees wondered what other schools were doing about the same or similar issues on their campuses.	Employees are not given a platform for communication with other institutions about these changes and wonder how similar schools handle them.
Sexual/Religious Identity	The navigation of one's religious identity in conjunction with one's sexual identity (regarding one's orientation, gender, or one's sexual decisions and behaviors).	A student wonders if they can remain Catholic if the Catholic Church does not approve of their sexual life.

were often identified as conservative bishops), the less likely a change around sexuality would occur. One participant articulated:

> [Relationship with the local bishop is] still a relationship that most colleges pride and would like to keep a very positive relationship with. And it's no secret under the prefecture of Pope John Paul II and Pope Benedict the XVI, that bishops were appointed because of their commitment to, and their skill in, reinforcing a very traditional understanding of Catholic sexual morality. So that meant that, you know, Presidents were trying to keep a very positive relationship with the local bishop, but also trying to be faithful

to their mandate as Catholic institutions for higher education—to foster free and open discourse on issues of human knowledge including human sexuality—but were in sort of tension with the local bishop and that kind of relationship.

In instances of bishops with conservative or traditionalist views on sexual morality, the less involved the bishop was, the higher the likelihood that a change would occur. When bishops were noted as particularly supportive of these changes, the proximity of their involvement did not impede these changes.

Closeness to Student Experience

It often seemed that the people interested in making a change or really understanding why a change needed to occur had the most direct student contact. The converse of this principle meant that higher-level administrators or people who did not understand the student experience were much more resistant to change. One participant synthesized their experience of this by saying, "It was my experience that the closer administrators were to the reality of student life, the more they were open to and receptive of efforts to promote honest informed and direct discussion of human sexuality and Catholic teaching."

Representation/Visibility

Another common theme was the representation or visibility of sexual minorities on campus. When there were not many LGBTQ people publicly visible, any out advocates, or representation anywhere in university life (i.e., institutional statements of support), it was harder for change to occur around sexual orientation in the institution. This also included visible places to go to be safe, such as safe space stickers or LGBTQ centers. One participant expressed the need for visibility in advocacy work, noting, "I also know of some other out people on campus who were doing some advocacy work, so for me it was really important to have them at the table and also I only represent one experience with the LGBTQ community."

Out Faculty/Staff/Administrators

Continuing the theme of representation or visibility, many participants specifically discussed having out people in leadership roles as particularly influential in the change process. Visibility of other students is important, but visibility of those employed by the university was often sent a different message—one of commitment in a more real way for participants. When recalling one university administrator's journey, a participant said, "I think eventually she came out as a sexual minority, she identified as bisexual. And that maybe ruffled a few administrators, but it really—she had become kind of a focal point for students who felt ostracized."

Respect/Trust

A component of respect and trust that employees had with the university also played a significant role in how change occurred. Some changemakers were frequently silenced or ignored, which did not breed a relationship of trust and respect between the employee and the institution. On the other hand, some employees discussed feeling heard by the university and in turn responded with patience, saying that they understood that there was a process involved in achieving a particular change. One administrator said about their campus, "So here, you're kind of walking in to that culture, you got to respect that culture and of course you want to because …we have very universal values." Another participant said, "So the Catholic school, you're always wanting to be respectful of your own greater context even though you may or may not agree with all those teachings and those traditions." Even if there were culturally Catholic barriers slowing a change, participants expressed more patience for the institution when they felt heard and connected to their university.

Politeness

Similar to the concept of respect, some participants identified being polite as instrumental to the change process. This code was originally in quotes because when this concept was employed, it was often mentioned in opposition to other types of activism. The participant pejoratively described those types of communication as "over the top" or "in your face." One participant suggested this as a key theme in why a change worked on their campus:

> [Board members] were on board and because I think I wasn't proposing anything too radical. There was wide support but I think that was because of the way that I approached it. If I would have gone in there with a very progressive, advocate kind of approach and I said, "This is wrong. We don't support gender diversity and we've got to make a big statement here blah-blah-blah." I don't think they would've supported it.

This theme was most often mentioned in contrast to communication strategies that buck against the cultural norms of communication. It is important to note the level of respectability politics at play here—"politeness" was held as a value after an institution had encountered what they deemed to be impolite, rude, or otherwise disrupt the institutional culture's standard communication.

External Atmosphere

Another common theme that affected change involved the external atmosphere. Including the university's geographic environment (discussed in later chapters), this theme refers to widely known, influential events or circumstances. Often, historical events such as the murder of Matthew Shepard or the legalization of gay marriage would be cited as influential to the change process on their campus. One participant described why students are raising concerns about sexuality by saying, "They are also living in a culture where discussions on these [sexuality] issues have changed and have changed at a break-neck pace." This participant continues after describing cultural changes, saying that all of this is happening

> in the midst of a culture that's going through seismic changes, and it adds to support human sexuality in general—and gay and lesbian issues in particular—because all that coming together creates the situation in which these became issues that Catholic institutions had to deal with.

Negative Public or Media Attention

Frequently discussed as either helpful or hurtful to change was the negative public attention or negative media attention. Universities wanted to avoid negative attention from scandals, such as firing employees because of their orientation but also wanted to avoid negative media attention from conservative outlets should they support LGBTQ students or allow a conversation about sexual health on campus. In a situation that a participant coded as helpful, they said,

> I think the other thing that helped was the College had a lot of egg on its face from the [previous public dis-invitation of a speaker]. And so I think they are attuned to get it right. They recognize now that they really acted badly. Which is good on them. You know, I think that's a good thing. But then also I just think they're just more careful about how they engage in [issues of sexuality].

While this theme could exist as a type of atonement for previous transgressions as described above, it can also exist as a catalyst to sweep issues under the rug or try to ignore an issue.

Sexual Shame

The concept of sexuality being shameful or being shamed by others, such as shaming a victim of sexual assault for being in a sexual situation, also presented as a theme in interviews. Most frequently, this was in reference to poor management of sexual assault reporting or sexual health conversations or information. Concerning the reporting of sexual assault, one participant said:

> So if someone is a victim of a sexual misconduct in some way, you have to not only get through the shame and embarrassment and fear and all the other things that are so common in any victim of these kinds of things but I think we have an additional layer too about morality: Can I talk about this? Will I get in trouble? And are my parents going to find out? Will this be okay at the University, can I admit this? Am I going to be shamed beyond what I already feel? Will I just be chastised for being sexual? Will anyone care to listen to my particular story? So, that is something we've uniquely had to respond to in our education for staff and faculty.

While sexual shame exists as a common theme in American culture, participants discussed the very specific experience of Catholic sexual shame creating a unique environment and a factor to specifically address when effecting change.

Legality

When a matter of change around sexuality was required by law, the change often occurred much more quickly. One participant described the leadership's interaction with this component by saying, "The leadership is trying to walk a fine line between their faith, what they believe in, their value system and what's the mandate [of] the state [in which] they are operating." It may not be a surprise that legal matters would motivate a change, but this theme also encompasses religious institutions seeking a religious exemption from certain legal matters.

Hostile Environment/Safety

Frequently in relation to LGBTQ students, faculty, or staff, the hostility of an environment or the safety of sexual minority individuals came up as important reasons to enact change. One participant recalled the reaction from someone on campus after safe space training stickers were being displayed:

> Once you started to see some more symbols on campus, ally symbols and things of that nature there were some—I wouldn't say hate crime or anything of that nature—but some disrespect towards the programs that were being provided with the symbols on campus, things of that nature and it's mostly from word of mouth or how people reacted to it.

Safety of students in matters of discrimination have been increasing in visibility in recent years. This theme was a concern on nearly all of the campuses, though individual experiences may have varied.

Lack of Resources

It was a common theme that for issues of sexuality, many universities lacked appropriate resources. This not only means resources for sexual health, but resources like time, money, space, work force, etc. Only one university in this study reported adequate resources to address the needs of students around sexuality. When discussing the small size of the university, one administrator said:

> At a small Catholic college, you're going to mix those [LGBTQ+] groups together. And we're a small school, man. So we don't have an office dedicated to—really any kind of student support outside of your typical academic student support, and like your career services and campus activities. So we don't have like a diversity office, we don't have an inclusion office, we don't have a women's center, we don't have an LGBTQ center. Like those things because we're so small they're just not a reality. So everybody kind of pitches in.

At times, this lack of resources may result in a university placing the entirety of the burden of cultural change solely on the backs of minority students, or on select few faculty or staff interested in helping.

Pushing the Envelope/Persistence

The theme of persistence, or what some participants described as "pushing the envelope," was often mentioned when working toward change around an issue. Whether they encountered miscommunication within the organization, or openness and curiosity of the university, persistence in varying degrees was often present. On the topic of gender-inclusive housing, one participant said:

> We're by no means done. I think just because we have some gender inclusive practices, I think we have to work on some campus culture and some campus climate and education still, since things are so rapidly changing with these populations. So I definitely don't see us ... sitting back after gender inclusive housing is launched saying our job is done when it comes to this issue. I think it's still pushing the agenda forward and advocating, we still have some policies that, you know, need to be updated.

Catholic Identity Navigation

A common theme was the way changemakers navigated the Catholic identity of the university. Some participants accepted it and found it helpful, others approached it with respect and worked within the structure, and still others found it a nuisance and tried to work outside of or around it. There were a variety of approaches to this with no clear pattern in reasons why changemakers navigated this the way they did. Put simply, one participant said, "I think that point is so important: how do you honor Catholic teaching, but have a true, honest experience here for your students. It's absurd to pretend that [the human experience of sexuality] is not happening here." There is more on this theme in later chapters on communication and hopes for the future.

The Institutionalization of Change

When a change occurred, whether it persisted or not was largely dependent on if the change had become institutionalized. Money, resources, space, an administrative position often signaled an institutionalization of the change. If the change was only person-dependent, it often ceased once a key change agent left the university. Many participants understood this and attempted to institutionalize as much of the change as they could. One participant who had been involved with change around sexuality in Catholic higher education for many years said, "I think there's a difference between institutions or ... Catholic campuses that have adapted openness with respect to human sexuality at its institutional value versus those are highly dependent upon individual personnel." As mentioned above, this dependence can also lead to over-burdening and contribute to burnout.

Curiosity About Other Schools

After the interviews, several participants asked me what other schools are doing around issues of sexuality. One participant expressed this curiosity, saying:

> I do think it would be interesting to know how other people are doing out there .... I don't know how it's going. So I don't know if, you know, are the bishops—have they calmed down on these issues for other [campuses]? Is it cyclical? That would be interesting to know.

There seemed to be no central place for employees of Catholic colleges and universities to go to share ideas and talk about better types of change. There have been conferences on the matter of LGBTQ issues in Catholic higher education in the past, but nothing consistent enough for participants to access.

Sexual/Religious Identity

Though vague and not often mentioned, some participants identified the navigation of a religious and sexual identity. Whether this was a sexual minority identity or an identity garnered from one's sexual decisions, the dynamic of sexual and religious identities was at play. One participant said simply, "I think for many of our students, the biggest issue is now—how can they be their authentic selves, but also have that love for Christ, you know, then they're Christian."

The Broader Picture

I mentioned that these themes were apparent when comparing all of the interviews. Not every theme above was present in every interview, but of all of the data, these were common themes relating to the environment of sexuality change and Catholic higher education. These catalyst themes appeared to have some importance in the change process around sexuality. Some of the themes were described in great detail, and some only mentioned in passing. In the coming chapters, you will see some of these themes present in various other sets of themes (i.e., Catholic identity in communication strategies, out faculty and staff as a support to change). But the above themes are meaningful when examined as a "big picture" of factors related to change because they help paint the picture of the common factors associated with change around sexuality in Catholic higher education. Some of these themes may be more or less present on particular campuses. While I discuss theological insights for the various other groups of themes in future chapters, I will take this time to focus on what can be seen as the root theological concern undergirding this book: sexuality as a theological good and how the empirical data from this study plays a part in that discussion.

Theological Insights: Sexuality as a Theological Good

In an article titled "Organizational Research as Practical Theology," Kent Miller (2014) described how one can do practical theology through organizational research engaging with empirical data, social theories, and theological traditions. I will examine the empirical data and social theories in light of theological traditions to give some background for how many of these participants see organizational change regarding sexuality—or insights theology can offer to the data we see in each section. The above themes (and themes throughout this book) are situated in the context of a Catholic organization. In order to better understand how this cultural context gives meaning to the data we see presented here, we look to history. In order to understand how this data represents religiously problematic practices, we look to theology.

Sexual shame is a deeply rooted and far-reaching phenomenon that has plagued the Catholic Church for centuries. Despite much of the theology about sexuality being *good* within the human experience, there still exists much fear and shame about sexuality. First let's look at some of the ways this topic is discussed in Catholic theology, some of the highlights of sexuality as good, and why sexual shame is contrary to how we should feel about our sexuality.

Sexuality in Catholic Theology

Catholic theologians Todd Salzman and Michael Lawler (2008) write a great deal about Catholic sexual theology and ethics in their book *The Sexual Person*. In it they describe the landscape for the dialogue about Catholic sexual theology. Sometimes, sexual theology is discussed as a "theological anthropology," or theology of bodies, humanity, and how those relate to God. In their book, Salzman and Lawler will discuss this as *sexual anthropology*—a theological anthropology regarding sexuality. They note two different ways of doing sexual theology (i.e., writing about/conceptualizing)—Traditionalist and Revisionist. They describe these types of Catholic anthropology as follows:

> Catholic Traditionalist sexual anthropology emphasizes classicism, the universality of basic goods and human "nature," absolute

norms, and an act-centered morality. Catholic revisionist sexual anthropology emphasizes historical consciousness, the particularity of basic goods and the human person, norms that reflect this particularity, and a relational-centered morality.

(p. 93)

This distinction between an act-centered and relational-centered morality is an important one when considering sexual theology. Many people are taught that the Catholic Church says various sexual acts not performed in marriage or related to the end of procreation are bad in all circumstances and should be condemned. A good illustration of a traditionalist, act-centered morality is the concept of *"penitentials"* or manuals used in 6th-12th centuries that named an act/sin and the corresponding penance which priests should prescribe when hearing confessions (see Brundage, 1987, p. 152; Payer, 1984). A relational view of sexuality considers much more of the complexities of the human person, wrestling with the reality that humans actions all exist in a context, giving them various meanings. Relational-centered morality stems from a revisionist sexual theology. Put simply, it is the fundamental view of how we examine humans and their sexual nature has been critiqued and is being better articulated with a fuller understanding of the human person. Many Catholics are not taught of this sexual theological dialogue that has been happening for decades (for more on revisionist theology, see Tracy, 1975). And while there is too much to include in detail here, I will outline some key aspects of sexuality as a theological good as a foundation to support the type of change I advocate for in this book. Let's turn our attention now to the goodness of sexuality in Catholic theology.

Sexuality as a Theological Good

The Catholic Church has many documents discussing sexuality as a fundamental aspect of humanity—some of them named in Chapter 2 of this book. While there were shifting theological views prior to the Second Vatican Council (a meeting of bishops that caries much authoritative weight in the church, sometimes called "Vatican II"), documents that came from this council of the church played a meaningful role in our understanding about sexuality (Salzman & Lawler, 2016). It is through *Gaudium et Spes* (para. 51) that Salzman and Lawler (2016) note a shift from sexual acts alone to sexual acts in the context of the "nature of the human person." Since the 1960s, there have been many church teaching and theologians that discussed the goodness of human sexuality. Let's consider a few of them here.

In Catholic teaching, we see in the *Catechism of the Catholic Church* (2000)—a summary of church teachings—that sexuality is a source of joy and pleasure (#2362), and that being made in the image of God (*Imago Dei*) is an essential teaching to the goodness of our bodies as sexual humans. In the 1970s, a team of Catholic theologians wrote a book called *Human Sexuality: New Directions in American Catholic Thought* (Kosnik et al., 1977). The premise of the book is based on the goodness of human sexuality, noting its complexity within the Catholic tradition. Kosnik et al. are critical of forces that have helped shape Catholic attitudes toward sex. They note that "inadequate knowledge of biology, as well as religious taboos, the tradition of subhuman treatment of women, and a dualistic philosophy of human nature have all left a distinct imprint upon Catholic thinking" (p. 1). As a notable work in the field of Catholic sexual theology, this work offers critiques and new ways of looking at human sexuality through a Catholic lens. Even in the 70s, for example, the authors note the pastoral need to accentuate the goodness and sacredness of human sexuality, and that "expressions and approaches that are fear-dominated, consequence-oriented, and sin-centered should be avoided" (p. 173).

In her book *Body, Sex, and Pleasure*, Christine Gudorf (1994) takes a bold theological step by examining sexual pleasure as grace and a gift from God. She observes sexual pleasure is *good* because it was deliberately created by God, and observes that just as pain can cause distortions to the human body, pleasure can bring with it relief and joy, maximizing our experience of our bodies. Gudorf contrasts the goodness of our human bodies and sexuality against the backdrop of sexual violence and violation, that the body *is* the self, and that with human inviolability comes the right all humans have to remain unviolated in regard to our sexuality.

Margaret Farley's (2006) book *Just Love* stands out as a work dedicated to making sense of Catholic sexual ethics in the world today. In the beginning of the book, she notes plainly: "it is, after all, a good thing to move beyond fear and shame generated by irrational taboos and beyond complacency built on ignorance" (p. 8). Farley looks at seven sexual norms in this relational reality of humanity; (1) do no unjust harm, (2) people must have free consent, (3) the mutuality of sexual interaction, (4) equality in sexual relationship, (5) commitment between partners, (6) fruitfulness of what sexual relationship can bring, and (7) social justice aspects of our sexual relationships. She pulls from the theology of Karl Rahner to discuss humans as *embodied spirits*, or *inspirited bodies*—a unity of both body and spirit that cannot be separated, a unified incarnation that gives us meaning in the world and a special connection to the triune God, our bodies, and the other embodied spirits around us.

We continue to see a rich Catholic theological dialogue about sexuality throughout the discipline. We see theologians like Mary Hunt (2005) discussing justice in conversation with sexuality as a conduit for social change; John R. Sachs (1991) naming erotic desire as a powerful expression of our interdependence with others; M. Shawn Copeland (2010) noting the importance of sexuality for generous, generative, and full living, that our embodiment calls for the integrations of sexual energies and drive rather than its repression (p. 62); and Patricia Beattie Jung (2005) and Elizabeth Antus (2018) discussing the wisdom we gain from a theological understanding of women's experience of sexual pleasure (or lack thereof). There is a rich dialogue about the goodness of this mystery of human sexuality in the Catholic tradition. Many people are not aware that there are many in the world of Catholic theology articulating this beautiful aspect of humanity. This is only a brief look into that dialogue. As Michael Lawler and Todd Salzman summarize in their article on "The Mystery of Sexuality," "human sexuality demands ongoing analysis to be, first, better understood physically, psychologically/emotionally and spiritually/relationally in order, second, to be better understood theologically as…revelatory of the incomprehensible God" (p. 162).

These scholars are all Catholic scholars, but there are also great theological insights from scholars in the broad field of Christian sexual ethics and theology (e.g., De La Torre, 2007; Jordan, 2002; Jung et al., 2005; Nelson, 1978, 1983; Ott, 2007; Stayton, 2020). Learning about the mystery of human sexuality from other traditions is not only good, but necessary according to Mary Hunt and Patricia Beattie Jung (2009):

> adequate and meaningful ethical and religious reflection on sexuality in the future will need to be done in ways that move well beyond parochial limits. Exclusive reliance on one's own cultural or religious tradition, or even common (mis)understandings of the meaning of those traditions, will prove insufficient.
>
> (p. 165)

There is much good in the Catholic tradition about sexuality and still much listening Catholic leaders must do about Christian sexual theology.

Describing the difference between traditionalist and revisionist sexual theology, Salzman and Lawler (2008) note "although being part of the same Catholic tradition as traditionalists, revisionists have a fundamentally different interpretation of the multifaceted dimensions of human sexuality" (pp. 102–103). One thing is true of Catholic revisionist sexual theology (and Christian sexual theology, more broadly)—it engages with the complex, relational reality of human sexuality in ways that relate more directly to the humans in this study and those that make up Catholic universities. Catholic theologian Joseph Selling critiqued an act-centered morality as having "done tremendous damage to our understanding of human sexuality and any efforts to build a positive, human, integrated and community-building sexual ethics. The preoccupation with individual acts has blinded us to the big picture" (p. 152). This is not only true of a theological preoccupation with act-centered views of sexuality, but has a tendency to foster feelings of shame about sexuality outside of the theological world as well. Let's briefly turn our attention to sexual shame and, despite its popularity, its nature as contrary to how God designed us.

Sexual Shame

Christian ethicist Mark Jordan (2002) discusses the pervasiveness of sexual shame in his book *The Ethics of Sex*. He notes,

> those of us raised in Christian or post-Christian societies are likely to have been raised within family systems affected by theological shames. We can hear in Christian condemnations not just the voice of the church, but the voice of our parents.
>
> (p. 152)

Jordan is identifying the nature of sexual shame passed down from theology to church to parishioners and their children. For decades now, a religious narrative of sexual shame has been linked directly to sexual dysfunction and even preventing people from engaging helpful therapeutic strategies (Simpson & Ramberg, 1992). This has given rise to clinical literature discussing Christian sexual shame and how to overcome it from a therapeutic lens (i.e., Dale & Keller, 2019; McClintock, 2001; Sellers, 2017). Some of these scholars discuss theological aspects of sexual shame as contrary to how humans are created (with a sexuality imbued with a goodness of desire) and shifting from a sex-negative narrative to a sex-positive one.

This examination of sexual shame is not only discussed in the sex therapy world, but has also been described in theological circles in recent decades. Just as Kosnik et al. were suspect of a fear-dominated approach to sexuality in the 70s, we see the US Catholic bishops raise suspicion of it as well. The United States Catholic Conference (1991) noted that in teaching about sexuality, excessive feelings of shame, guilt, or discouragement should be avoided:

> In attempting to present the principles of sexual morality to children and adolescents, the Church strives to assist the young to

become aware of Catholic teachings without, at the same time, creating excessive feelings of guilt, shame, or discouragement. In the past, too many adolescents have withdrawn from the practice of their faith and disparaged the Church rather than facing their shortcomings and seek forgiveness, since their exaggerated feelings of guilt seemed, to them, unbearable.

(p. 19)

It is no secret that Catholic theology has historically had a fear-based sexual shame problem. The message that we see helps calm the fear of sexual shame as an understanding that our sexuality is a gift from God—not to be avoided or feared. Because we are embodied spirits made in the image of God, a rejection of our sexuality would be a rejection of what James Nelson (1978) calls our "body-selves." While it may be a popular idea, the concept that the body and soul are at odds (leading to "sexuality as bad") is not only incorrect, but a very un-Catholic way of operating around sexuality. What we will see in the chapters to come will be the effects of a fear-based reaction to sexuality at the institutional level in Catholic higher education. At times, without stopping to ask or understand the situation at hand, employees will assume something regarding sexuality cannot be done simply because they are a Catholic institution.

Conclusion

This chapter has been a broad overview in a couple of ways. The catalyst themes that arose from the data in this study were an overview of themes that were present in the process of change around human sexuality at Catholic colleges and universities. Depending on the institution, these themes may be more or less present. We also overviewed the dialogue around Catholic sexual theology, how sexuality is a theological good, and how shame and fear about sexuality are contrary to our embodied human goodness.

The present study was about employee change efforts regarding topics of sexuality at Catholic institutions of higher education. Pope Francis (2015a) reminds us in his encyclical *Laudato Si'* that an integral ecology is needed to respect humans in their social dimensions. Empirical data from the current study can help give voices to the changemakers in ways that can inform the dialogue of this change process. We see that Pope Francis (2015c) calls Christians to change with the times. He encourages us to be open to the challenges of the present, and that Christian doctrine is not a closed system, but is living and able to enliven (Francis I, 2015b). The participants of this study embody this call for change faithfully, for the common good.

To follow the logic from our above theological examination, we see (1) sexuality is good, (2) revisionist theology that considers the many wisdoms brought about through a relational lens, (3) empirical data can help us understand these relationships, and (4) that there is a call for staying committed to understanding and listening, addressing the needs of the church in the changing times. It is through this study data and theological reflections through this book that I hope Catholic institutions can dialogue with life's complexities and change for the good of all. Let us turn our attention now to a more focused categorical grouping of the themes present in the data.

References

Antus, E. L. (2018). "Was it good for you?": Recasting Catholic sexual ethics in light of women's sexual pain disorders. *Journal of Religious Ethics, 46*(4), 611–634. https://doi.org/10.1111/jore.12238

Brundage, J. A. (1987). *Law, sex, and Christian society in medieval Europe*. University of Chicago Press.

Catechism of the Catholic Church. (2000). (2nd ed.). Libreria Editrice Vaticana.

Copeland, M. S. (2010). *Enfleshing freedom: Body, race, and being*. Fortress Press.

Dale, B., & Keller, R. (2019). *Advancing sexual health for the Christian client: Data and dogma*. Routledge.

De La Torre, M. (2007). *A lily among the thorns: Imagining a new Christian sexuality* (1st ed.). Jossey-Bass.

Farley, M. (2006). *Just love: A framework for Christian sexual ethics*. The Continuum International Publishing Group Inc.

Francis I. (2015a). *Laudato si'*. http://www.vatican.va/content/francesco/en/encyclicals/documents/papa-francesco_20150524_enciclica-laudato-si.html

Francis I. (2015b, October 23). *Pastoral visit - Florence: Meeting with the participants in the fifth convention of the Italian church*. https://www.vatican.va/content/francesco/en/speeches/2015/november/documents/papa-francesco_20151110_firenze-convegno-chiesa-italiana.html

Francis I. (2015c, November 10). *Times change: Morning meditation in the chapel of the Domus Sanctae Marthae*. https://www.vatican.va/content/francesco/en/cotidie/2015/documents/papa-francesco-cotidie_20151023_times-change.html

Gudorf, C. E. (1994). *Body, sex and pleasure: Reconstructing Christian sexual ethics*. The Pilgrim Press.

Hunt, M. E. (2005). Just good sex: Feminist Catholicism and human rights. In P. B. Jung, M. E. Hunt, & R. Balakrishnan (Eds.), *Good sex: Feminist perspectives from the world's religions* (pp. 158–173). Rutgers University Press.

Hunt, M. E., & Beattie Jung, P. (2009). "Good sex" and religion: A feminist overview. *Journal of Sex Research, 46*(2–3), 156–167. https://doi.org/10.1080/00224490902747685

Jordan, M. D. (2002). *The ethics of sex*. Blackwell.

Jung, P. B. (2005). Sanctifying women's pleasure. In P. B. Jung, M. E. Hunt, & R. Balakrishnan (Eds.), *Good sex: Feminist perspectives from the world's religions* (pp. 77–95). Rutgers University Press.

Jung, P. B., Hunt, M. E., & Balakrishnan, R. (Eds.). (2005). *Good sex: Feminist perspectives from the world's religions*. Rutgers University Press.

Kosnik, A., Carroll, W., Cunningham, A., Modras, R., & Schulte, J. (1977). *Human sexuality: New directions in American Catholic thought*. Paulist Press.

McClintock, K. A. (2001). *Sexual shame: An urgent call to healing*. Fortress Press.

Miller, K. (2014). Organizational research as practical theology. *Organizational Research Methods, 18*, 276–299. https://doi.org/10.1177/1094428114559216

Nelson, J. B. (1978). *Embodiment: An approach to sexuality and Christian theology* (Revised ed.). Fortress Press.

Nelson, J. B. (1983). *Between two gardens: Reflections on sexuality and religious experience*. Pilgrim Press.

Ott, K. M. (2007). Rethinking adolescent sexual ethics: A social justice obligation to adolescent sexual health. *Journal of Lutheran Ethics, 7*(2). https://www.elca.org/JLE/Articles/530

Payer, P. J. (1984). *Sex and the penitentials: The development of a sexual code 550–1150* University of Toronto Press.

Sachs, J. R. (1991). *The Christian vision of humanity*. The Liturgical Press.

Salzman, T. A., & Lawler, M. G. (2008). *The sexual person: Toward a renewed Catholic anthropology*. Georgetown University Press.

Salzman, T. A., & Lawler, M. G. (2016). Vatican II and sexual ethics: Past, present, future. *Toronto Journal of Theology, 32*(2), 297–313. https://doi.org/10.3138/tjt.4202g

Sellers, T. S. (2017). *Sex, god, and the conservative church*. Routledge.

Simpson, W. S., & Ramberg, J. A. (1992). The influence of religion on sexuality: Implications for sex therapy. In R. M. Green (Ed.), *Religion and sexual health* (Vol. 56, pp. 155–165). Springer.

Stayton, W. R. (2020). *Sinless sex: A challenge to religions*. Luminare Press.

Tracy, D. (1975). *Blessed rage for order: The new pluralism in theology*. Seabury Press.

United States Catholic Conference. (1991). *Human sexuality: A Catholic perspective for education and lifelong learning*. United States Catholic Conference.

Chapter 4

The Landscape for Change
Key Areas of Change and Reactions

> What did participants think needed changing? How did they see themselves and their motivations in these efforts? What reactions did they encounter when embarking on this changemaking process?

In this chapter, we will look at three factors that contributed to the dynamic of change: (1) key areas for change noted by participants, (2) how participants contextualized their efforts, and (3) the reactions they encountered in the process. These components were instrumental in creating the framework discussed later in Chapter 8.

One of my research questions for all participants was: "What do you think needs changing?" Answers varied greatly, but many focused on LGBTQ issues, policy issues, curricular concerns, gender diversity, discrimination, or sexual health. As I got answers, I also wondered how people reacted to these changes participants were trying to help make. In this chapter, I will describe the key areas people felt needed to be changed in their time at universities and the reactions they encountered throughout the process. An important note here is that some participants had been working in their positions for less than 5 years, and others had worked in their positions for 15–20 years or more (those I liked to call "mega sources"—sources chock-full of institutional memory and experience making change). This means some of the content people felt needed to be addressed could have also spanned decades. This is not an exhaustive list of things that need to be changed at Catholic colleges and universities, but these are the most common themes brought up in this study across 17 different institutions.

Key Areas of Change

My first research question was: "What do Catholic higher education faculty/staff/administrators identify as key areas needing change?" Thirty out of the 31 participants had been involved in several different types of changes on their campus. I coded the types of changes that were discussed into 17 themes that I grouped into 6 major categories. Types of changes that participants named included LGBTQ student life on campus, including changing the hostile climate (e.g., instituting safe space trainings) and resources for LGBTQ student groups; policy issues around Title IX/sexual assault, and other sex-based policies like parental leave and partner benefits; curricular concerns about including courses on sexuality and academic freedom around issues of sexuality; issues of gender diversity, such as gender diversity in leadership, gender-neutral bathrooms, gender-inclusive housing, and managing dynamics with transgender students on campus; discrimination such as non-discrimination clauses or employee discrimination; and student sexual health (including dorm visitation, sexual decision-making and healthcare concerns such as birth control, abortion, condom distribution, etc.).

LGBTQ Student Life on Campus

While there were many intersecting areas of change, the most common themes revolved around making the campus more inclusive of LGBTQ students. This included a change in climate of the treatment of LGBTQ individuals as well as finding space and resources.

Climate Change

The need for a change in climate around LGBTQ students and orientation was a common area that participants cited in their experiences of change. Students were being bullied, harassed, and demoralized through various facets of the community. Whether it was with fellow students, faculty, staff members, administrators, or from institutional policy, participants identified a need for a climate change. One participant said:

> Our campus culture and climate [around LGBTQ visibility and support] wasn't very strong. Because a lot of our students who identified as part of the community would be witnesses to slurs and just outing by professors in general as well ... even employees who identify as part of the community [experienced this discrimination].

Other needs for a change in climate simply came from the fact that many university professionals and students were not aware of how to support LGBTQ students. One participant discussed the way they attempted to amend this:

So then the university started to take on more of a change in helping the students become more educated. Becoming more of an ally to students and also to start building programs around students, *for* students so that they can feel more comfortable on campus. I think the specific idea was that students who may have had specific sexual orientations or needs—that the university was not supportive of that, we were losing those students as opposed to embracing those students.

A recurring theme in this category was the presence of a safe space or safe zone training. These trainings are designed to inform various members of the campus about issues of sexual orientation and gender diversity, ultimately making the campus more aware of the experiences of sexual and gender minorities. One participant articulated:

We have what we call Safe Zone training on our campus and you know it's one of those things where I think in the very beginning when it started it might have been quote unquote "same old choir people" who're like, "yes let's do this, lets sign up for this and you know get retrained every year" but now I mean I don't even know how many people ... most offices you go in ... you see the banner for the safe zone training ... that's part of their programming for the regular university orientation.... So the conversation is being had all throughout campus and different places so it's not a, you know ... students are very aware of it, you know? And they know who to go to if there's ever an issue and they feel more comfortable having a conversation.

Some participants discussed the safe zone or safe space training as important for climate change, others discussed this training as the focus of the change—the change was to get a training onto campus in the Catholic environment.

LGBTQ Space and Resources

Often accompanying the need for a change in climate was the search for resources for LGBTQ students around issues of sexuality. Participants who identified this area of change discussed a need for more resources or a resource center about sexuality. One participant recounted:

[The LGBTQ student group] didn't have a space on campus. They had meetings but they didn't have a room that they met in, they had a classroom that was rotated every semester.... Membership to this organization was kind of in flux, the leadership was kind of weak.

Many participants had the experience of filling (or attempting to fill) the need for LGBTQ students to have a space on campus or the resources they needed to successfully exist as a student group. Several participants discussed issues of space, a resource center, or office specifically designated for sexuality as important to the lives of students and student groups that organized around sexual identity. Educational or social student group events were also seen as important components to LGBTQ student life.

Policy Issues

Other key areas for change involved various institutional policies around sexuality. Most frequently discussed was sexual assault and Title IX policy, but participants also discussed other sex-based policy such as parental leave and same-sex partner benefits.

Title IX/Sexual Assault

When discussing their experience in the area of Title IX and sexual assault prevention, one administrator said:

> We implemented all new sexual harassment and sexual assault policies—before all this Title IX guidance and the 2011 dear college letter came out, so we were way ahead of that. But that was prompted by a complaint from the Department of Education office for civil rights investigation.... I've implemented policy around sexual assault, broadened education around direct education for students around these sexual assaults, we've done a ton of education for employees related to sexual assault, sexual harassment. So I have a lot of experience there.

Because of its proximity to possible litigation and liability, Title IX compliance and sexual assault education was a common area of successful change when it was discussed (see *legality* theme in Chapter 3).

Other Sex-based Policies

The other two areas only mentioned in passing involved parental leave for both men and women at one institution and receiving same-sex partner benefits for health insurance. While some institutions avoided using terms such as "same-sex partner," some employees felt supported and affirmed by the decision:

> I think partly it was symbolic. So it was one way that the university could recognize our relationships on some kind of an equal level.... It was also a recognition that, financially, we were at a real major disadvantage because [my partner had] to carry an individual private policy, whereas other people at [the institution] who were married were not in that situation. So I think there was a real honest sense of (1) acknowledgement about our relationship, and (2) a real sense that we were at a disadvantage financially in terms of—I think health care which perhaps is one of the things that employers are most direct in providing people in relationships.

While the avoidance of the term "same-sex partner" in the policy did not bother some people, it should be noted that this practice (that I term *language sensitivity* in Chapter 6) can also contribute to erasure, contributing to the lack of *representation or visibility* noted in Chapter 3.

Curricular Concerns

Another common area of change discussed by participants was effecting a change in the curriculum or around academia in some way. Many participants saw the need to learn about sexuality as an integral part of their identity as a Catholic institution. Whether it was in a class that critically examined one's own sexuality and decision-making, formalized courses in LGBTQ history and literature, or classes that study and dialogue about sexual behavior and sexual ethics, participants often discussed their experience of incorporating issues of sexuality into the curriculum. One participant identified the university's concern when they first expressed a need for the course, saying: "I found out that the Theology Department ... was not open to that kind of course, they were very nervous about it, they did not think that it was a course that they could sponsor." Another faculty member identified resources that other faculty members could use to incorporate LGBTQ+ issues as well:

> So we held two formal workshops and then we were able to grant stipends to faculty who proposed and then actually did incorporate issues related to the LGBTQ+ community in existing courses and that was a way to kind of leaven our curriculum.

Issues of Gender Diversity

Another key area of change participants discussed I themed broadly as issues of gender diversity. With the exception of one interview that focused specifically on the inclusion of women in leadership positions, these topics almost exclusively focused on topics of gender-inclusive housing or bathrooms. By virtue of my inclusion criteria, it was expected that this would commonly be represented as most of higher education is also managing gender diversity in these areas (Hobson, 2014; Willoughby et al., 2012). Gender-inclusive housing and gender-neutral restrooms were discussed by participants as very common themes. However, some participants attempted to use language that avoided or negated the experience of transgender and non-binary individuals. For example,

> I brought the proposal and we named it, instead of naming it, like a ... we talked about it as "transgender bathrooms" but really what we were talking about is basically, any gender bathroom. And so in this case I decided to call them family bathrooms.

As noted in the sex-based policies above, situations like this were manifestations of language sensitivity discussed in Chapter 6.

In addition to including women in leadership positions, gender-inclusive housing, and gender-neutral bathrooms in this category, participants often discussed having to figure out accommodations for transgender students on campus. When discussing the difficulty they had incorporating transgender individuals into the prescribed gender binary on campus, the participant said, "so there's, like, the ... question, about how we incorporate those kinds of things with our ideas and principles and things like that, in accordance with what the law says." It seemed that some participants did not exactly understand the issue, did not understand transgender individuals, or expressed some confusion about how to understand gender identity (though many participants working for these changes most certainly *did* understand these things). Some participants were concerned with the existing structures: "have we had to make changes, there, I mean ... that would really shake us up a little bit with how we handle, you know, residence halls and housing and bathrooms and these kinds of things so..." A couple of participants were unclear about how to understand the concept of gender identity. When talking about the increasing focus of LGBTQ+ student organizations, one participant said:

> I don't even understand what they're talking about. So to get the population to understand these things that they want to push, they're hurting their own agenda, by confusing, there's too many things—[the woman overseeing the student organization] says it's just too many things in there [referring to the acronym LGBTQ+]. We're no longer talking about gay or straight, we're talking about all these other things that people just don't know about and so

it's kind of now hurting a little bit, the student group, you know? I think that that's the big thing, that's where you would get the gender-neutral bathroom, the gender-neutral resident hall wings and things, it's just too hard to do that right now anyway.

It may be worth noting here that in this case, the "issue" of gender diversity included employees' inability or lack of opportunity to understand how gender identity works.

There were also a number of well-informed participants who understood how to accommodate gender diverse students, but articulated difficulty working within the system:

> I think gender identity is important and I think many Catholic institutions will say that, although it's separate from sexuality, its related to sexuality and I think many Catholic institutions recognize two genders, male and female, and I think that's not helpful to people who may find themselves to be transgender or transitioning or on spectrum or outside of the binary.

There was only one institution that had very little difficulty working around the inclusion of gender diversity on their campus.

Discrimination

A key area of change for universities involved issues of discrimination. Changing the non-discrimination clause or attempting to change instances of employee discrimination were both coded under this discrimination theme.

Non-discrimination Clauses

Most often, this area of change involved including sexual orientation and gender identity in the non-discrimination clauses of the university. One faculty member participant recalled:

> The students had successfully protested and lobbied and used their leverage to get the College to modify its statement on non-discrimination to include gender identity and sexual identity.... So that's official now, the Board agreed to that as a way to sort of hold off more protests from the students and I think that's had a serious knock off effect that only now it's starting to be seen.

Student protest for policy change around this issue was not uncommon in the broader experience of Catholic higher education (see

Archbold, 2012; Dionisopoulos, 2013; Nelson, 2012, also noted as *student protest* in Chapter 6).

Employee Discrimination

Participants also spoke of the discrimination of employees as an area that needed change. Expressed by a participant in a faculty position:

> There are still some campuses where people fear that if they're known as being openly gay or lesbian or trans, that that could impede the prospect [of] either being promoted in a non-academic position or being promoted with tenure in an academic position.

This fear of discrimination also spread into graduate students' work on issues of sexuality—being concerned with facing discrimination should their curriculum vitae or resume contain issues of queer studies or sexuality.

Staff members also expressed a concern for discrimination:

> You can be fired at any moment, there's no protection for staff, I'm in a state where I can be fired at any moment for being queer, I'm young, and I don't have a doctorate, right? ... you're so vulnerable so when you think about people trying to do this work on other campuses, you have to have somebody that is just like not—just going for it and I think that's really a lot to ask of somebody.

Much of the fear of discrimination and retaliation here is noted as a barrier to change, elaborated on in the next chapter.

Student Sexual Health

Another key area that arose in the interviews involved student sexual health concerns. This topic often included issues of student sexual activity in dorms, sexual decision-making, and healthcare concerns such as birth control, abortion, and condom distribution.

Dorm Sex

Some participants discussed changes around the sexual lives of students, including how college students make sexual decisions and how policies on dorm visitations related to their sex lives. One participant outlined the predicament:

> [Statistics] show that these students are sexually active—the ones who are certainly identifying as heterosexual. And there's a lot

of it. College is like that, institutionally. You know, there's no sex ed, there's no ... It causes a lot of problems from a student-welfare point of view—a LOT of problems—because it really ties the hands of counselors and administrators when it comes to talking about healthy relationships. You're not supposed to say, as an administrator, a healthy relationship involves safe sex. You're not supposed to be having sex. So there are those problems there.

Sexual Decision-making

Student sexual decision-making was often discussed in conjunction with the hook-up culture. While some participants were interested in starting conversations with students about the hook-up culture, one administrator expressed difficulty in engaging with the conversation:

> One thing that I was really interested in ... was the idea of the hook-up culture. I didn't really end up doing a whole lot of programming or efforts to make any changes in that area, it's just too damn hard.

The participant, however, did not describe why it was a difficult task.

Healthcare

Issues of healthcare were another recurring theme. Whether it involved including birth control or abortion on the student healthcare plan or the distribution of condoms, these more concrete issues of sexual health were seen as big issues over which participants felt like they had little control. One faculty member expressed concern with the inability to distribute condoms on campus: "So on the one hand, it's lovely to walk out [and see LGBTQ-focused events] on the quad. But, by refusing to put condoms in the dormitory restrooms, we're encouraging unsafe sexual behaviors that put young people's lives at risk."

Other participants felt powerless and accepted the fact that the university was "never" going to allow condom distribution on campus. About student sexual health, another participant said:

> And so, you know, that's really been a concern and so actually for the first time, a student—usually the student will come and talk to me about, "well we want baskets of condoms." I'm like well that's not going to happen, but tell me why that is so important.

Contextualized Efforts

My second research question asked: how do Catholic higher education faculty/staff/administrators contextualize their efforts to create change around sexuality issues within their institutions? Data on how participants have contextualized those efforts, however, were not clearly or consistently articulated. The interview question of "why did you think the change was so important" did not garner much attention or response. It seemed as if participants felt it was obvious why things that were harmful to people should be changed (and in their defense, it is fairly obvious). This "obvious" factor is evident in responses like: "it's pretty hard not to see that there is a need for sustained intervention in Catholic higher education institutions …. [It] ends up with a lot of nervousness when it comes to dealing with these issues." Or "when I came I saw that people were saying we couldn't talk about sexuality because we were a Catholic institution and I found that to be completely erroneous."

Even still, at least 13 of the 31 participants clearly conceptualized their role as someone to advocate for the students who could not advocate for themselves or mentors for the students to empower them in their educational journey. One participant summed up the need:

> I think that we need to stay abreast of these situations and up-to-date and supporting individuals who may be experiencing any number of changes or experiences that relate to their sexuality. So I think that it's important just to, you know, from our stand point to continually support our students and stay up-to-date on what things we should and maybe shouldn't be doing as it relates to sexuality in this day and age.

Other faculty members discussed teaching classes on issues of sexuality. They talked about their passion for the subject and how it can help students better understand sexuality. Other participants discussed more affective reasons for the importance of the change—whether it stemmed from their own hurt of experiencing discrimination or sensitivity to similar issues of oppression such as sexual shame around sexual assault. One participant replied to why the change was so important:

> [It is important for] student quality of life and for campus climate, I mean there was a lot of anti-gay cultural things going on both in and outside of the classroom, students who were questioning their sexual orientation or were out were very obviously—I mean even beyond macroaggressions. They really were condemned. Sometimes straight out in a classroom with a professor saying you're going to hell. It was a pretty ugly climate, again, it's a Midwestern Catholic University. But those students really had a tough time and I really felt for them.

Similarly attuned to the pain of others, and looking to their Catholic roots as a reason for change another participant said:

> I saw the restraint under which the students met and I saw the kinds of harassment and bullying that they experienced in their lives and I thought this is not how any student should live, this is not just, it does not align with the Christian principles of love; it doesn't even align with Roman Catholic principles of respect and dignity for every individual.

One participant discussed their role and the need to be leaders on the issue of sexual assault awareness:

> We needed to be a leader on the campus ... and so I think people like that vision of being responsible—of doing everything we possibly could to prevent sexual assault and create a healthy sexuality on campus, it's part of the ethics of care [a tenet related to the Catholic mission of their institution].

This participant viewed sexual assault awareness and healthy sexuality as important for caring for humanity, contextualizing their institutional change around sexuality as an issue of human dignity—part of the mission of the church. Much like this participant, others described their role as engaging and upholding the Catholic nature of the university by addressing these issues. Several responses echoed the following:

> So hearing those kinds of [sad] stories from students, it was really like, we had to do something, there wasn't really any other answer, but you know we can't sit there and say that we are Catholic University that cares for people and—in my mind anyway— ... these questions from the students would be right there in front of me, saying, "you say, that we are a welcoming church that we welcome the poor, we welcome this, we welcome that, but where do you welcome me?" And so those questions really resonated with me as, like, a good question and a good self-reflection for myself. Who do I welcome and *how* do I welcome?

Overall, the participants contextualized their efforts in terms of working toward a justice that was being overlooked. Whether they worked within the framework of Catholicism or simply treating people in a just way, participants saw themselves as doing work that needed to be done to prevent harm, discrimination, or further damage to people.

Reactions/Responses

Reactions that changemakers experienced from other university employees or offices also had culturally relevant factors to the Catholic context. Reactions to change efforts varied greatly. These reactions experienced by participants influenced the type of method (see Chapter 6) they would use to effect change at the institution. People responded supportively or with resistance. When responding with resistance, I coded the reason for the resistance as well as the resistant outcome or actions taken.

1. Supportive Responses

    Several participants reported certain people in the university (i.e., the student life staff, residence life staff, the student body, individual supervisors, etc.) or virtually the entire university community responding in some positive way. When discussing updating a safe space training to make it more relevant to the university context, one participant said, "I think once we rolled it out, [everyone] has been very supportive. I don't think we got any question about—if anything, people were wondering when a safe space [training] was going to be happening."

    Supportive responses occurred with a variety of changes from safe space trainings, to educational initiatives, to curricular changes. Another participant described getting a curricular approval at their university:

    > We had to go through that approval process for a new interdisciplinary minor, it went up through the ranks at [the university], through the curriculum committee, through the council of deans and up to the president and it was approved without any resistance and with a great deal of support.

2. Resistant Responses

    A majority of the study participants reported some type of resistance associated with their change regarding an issue around sexuality. Changes around sexual assault policies or trainings were most frequently reported to have no resistance, even in more conservative environments. I have coded resistance in two ways: the reasons for resistance (fear/nervousness, misunderstanding, mission/identity incongruence, and perceived scandal) and resistant (in/)actions (silence/avoidance, rescinding offer, and church hierarchy involvement).

Reasons for Resistance

Participants met resistance at many different levels and from many different facets of university life. These reasons often overlap and are not mutually exclusive. For the sake of contextualizing the landscape of changemaking, I have coded these reasons for resistance into four groups: fear/nervousness, misunderstanding, mission/identity incongruence, and perceived scandal. A brief definition and description of each can be found in Table 4.1.

Fear/Nervousness

The most commonly cited reason for encountering resistance was because of fear or nervousness. Fear was coded as a barrier to change when experienced either by the changemaker or others. Fear of losing one's job can be enough to prevent a change. When fear is coded as a reason for resistance, the discussions appear more ambiguous. About a president's motivation toward offering same-sex partner benefits, one faculty member noted: "[The president's] predecessor had told us on numerous occasions after we had demonstrated … that he did not want to be the first president of a Catholic school to give domestic partner benefits." Of what the president was afraid remained unclear.

Similarly, one administrator identified fear of getting backlash from more conservative Catholics, saying that they did not want to "put out there into the world that, okay [our university] now has transgender bathrooms and the reason why is because then that's going to raise some red flags with some conservatives."

Some employees experienced fear involving termination or fear of backlash from conservative constituents. Some participants also reported a fear of people calling in under false pretenses to deceive the employee to get information and somehow denounce or slander the university in some way (i.e., a blog post, conservative magazine article, report to the bishop, etc.). One housing professional recalled: "And I think we didn't know whether the student was transgender or somebody was inquiring maybe for negative reasons or somebody was 'testing us' to see if we were really Catholic, you know, that sort of thing." I occasionally encountered the same type of skepticism when seeking study participants. Fear often coincided with the other three reasons for resistance—misunderstanding, the change seen as against a Catholic identity, and an apparent scandal.

Misunderstanding

Another common source for resistance was misunderstanding what the change was about or generally being uneducated about sexuality.

Table 4.1 Resistant responses to change around issues of sexuality in Catholic higher education

Theme	Definition	Example
Reasons for Resistance		
Fear/Nervousness	Fear or nervousness (either vague or specific) about dealing with a change related to sexuality at a Catholic institution.	A president afraid of public backlash for a change; employees fearing job termination; administrators being afraid to be the "first" university to make that change.
Misunderstanding	Misunderstanding what the change was about or being uneducated about the given sexuality topic.	A dean not understanding what a drag show entails; administrators associating everything about LGBTQ+ student organizations with sexual activity.
Mission/Identity Incongruence	Perception that the change was at odds or incongruent with the Catholic mission/identity of the institution.	Preventing a presentation on sexuality because "talking about sexuality is against Catholic teaching"; dissolving a queer student organization because it "goes against Catholic teaching."
Perceived Scandal	Perception the change would bring public attention in which the change would be interpreted as 'scandalous.'	A president not allowing a change because they think the public well get confused; preventing a public view of support for Pride to avoid the public thinking the school "socially endorses homosexuality."
Resistant Actions/ Inactions		
Silence/Avoidance	Requests for change being met with silence from those in a place of power to allow it. Avoidance of the changemaker attempting to effect the change.	A residence life member asking an administrator about transgender accommodations and being ignored; university leadership pretending an administrative decision with harmful effects never happened.
Rescinding Offer	Taking back an institutional offer (e.g., job, award, invitation) because of something regarding sexuality.	Upon learning that a speaker who was invited to give a talk wrote on matters of sexual health, a dean reaches out to rescind the invitation.
Church Hierarchy Involvement	The local bishop is involved (or a threat is made to involve the bishop) to dictate that a change should not happen.	Bishop calls a university president to request a scholar publicly dissociate from the university; faculty member threatening to call the bishop if a change is enacted.

One faculty member reflected on the administration's reaction when hosting a "big gay" student event:

> For them big and gay meant big old penises and on big old gay men.... [It] has been [the administration's] prescription that anything related to [the LGBTQ student group] means sex.... That's true for some external constituencies to the university as well.

Similarly, a faculty member reported on feedback from a drag show the student group was planning to implement. The participant said, "I was reading about the opposition to the drag show, it's almost just completely about that it promotes a gay lifestyle." It was clear to the participant that the resistance was coming from a misunderstanding about what the student events would be about.

Misunderstanding from the administration was also reported by another participant when trying to form an LGBTQ student support group. When talking about the initial steps of forming the group, the participant said:

> That was met with resistance from the administration when we first proposed it, because the fear was that this was going to be a hookup group that the only reason students were wanting to do this was so that they could hookup with other students who were identified as like themselves.

While the administration misunderstood the student group to be a sexually driven social group, drivers for change eventually educated the administration on how a student group around orientation and gender identity can be a supportive, educational experience for college-aged students.

Mission/Identity Incongruence

Another reported reason for a resistant reaction involved the perception that these things cannot happen at a Catholic university—that supporting any same-sex concept or discussing sexuality is against a Catholic identity. One participant recounted getting calls from parents about a sexual and gender minority informational event, "So I was getting calls from parents of students, saying that they heard that we were putting on a week of programs that supported a gay lifestyle [and] how can we do that as a Catholic University?"

A strong critique of this Catholic identity often came from faculty members or other university constituents. A campus minister identified this type of resistance they experienced from faculty members on campus:

> There were some faculty and administrators who were very conservative in their thoughts and their ideas about the whole sexual identity piece and this was a Catholic University and this is the blah, blah, blah ... that they are intrinsically evil, all that kind of stuff that you would get.

While another participant recalled some feedback they got when effecting a change around supporting LGBTQ students in residence life:

> We did have some backlash I would say from some faculty members who didn't see that this was something that as a [Catholic] Institution, we needed to reflect on because we were identified as a Catholic institution and based on Catholic teachings it goes against what a lot of the teachings proclaim.

A small but important theme was present in this study—people interpreting the Catholic identity as *against* supporting sexually and gender diverse people. This was likely a driving force in the few cases of resistance from conservative Catholic student groups reported by participants.

Perceived Scandal

Some administrators exercised caution, trying to prevent the perception that they were doing something scandalous. The fear of having something appear scandalous is a long-standing concern for the Catholic Church. The *Catechism of the Catholic Church* outlines the term "scandal" as something extremely problematic that "lead[s] others to evil" (para. 2284). Though later, one participant and priest noted that by scandal, the church means something that would lead others to evil while Catholic institutions interpret scandal to mean a "public relations nightmare." This concept is reflected in reactions encountered by participants—fear of "creating scandal" around an issue of sexuality. Participants talked about not doing anything that might send a message by which the public may get confused. One participant recalled being told that the newly formed student group should "not do anything that could be considered a social endorsement of homosexuality." Something as simple as citing a Planned Parenthood resource on sexual health information could also have been seen as support for the organization, creating a "scandal" for the Catholic university.

Resistant (In/)Actions

From any of the above listed reasons, participants noted the resistance they encountered being active or passive such as encountering silence or avoidance of the issue, an offer being rescinded (i.e., an award or employment position), or church hierarchy involvement.

Silence/Avoidance

One oft-cited response involved silence or avoidance from administration or people necessary for the change to become a reality. After experiencing this reaction, one participant referred to this phenomenon: "And this was indicative of what I think of as the time of silences. And what are we silent about? We're silent about the things that we're afraid of, that we don't want to happen."

On the topic of getting services for a transgender student, one faculty member mentioned that they "think [the university] was kind of mum on it, like they weren't commenting when they were asked to comment.... There's just kind of this air of secrecy over many topics on campus."

A similar air of secrecy was reported when one administrator was asking how to respond to student inquiries about sexual health. They said, "There was some question about what happens when students want to have conversations around sexuality and so basically the message that I was giving was, oh, you know, we don't talk about that."

Reporting on a situation in which the administration took harmful actions against the resource center for sexuality on campus, a faculty member identified a similar reaction—that "they just acted like none of that had happened, which it did." Whether it was explicitly being told to be silent, not returning e-mails asking for permission, or avoiding situations of change, several participants identified silence or avoidance as a response they had encountered.

Rescinding Offer

Occasionally, there have been times when a university was granting an award to an individual or signed a contract with a new employee and rescinded the offer (or was forced to rescind the offer) over a matter of sexuality.

Several participants discussed accounts of job offers, various awards, or speaking engagements being rescinded. One participant identified a time when their student group was told not to give an award for service to the LGBTQ community to the person they had chosen:

> The question was could we give an award to somebody who was basically working, basically, at cross-purposes to the church....

And the answer was like "no. You can't. You can bring that person to speak, you could talk about it in class, you could have a panel discussion, you bring a movie, but you can't give somebody an award."

The participant not only had to rescind the offer for the award, but had to rescind the offer for the person to speak on campus. This was a result of another faculty member threatening to call the bishop should the speaker come to campus.

Church Hierarchy Involvement

A less reported but highly feared action of resistant responses was getting the church hierarchy involved. This often looked like calling the local bishop and could occasionally result in ecclesiastical investigation. One health services participant recalled the bishop giving orders about what can or cannot be included in the insurance plan. The participant identified having to comply because of the bishop's involvement.

Bishop involvement (or episcopal intervention) was also described regarding issues of academic freedom. One faculty member discussed engaging in public discourse on sexuality. A statement the participant made was published in a local newspaper and said "as [the bishop] read that, he called our president and the president called me down and asked me to publicly disassociate myself with [the university] anytime I engaged in any type of public scholarship."

Discussion

Key Areas of Change: A Changing World Not Easily Ignored

The key areas identified in the results section above were issues participants found to be important areas of change around sexuality in Catholic higher education today. To group them even broader into issues of orientation, gender identity, sexuality knowledge, and discrimination, these topics likely entered participants' minds because of how they interpreted the phrase "issues of sexuality" when agreeing to participate in the study. Topics of orientation and gender identity seemed to take most of the focus on each of these campuses. This is likely because of the association of the word "sexuality" in this study—participants thought more about sexual behavior-related concepts or gender identity. Sexuality is a term often reduced to refer solely to genitals or orientation (maybe also gender identity). Morey and Piderit (2006) discussed the Catholic university culture as having important connections to the dominant US culture and US university life. It is likely that these topics are present because other universities in the United States have been dealing with them as well (Cramer, 2002; Greytak et al., 2009; Sausa, 2002). Though one participant did note that they had dealt with issues of safe space training 15 years prior at two different public intuitions, claiming the Catholic intuitions seem to be lagging behind.

Overall, the key areas of change identified by participants were largely similar to that of most non-Catholic institutions of higher education (Cramer, 2002). The fact that LGBTQ student concern is quite prevalent at these universities coincides with the previous literature, as most studies focusing on issues of sexuality in Catholic higher education tend to be about lesbian and gay student experiences (Fry, 2013; Getz & Kirkley, 2006; Hughes, 2015; Love, 1997, 1998; McEntarfer, 2011; Miceli, 2009).

An area less explored by the research literature, however, is the experience of transgender identities in Catholic higher education. Participants frequently discussed addressing best practices in providing services to transgender or gender non-conforming students. The experience of transgender individuals in Catholic higher education has been vastly understudied and requires much more attention, as evidenced by the participants' concerns about how other schools are managing policy around gender in a Catholic setting.

Conceptualizing Their Efforts: Not Alone

The ways in which participants described their motivations suggests that they largely conceptualize their efforts as doing good and important work. Many people framed their role as mentor, advocate, and as caring for humanity. Some participants were not clear about or did not identify their motivations. Participants who discussed advocacy or mentorship often included their Catholic faith as a source for this motivation. Catholicism as a driving cause for this advocacy and change would be consistent with findings in previous studies. In a dissertation study on LGBT issues in a Jesuit university, Hughes (2015) cited the Catholic faith being an important factor for students, faculty, administration, and staff in their efforts to make campus life more accepting of LGBT individuals, also supporting Love's (1997) finding.

The experience of using the Catholic faith to support LGBT individuals has also appeared on more popular and practical book lists in recent years. A recent book by a Jesuit priest, Fr. James Martin (2017a), discussed the intersection of Catholicism and LGBT individuals. This may be a helpful resource for changemakers interested in learning more about how the Catholic Church can support

LGBTQ+ individuals. Martin described ways that Catholic leaders and representatives can address harm done to LGBT individuals by the church. The book, however, does not come without critiques. Martin said that his critics feel the book has gone too far or not far enough (Martin, 2017b). In the conservative magazine *Crux*, Fr. Dwight Longenecker (2017) critiqued the book as having gone too far, claiming that recognizing LGBT people is dangerous and he advocated for the use of groups accused of supporting conversion therapy (Coffin, 2012). In another magazine, the National Catholic Register, Fr. Landry (2017) discussed the book's shortcomings by not engaging church teaching directly—the source, Landry said, of a lot of pain for LGBT individuals. For changemakers who are learning about the experience of LGBT individuals and the Catholic Church, Martin's book may be a useful source of motivation or guidance. It may be important to note that many LGB Catholic (or former Catholics) in my own life found this book to be the "bare minimum" or "too little, too late"—expressing disappointment that Martin's call for basic human dignity is seen as a ground-breaking movement. While the book may be useful to some people working in the field, know that it exists in a context that has caused much hurt and pain to LGBT persons. This may help readers view this book as just one small step toward a loving dignity LGBT people may rightly feel they deserve from the Catholic Church.

Reactions: Dynamics with Much to Tell

I coded the reactions that participants encountered as either supportive or resistant. Participants identified positive reactions often described as "no resistance" or identified ways people approved—accepting the change happily, verbal support of the changemakers, and working to make a change a reality. I did not analyzed details of this type of reaction in depth because a supportive reaction is not a barrier that needs to be overcome. Participants noted that some people in their social circles outside of university life did not believe supportive change around issues of sexuality could take place in a Catholic institution. Love (1997) discussed "contradictions and paradoxes" of change for LGB students at religiously affiliated institutions such as leaders that could not lead, LGB people may have a strong Catholic identity, and that support could come from campus ministry or departments of religious studies. In the same paradigm, some people may view a Catholic institution accepting a change with no resistance as a paradox. For some, a comforting insight from this study is that some Catholic institutions do not find difficulty in adapting to the acceptance and support of LGBTQ+ persons.

With resistance, however, various methods of communication needed to be employed. Types of resistance included silence or avoidance, or more active roles like rescinding an offer from a speaker or potential employee or getting the church hierarchy involved. In the particular university he studied, Hughes (2015) discussed what he called a culture on non-confrontation, referring to how students responded to resistance from administration, and less about how the administration was responding to a change. The present study focuses on the administration's silence or avoidance of the topic of change. Silence and avoidance were employed by administrators on a wide variety of topics. One reoccurring topic involved issues regarding transgender students. One participant speculated administration's silence was due to the fact that no other (Catholic) campus has resolved how to manage housing for transgender students (to their knowledge), leading to the void of direction. This could indicate a type of culture in between the espoused culture (values the university openly claims) and the shadow/un-espoused culture (the unwritten rules—the things you don't say out loud, but everyone operates on) identified by Morey and Piderit (2006). This in-between culture can be seen as a nebulous culture where a given value is not universally operated on in the shadows, but it is also not clearly espoused by the university. This type of neglectful permission—or permission-by-omission response—allows the administration to escape a certain sense of culpability should conservative constituents raise this as an issue, while also meeting the needs of students. Hughes' category of "stalling behaviors" as a barrier can fit into this category, but does not completely encompass this experience as some people may not have intentionally stalled to prevent a change, but merely avoided addressing the matter to omit involvement in the change.

The more active roles of resistance involving rescinding offers and getting the church hierarchy involved appear to be only two types of methods described in the interviews. Hughes (2015) discussed controlling behaviors as a type of power dynamic including bishop involvement (also true for Love, 1998) or forcing LGBT groups to work with campus ministry. The present study supports the findings of Hughes and Love that hierarchical involvement can impede the process for effective change around issues of sexuality. The active resistance of rescinding offers occurred frequently enough in participant interviews that it demonstrates the need to identify this as a possible reaction, more than just the church hierarchy exerting power—the administration was also exerting power over the situation. Whether the administration was forced to do so by the bishop, for fear of donors withholding funds, or for other reasons remains unclear. But what can be garnered from this data is the focus on the dialogue between the institution and hierarchal church. Some participants spoke of comfort with their president's commitment to talking with the bishop. It is possible that the dialogue between a bishop and university administration offers more insight into how these colleges and universities may best support their LGBTQ+ constituents.

Some people may be resistant to change for a number of reasons—misunderstanding, underlying assumptions about scandal, mission incongruence, or repercussions. The reasons for resistance will help determine the types of communication that can overcome these barriers. The reactions here combined with the communication strategies in Chapter 6 will pair to offer a helpful framework for effecting change at an institution in Chapter 8. Each campus has a number of cultural factors that will determine the best combination for effective change around issues of sexuality. The key to effective change will be finding the combination of methods that work best with the institutional culture.

Theological Insights: Discrimination and Communal Redemption

While there are many theological themes we can pull from the data in this chapter, I want to focus specifically on a theology of discrimination in relation to these resistant reactions and communal redemption in relation to how university structures (and those who uphold them) mistreat people with regard to sexuality, and specifically sexual identity. Put simply, discrimination as institutional sin and communal redemption is the process through which our institutions can better serve all of God's people.

Many of the key issues that changemakers were attempting to solve seemed to be addressing inclusion or discrimination in some way. The concerns of discrimination paired with the resistant reactions changemakers met from their colleagues paint the picture of a very important problem in Catholic culture—the use of the Catholic faith (or the tendency of those in the Catholic culture) to exclude, condemn, or avoid honoring LGBTQ+ peoples and overall sexuality information in the institution. Let's briefly consider the theological insights the church has to offer about this phenomenon.

We often see people using Catholic teaching on sexual orientation and gender identity to defend Catholic institutional discrimination of LGBTQ+ peoples (e.g., Herriot & Callaghan, 2019; Hughes, 2019). This may look like active discrimination—job terminations, denied requests for policy changes or inclusion, etc.—or more passive discrimination in the silence or avoidance of discussing LGBTQ+ people and associated needs. In an article about youth ministry, Arthur David Canales

(2016) refers to this as an "eyes wide shut" approach—the almost non-existence of ministry to LGBTQ youth, failing to "cater to, actively attract, or tolerate LGBTQ youth" (p. 61). This is part of what I term "Catholic erotophobia" or the fear of/distancing from the topic of sexuality in Catholic culture. University and colleges with such an *eyes-wide-shut* approach to LGBTQ peoples and their needs are actively choosing exclusion and avoidance over institutional inclusion, which, in a theology of organization, results in choosing not to invite the inclusive love of God into relationships at an institutional level.

The official Catholic teaching on discrimination, however, is in direct contradiction to the very exclusion being enacted by members of these institutions. The *Catechism of the Catholic Church* (2000, #1935) explicitly names the equality of persons as the basis for not discriminating against others. The *Catechism* cites the conciliar document *Gaudium et Spes* when naming "every type of discrimination, whether social or cultural, whether based on sex, race, color, social condition, language or religion, is to be overcome and eradicated as contrary to God's intent" (Paul VI, 1965, para. 29). This condemnation of discrimination was a key point in Fr. James Martin's (2017a) popular book *Building a Bridge: How the Catholic Church and the LGBT Community Can Enter into a Relationship of Respect, Compassion, and Sensitivity*. In it, Martin quotes Australian Bishop Vincent Long (2016) on being an inclusive church:

> We cannot talk about the integrity of creation, the universal inclusive love of God, while at the same time colluding with the forces of oppression in the ill-treatment of racial minorities, women, and homosexual persons. It won't wash with young people, especially when we purport to treat gay people with love and compassion and yet define their sexuality as intrinsically disordered.
>
> (para. 33)

Indeed, in a response to a letter Fr. James Martin wrote the Pope seeking answers to questions commonly asked by LGBT Catholics, Pope Francis replied that God does not disown any of God's children and that the onus of rejection is on people within the church, not grounded in the nature of the church (Bordoni, 2022). When people attempt to use Catholic teaching as a basis for discrimination and exclusion, they are opting to focus on ways to exclude others from a community dedicated to serving humanity rather than bring people together in ways that honor human dignity. Every time someone is fired from a Catholic institution for being gay, told that one's Catholic identity is forcing this discrimination, or ignoring requests for help from sexually and gender diverse people, that person is enacting the very discrimination condemned by the church itself. Using an inclusive church—a Catholic (*Katholikos*: universal) Church *for everyone*—as a reason for discrimination is not only inaccurate and antithetical to the Catholic Church's mission in the world but creates an environment ripe for those in the dominant group to discriminate against people in the minority. The creation and upholding of this discriminatory environment should be a systemic concern for all Catholic institutions.

Given this theology of discrimination, resolution that fosters right relationship involves an institutional or communal redemption. Doing the work of dialogue and liberating people from oppression is—as we see employees named above—inspired by a liberating God. When an employee or group of people work for change to treat groups of people better, handle sexual assault cases with more dignity, or help an institution educate people how to better care for themselves regarding sexual health, an organization engages in a type of communal redemption. It institutionalizes an ethic of care that changes the ways it operates. Rosemary Radford Ruether (1983) discussed communal redemption like this:

> It is essential to understand redemption as a communal, not just an individual, experience. Just as sin implies alienation and broken community, so rebirth to authentic selfhood implies a community that assembles in the collective discovery of this new humanity and that provides the matrix of regeneration.
>
> (p.193)

Sin of discrimination that breaks community apart requires the redemptive practice of rebirth. A redefinition of institutional practice, a commitment to an institutional self that listens and works to include others. Ruether's words remind us that we—as community—must collectively join, in our most humane nature, with each other to regenerate a community that honors everyone. As Catholic institutions reflect on this practice of exclusion and avoidance, they are met with an opportunity to include LGBTQ+ peoples in ways that mend relationships, uphold dignity, and honor the gifts that sexually and gender diverse people bring to that community.

Conclusion

Throughout this chapter, we looked at the topics participants thought should be changed, how they saw their own efforts, and the reactions they encountered. These key areas of change were informed by cultural and historic factors that will change over time. For many in the world of Catholic higher education, I was told consistently by participants who worked in both Catholic and non-Catholic institutions that "the Catholic work is about 15–20 years behind the rest of the world" in terms of understanding issues of sexuality at an institutional level. While I don't believe this is true for all Catholic universities or every issue of sexuality, it did seem to be the general notion of participants. Whatever issues do arise, I believe these changemakers will be motivated by their love of God's creation, the Gospel, and human dignity to effect the necessary changes to ensure a safe and thriving environment for everyone.

We will return to theological insights about participants following their conscience when contextualizing these efforts in Chapter 7 where we will continue the conversation of changemakers' efforts and theological foundation regarding social sin and the right to information. For now, let's examine the themes of supports and barriers to effective change around topics of sexuality in Catholic higher education.

References

Archbold, M. (2012, September 27). Catholic college adds sexual identity to non-discrimination policy. *Catholic Education Daily.* http://web.archive.org/web/20131108193639/http://www.cardinalnewmansociety.org/CatholicEducationDaily/DetailsPage/tabid/102/ArticleID/1583/Catholic-College-Adds-Sexual-Identity-to-Non-Discrimination-Policy.aspx

Bordoni, L. (2022). *Pope to LGBT Catholics: 'God is father who does not disown any of his children'.* https://www.vaticannews.va/en/pope/news/2022-05/pope-letter-fr-martin-lgtb-outreach-questions.html

Canales, A. D. (2016). Ministry to Catholic LGBTQ youth: A call for openness and affirmation. *New Theology Review, 28*(2), 60–71.

Catechism of the Catholic Church. (2000). (2nd ed.). Libreria Editrice Vaticana.

Coffin, E. (2012). *Wolf in sheep's clothing: Courage and 'conversion' therapy.* https://www.huffingtonpost.com/ed-coffin/gay-conversion-therapy_b_1950880.html

Cramer, E. P. (Ed.). (2002). *Addressing homophobia and heterosexism on college campuses.* Huntington Park Press.

Dionisopoulos, T. (2013, October 9). Catholic college adds 'gender identity' and 'sexual orientation' to non-discrimination clause. *CampusReform.* http://www.campusreform.org/?ID=5144

Fry, J. P. (2013). *Lesbian and gay alumni perceptions of their acceptance in a Catholic university in the United States* (Publication No. 3575124) [Doctoral Dissertation, St. Joseph's University]. ProQuest Dissertations & Theses A&I.

Getz, C., & Kirkley, E. (2006). Shaking up the status quo: Challenging intolerance of the Lesbian, gay and bisexual community at a private Roman Catholic university. *College Student Journal, 40*(4), 857–869.

Greytak, E. A., Kosciw, J. G., & Diaz, E. M. (2009). *Harsh realities: The experiences of transgender youth in our nation's schools.* GLSEN.

Herriot, L., & Callaghan, T. D. (2019). Possibilities for trans-affirming policy potential: A case study of a Canadian Catholic school. *Journal of Catholic Education, 22*(3), 58–84. https://doi.org/10.15365/joce.2203042019

Hobson, A. (2014). Designing and implementing a successful gender-neutral housing community. *Journal of College and Character, 15*(1), 33–38. https://doi.org/10.1515/jcc-2014-0005

Hughes, B. E. (2015). *"Who am I to judge?": How a Jesuit university addresses LGBT issues on campus* (Publication No. 3706207) [Doctoral Dissertation, University of California, Los Angeles]. ProQuest Dissertations & Theses A&I.

Hughes, B. E. (2019). "You're not like everyone else": Sexual orientation microaggressions at a Catholic university. *Journal of Catholic Education, 22*(3), 14–35. https://doi.org/10.15365/joce.2203022019

Landry, R. (2017). *Building the right bridge toward the kingdom: Sexually active gays and lesbians—and all others who are engaging in 'porneia'—need conversion, not affirmation.* http://www.ncregister.com/blog/fatherlandry/building-the-right-bridge-toward-the-kingdom

Long, V. (2016). *Bishop Vincent Long OFM Conv delivers 2016 Ann D. Clark lecture.* https://parracatholic.org/bishop-vincent-long-ofm-conv-delivers-2016-ann-d-clark-lecture/

Longenecker, D. (2017). *Father James Martin on LGBT community: A bridge too far?* https://cruxnow.com/commentary/2017/06/17/father-james-martin-lgbt-community-bridge-far/

Love, P. G. (1997). Contradiction and paradox: Attempting to change the culture of sexual orientation at a small Catholic college. *Review of Higher Education, 20*(4), 381–398. https://muse.jhu.edu/article/30031

Love, P. G. (1998). Cultural barriers facing lesbian, gay and bisexual students at a Catholic college. *Journal of Higher Education, 69*(3), 298–323. https://doi.org/10.2307/2649190

Martin, J. (2017a). *Building a bridge: How the Catholic church and the LGBT community can enter into a relationship of respect, compassion, and sensitivity.* HarperCollins Publishers.

Martin, J. (2017b). *Stepping out onto the bridge: Father James Martin responds to conversation surrounding his L.G.B.T. Book.* https://www.americamagazine.org/faith/2017/06/19/stepping-out-bridge-father-james-martin-responds-conversation-surrounding-his-lgbt

McEntarfer, H. K. (2011). "Not going away": Approaches used by students, faculty, and staff members to create gay–straight alliances at three religiously affiliated universities. *Journal of LGBT Youth, 8*(4), 309–331. https://doi.org/10.1080/19361653.2011.607623

Miceli, M. J. (2009). *Coming-out at Catholic and non-Catholic colleges and universities* (Publication No. 3355077) [Doctoral Dissertation, Johnson & Wales University]. ProQuest Dissertations & Theses A&I.

Morey, M. M., & Piderit, J. J. (2006). *Catholic higher education: A culture in crisis.* Oxford University Press.

Nelson, L. A. (2012, April 26). How Catholic? *Inside Higher Ed.* https://www.insidehighered.com/news/2012/04/26/tensions-over-social-issues-front-and-center-several-catholic-colleges

Paul VI. (1965). *Gaudium et spes: Pastoral constitution on the church in the modern world.* http://www.vatican.va/archive/hist_councils/ii_vatican_council/documents/vat-ii_const_19651207_gaudium-et-spes_en.html

Ruether, R. R. (1983). *Sexism and god-talk: Toward a feminist theology.* Beacon Press.

Sausa, L. A. (2002). Updating college and university campus policies: Meeting the needs of trans students, staff, and faculty. In E. P. Cramer (Ed.), *Addressing homophobia and heterosexism on college campuses* (pp. 43–55). Huntington Park Press.

Willoughby, B. J., Larsen, J. K., & Carroll, J. S. (2012). The emergence of gender-neutral housing on American university campuses. *Journal of Adolescent Research, 27*(6), 732–750. https://doi.org/10.1177/0743558412447852

Material from this chapter can also be found in the following source:

Levand, M. A. (2021). Communication strategies and responses to change around issues of sexuality in Catholic higher education. *Profesional de la Información, 30*(5), 1–14. https://doi.org/10.3145/epi.2021.sep.04

Chapter 5

Difficult or Easy?
Themes in Supports and Challenges Faced by Changemakers

> What did people find to be most helpful in the change process? What did people find to be the biggest barriers when trying to effect change?

In this study, this question was a big one. Participants gave great information about what was helpful or not so helpful when trying to effect change. It is important to remember that these include themes from across several different institutions. This means that some themes were more present at some institutions than others. And the type of institutional culture also influenced the types of supports and barriers in the process. Comfort with sexuality, in general, geo-political environment, institutional culture, and even individual people were all factors that impacted how changes happened. This chapter is a look into the biggest barriers to change and themes people noted were most helpful. These themes can be found in brief in Table 5.1.

Barriers/Challenges in Change Efforts

Several themes occurred as barriers to effective change around issues of sexuality in these institutions of Catholic higher education. These themes can be grouped into four general themes: fear (i.e., of job termination, of the administration, of the local bishop), conservative constituents (i.e., faculty/admin, student groups, donors, parents, public defenders of Catholic orthodoxy), administrative resistance, and organizational barriers (i.e., language issues and poor organization).

Fear

One of the most commonly articulated barriers to change was fear. Whether it was fear of the change by members of the community, fear of retaliation by administration, fear of job termination, or fear of the local bishop, fear played a significant role in why a change effort may

DOI: 10.4324/9781003218159-5

118 Difficult or Easy?

Table 5.1 Supports and barriers to change around issues of sexuality in Catholic higher education

Barriers

Main Theme	Subtheme	Example
Fear	• By members of the community (general fear of the change) • By changemakers of the administration • By changemakers of job termination • By changemakers of the local bishop	A dean being afraid of negative public attention; employees fearing job termination; administrators being afraid to be the "first" university to make that change.
Conservative Constituents	• Conservative faculty/administrators • Conservative student groups • Conservative donors • Conservative parents • Self-appointed public defenders of Catholic orthodoxy	A faculty member opining about how supporting LGBTQ+ people is "not Catholic"; a president preventing a change for fear donors will stop donating money; a conservative dean preventing a week honoring diversity of sexual orientation on campus; parents calling to complain about an STI awareness campaign.
Administrative Resistance	• Official responses/collective administration reasoning • Lack of transparency • Dysfunctional leadership	Several administrators being under the wrong impression about a change; administrative decision-making processes that are hidden from changemakers or distanced from the conversation of change; leaders not leading effectively.

Organizational Barriers	• Language issues
	• Poor organization
	  ○ logistical/financial issues
	  ○ computer programs
	  ○ organizational miscommunication
	  ○ failure to communicate
		Avoidance or intentional use of certain words a particular audience may find off-putting; no funding for a resource center; a technical issue that prevents a more inclusive gender change in a system; a breakdown in communication between people or offices on campus about a change; members of a university not responding to direct questions about why a change cannot happen.

Difficult or Easy? 119

Main Theme	Subtheme	Supports Example
Principal Changemakers	• Students • Tenured faculty • Individual administrators/staff	A group of students advocates for an LGBTQ+ student group or function; a faculty member creates a course on sexuality and sexual health; a dean initiates an inclusive restroom policy.
Various Offices	• Office of residence life • Office of student life • Office of mission and ministry • Campus ministry • Counseling center • Theology/religious studies departments	Res. life staff hears the needs of students on campus and offers informational gender education sessions; student life offices advocate for a space for an LGBT+ student group; theology departments help write policy to institutionalize a change.
Supportive University Leaders/Constituents	• Higher administration buy-in • People religious (nuns, priests, etc.) • Financial donors/alumni • Board of trustees members	A president supports a change and offers to help the local bishop understand the change; a board member supports a campus climate survey about gender identity on campus; the priests/friars/nuns support a change for an LGBTQ+ student group.

Organizational Characteristics	• Mission/history/heritage
	• Open geo-political environment
	• Good organization
	  ◦ effective teamwork
	  ◦ effective social networking
	  ◦ good internal communication
		Part of the mission of the university was incorporated into a change effort pitched to the administration; a university has a strong culture of acceptance and support for student care, so getting a sexuality resource center was not difficult; a college situated in a diverse metropolitan context has no difficulty honoring sexual diversity on campus; a team of 3 people from various offices institutionalized a preferred name computer system in a relatively short amount of time.

be slowed or halted. Most broadly, participants identified the possibility of fear arising from the university as a whole. One participant recounted the support of LGBTQ students on behalf of the university:

> [It was] probably more towards 2011–2012 when the university started to take on some change and start to work with students to help them—to deal with either their sexual orientation, their biases, and also their educational level. I think at that time—earlier times—the university was scared to bring that to fruition, because of their affiliation with Catholicism.

Participants spoke of "the university" being afraid, likely referring to the university community. Whether they meant leadership or all members of the university remained unclear.

Other participants identified a general, vague sense of fear of the administration. When discussing the beginning of their university's support of LGBTQ students, one residence life administrator said:

> A lot of our students were afraid to come out to voice their opinion, to identify themselves in certain ways .... I mean, again it was very tough when I first started there, someone putting some type of informational bulletin board out about LGBTQ communities, you know, we had to question that first before that could even happen because we didn't know how administration thought about it. At that time it was like, you know, let's not push the envelope yet. Let's not get to that point because we don't know. We don't want to upset other folks. But by the time—5, 6 years later on—it's like, we had to make that change. Something had to happen, because there was a lot of students on our campus who were identifying themselves yet they didn't feel supported and they wanted to make that change.

There were several instances of participants recounting times that a fear prevented or almost prevented a change around an issue of sexuality. When recalling a conference about LGBTQ students and Catholic higher education, one participant noted:

> There were people coming from institutions where they were afraid to tell their institutions they were even attending, and they didn't. So, I mean that just sort of shows that Catholicism is not a monolith by any means .... [And] people's experience around these issues were all over the map.

Fear was also present in curricular changes about under enrollment or freedom of academic scholarship. Staff members identified fear of being fired for working on sensitive issues. One staff member identified an instance of being approached: "You know, I remember one person said this to me 'be careful about the fight that ... you're choosing, like, is it really worth it if it's going to jeopardize your job?'" These staff members described their confidence and determination as reasons preventing that fear from deterring them from enacting change.

Fear of the local bishop was also discussed as a common theme. The fear of the bishop often seemed to be experienced by the administration. Whether changemakers had direct interaction with the bishop around these issues or not, the threat was present in many participant interviews. One administrator suggested the care in which they had to go about effecting change: "And it just takes somebody who doesn't get it, a couple of phone calls, either to the religious order or the bishop and now all of a sudden you got a problem on your hands."

Conservative Constituents

Another group of barriers to change around sexuality consisted of various conservative constituents in the process. Participants most frequently mentioned conservative faculty or administration members, conservative student groups, conservative donors, parents, and what one participant called "self-appointed public defenders of Catholic orthodoxy."

Conservative Faculty/Administrators

Participants often discussed faculty members or specific administrators responding with resistance. Participants identified that some conservative faculty members might speak out against a change that supports LGBTQ students as "not Catholic" or against a Catholic mission. In a discussion of how a conservative faculty member was a barrier to creating a supportive climate for LGBTQ students, one participant mentioned that this particular faculty member wrote a strongly worded article about the support:

> And the students, to their credit, tried to engage him, and they were very thoughtful on how to do it, and ... what they were trying to accomplish. But I know that that kind of vitriolic opposition, which really does look a lot like, just, you know, near bigotry. That can be an obstacle. You know, cuz what it does is it reinforces—whether correctly or not— ... in the eyes of the students and definitely some of our faculty, that things have not changed as much as they have, so they can be discouraged in that respect.

When working with administration, one faculty advisor to the LGBTQ student group recalled a tense discussion between administrators and the student organization:

> Two Vice Presidents initially rejected the [student organization that] wanted to have a dance and the Vice President of student affairs in consultation with the Vice President for Mission and Ministry rejected. They declined allowing [the student organization] to have a dance and there ensued some really uncomfortable and unpleasant meetings ... the [student organization] advisor who was filling in that year said that he was told that LGBTQ+ persons will never be fully accepted on this campus.

It is important to note that the reason conservative administration is listed under this barrier (versus below, under organizational barriers) is because a resistant individual in administration may be reasoned with differently than a resistant administration. In this particular case, these same administrators later approved the student organization's event.

On more than one occasion, participants identified what they called (albeit, an ageist term) "old heads" as being a barrier to change. These were often identified as older administrators who had a particular way of governing that did not involve meeting student needs. Older faculty members involved in the LGBTQ+ life on campus but stuck in the routine of "how it's always been done" also fell into this group. Participants discussed these "older" constituents as resistant to change and attributed their age-dependent developmental worldview to that resistance. One participant knew the problematic message, and articulated this reality:

> The obstacles a lot of times were folks that have been at the college a long, long time. Folks that have been at college—and I'm stereotyping, to be really honest with you on that. Folks that have been here as a faculty or staff member a lot of times ... really had a vision of what the institution was [previously].

A less ageist way of discussing this may be as "old guard" or "stuck in an outdated way of doing things." This stagnation in ability to grow with the organization was nonetheless identified by some changemakers.

Conservative Student Groups

Though not frequent, a theme that appeared in a few interviews involved conservative student groups or student voices that spoke out against a change. These types of resistance were almost exclusively about support of students or events that recognize some type of same-sex interaction. Whether it is an LGBTQ student social event, a movie screened on campus, or the protest of a speaker, participants identified Catholic students or student groups as possible areas of resistance. One administrator recalled:

> You know, there were some groups—student groups—that were anti, you know, bringing about this type of teaching on the campus, because they decide they came here because of the Catholic teaching and this is not what they were taught.

Conservative Donors

Donors and alumni were also cited as barriers to effectively creating change around issues of sexuality on Catholic campuses. As one participant succinctly synthesized:

> Catholic universities are very sensitive to donors and it seems to be a truism that many donors tend, as a rule, to be more socially conservative in their viewpoint on political and social issues. So that would be of a concern for college presidents in terms of dealing with situations of human sexuality especially when they have faculty members and they have students who tend to be more liberal on these issue.

More specifically, a participant recalled a conversation had with the president of the university that seemed to reflect the president's navigation of this issue: "[The president] would say 'Look, I'm the president of a conservative ... Catholic University and we don't have a huge endowment ... I could build buildings if these rich conservatives give me money.' And he was very clear about that." The threat of donors to remove funding or alums' disapproval of the change appeared to be a common theme in barriers to change.

Parents

Parents of students also appeared to be a barrier or challenge when managing issues of sexuality in Catholic higher education. Over a quarter of the participants identified parents as playing some resistant role in an issue of sexuality on campus. A participant articulated:

> Navigating parents is challenging, I think sometimes our students ... are a little bit more progressive than our parents. And so when we present these changes on campus and, you know, students tell

their parents that they're happening, you know, it's a little bit challenging to get them on board.

Parent involvement or parents as a challenge seemed to vary by institution. The reason for this, however, was not discussed by participants.

Self-appointed Public Defenders of Catholic Orthodoxy

Originally coded as "watch-dog public," (or people from the public realm with no affiliation to the university that kept diligent watch of the university's dealings around matters of sexuality) this group was described by a participant as the "self-appointed public defenders of Catholic orthodoxy." This participant further explained:

> And by that I mean almost exclusively their concern is with matters of gender and sexuality and the websites exert a lot of pressure to police and to condemn what they conclude as deviancy from accepted corporate Catholic orthodoxy as they understand it. And that fear—they are a nuisance that Catholic administrators have learned to put up with, with varying degrees of success. At worst, they can create adverse publicity, which again, Catholic administrators are, at any event, they are loathe to have … negative publicity.

At least a third of the participants discussed the role of public defenders of Catholic orthodoxy in the experience of change around sexuality. Whether it was harassing letters to changemakers, public protests with slurs about the university, or just writing blog posts, participants described this component as a challenge when it came to making changes around sexuality. One participant said:

> [The external protesters] were not allowed on campus but they would picket outside the university on the day where they knew that the parents and donors would be here. So they would picket on freshman move-in day, homecoming weekend, and the press came for meeting here and they would hold signs like, "University, sodomy, and deprivation" and were crabby about this [change].

Administrative Resistance

Different than individual administrators being resistant to change is the barrier or challenge of having a resistant administration. This barrier to change was often more elusive than a single administrator that can be talked with privately or may leave the position. Participants spoke of the administration's resistance with generality. One faculty member hypothesized: "I would say that in general, that administrators ... who were more removed from student life would also be more resistant to, or more concerned about, venues that would foster discussions of human sexuality."

Another participant in residence life cited the presidential cabinet as a source of resistance. Other participants described the administration's reasons for resisting the creation of an LGBTQ student group because of "the fear was that this was going to be a hookup group" or "the fear of creating something that would be seen as the university supporting a gay lifestyle." This is likely a result of a select few administrators' concerns, but I find it important that this was reported as a general administration concern. Accounts of individual administrators yielded stories of greater depth, while accounts of the resistant administration tended to be vague, focused on official responses or a collective administrative reasoning.

Participants identified various types of administrative operational resistance such as a lack of transparency or dysfunctional leadership. A lack of transparency from leadership (resulting in a barrier to the change process) was mentioned at two different institutions. One experienced faculty member described the situation:

> And then this is where transparency was sort of annoying at the time. There was not an ounce of transparency. There were like five white guys in suits. And they all had these weird titles but no one ever saw them anywhere.... No one knew what their positions were but we knew they made all the decisions. And we never knew how or why. It was all kind of a dark room of white men and that upset a lot of us —just the process.

Other participants described situations of resistance from the administration because of what was identified as dysfunctional leadership:

> I think that one of the problems was that our investigation revealed intrinsic dysfunctional leadership. And that means that the people that are responsible for making the changes aren't going to, because they're the ones that are the problems.... So that would be the biggest problem, was expecting any change because of who the guy was at top.

These examples were not the majority of cases, but most certainly were part of the change process for at least 2 out of the 17 campuses in the study. There were other organizational barriers that inhibited change, but higher administration, when discussed, was discussed as independent from and much more systemic than the organizational barriers in the next section.

Organizational Challenges/Barriers

The remaining two themes were prevalent in about half of the interviews: language issues and poor organization. Participants noted that within a Catholic context, some people took issue with the language they used to discuss some topic of sexuality. What I coded as "poor organization"—poor communication, logistical issues, etc.—likely looks similar in organizations, religious or otherwise.

Language Issues

A recurring theme—whether around gender issues, same-sex partner benefits, or student groups—consisted of the words individuals used to discuss the change. This theme refers to the words participants intentionally used or avoided when talking about effecting change. When student groups began to form at some of the universities, advisors were specifically urged not to use words such as "advocacy" or "sexuality" in the title of a group, resource center, or in any advertisements for student events.

When navigating these issues, participants often described working around this issue by using less direct or more inclusive language. For example, at a number of universities, when changing policy to include same-sex partner benefits for employees, changemakers noticed that the administration preferred to use vague terms such as "domicile adults" for additional people on a health insurance plan. While this did include same-sex partners, it avoided the same-sex nature of the issue by applying it to a broader audience (i.e., anyone who lived in the same residence as an employee).

Another more recent example involved gender-neutral restrooms. As a way of avoiding further problems, one participant did not believe their administration would change bathrooms from binary sex to gender-neutral or -inclusive restrooms if they approached the board with that language. As a result, this administrator used the term "family bathrooms" to secure bathrooms that anyone can use. The administrator said:

> My preference is to take the issue and to solve it in a way that is productive and helpful to the student but also is respectful of the history and tradition of the college. So in this case I brought the proposal and we named it, instead of naming it, like a ... we talked about it as transgender bathrooms but really what we were

talking about is basically, any gender bathroom. And so in this case I decided to call them family bathrooms.

Poor Organization

The theme of poor organization encompasses logistical or financial issues, computer programs, organizational miscommunication, or failure to communicate at all (e.g., silence/avoidant responses). Participants would describe difficulty in the change process due to a lack of communication, not having enough time or resources, or uncertainty in deciding who should take the next steps. While examining gender inclusivity issues on campus, one participant noted:

> Just changing a sign is pretty easy, the process just drags out so much longer, and if people aren't like really passionate about it, it can stall out in various places. So they just kind of like, you know, you pass it along to the registrar, you figure this out, and okay, maybe they'll not remove it, or maybe they're busy and then it stalls there before it can go to ... the next step to work out. So that was a lot more difficult and a lot more dragged out to be honest.

More pertinent to change in the Catholic setting were the ways in which miscommunication occurred around issues of sexuality. Regarding permission for student organizations to have social events, one faculty member identified assumptions as a barrier to possible change:

> [The students] would go to a kind of a lower-level-like administrator, who had to give them the stamp of approval to advertise it for instance, and that person would say, "oh, my boss would never let this go on. We're not going to do that. That's not part of our identity as a Catholic University." And I would kind of make a phone call to, like, the vice president of student affairs, like the head of all of it, and he'd say, "Oh, that's a great idea, yeah let's do that." You know, and everybody below him assumes, well, that he wouldn't approve it. And then they just say no to the students.

Because of the assumed taboo nature of sexuality, some employees did not want to approach supervisors to ask permission, simply assuming a negative outcome. Whether around miscommunication, finances, or employee competence, basic logistics were often a barrier to change.

Areas of Help/Support in Change Efforts

Because of the vast experiences of participants, it was at times unclear whether a change was successful or in flux. There were certainly times when changes had clear successful or unsuccessful outcomes, but much more prevalent were people or entities that participants found to be helpful in the change efforts. There were four main categories, each with subthemes: principal changemakers, various offices, supportive university leaders/constituents, and organizational characteristics.

Principal Changemakers

The most frequently mentioned individuals responsible for change were the students, tenured faculty members, and individual administrative or staff members.

Students

Participants most frequently mentioned students as the drivers for change. This was evident in statements like "the students were pushing really hard for [change] and then sort of faculty started coming on board" and "it was because of students. Students were coming to administration and indicating that they did not feel support on this campus."

At times, the students took the lead on change with minimal guidance. Other participants described their role in supporting students' drive for change:

> [Students] were like "we want to do this!" And [the students'] voice is more powerful than ours [staff]. Like if you want to do this then y'all come up, and y'all find the host [for the event], and y'all find the space, and when you do this—we're here to give you resources, and we're here to like bounce ideas off of and actually give you a structure, and you're the ones that are actually creating. So I think it was very—the most important thing in getting the ball off the ground, getting people interested in it, advertisement, and even getting our performer [for an event] ... [the students] were the most integral piece of it.

Whether requiring support by staff or organizing efficiently on their own, students were seen as the most important agents of change around issues of sexuality.

Tenured Faculty

About a third of the participants in the study consisted of faculty members. When effecting change in higher education, having advocates with job security afforded by tenure is a logical choice for change around such a sensitive issue as sexuality. One participant described the experience of change around controversial issues:

> We have tenure so we can go ahead and start a conversation and get the ball rolling without fear of termination. And then that allowed other administrators to feel encouraged to participate, which allows the conversation to kind of spread across campus quickly and really efficiently.

Many participants recognized faculty's participation as critical to effecting change around sexuality, even if they were not the starters or driving force for change.

Tenure was explicitly or implicitly referenced as useful here. One participant recounted the explicit meaning of tenure in the process of change:

> So you know, I guess I could just say that, you know, fear kept the members [of the faculty council] maybe from being higher [in involvement] than they would have been. You know, just the fact that we happen to be doing this right after people found out if they got tenure or not. You know, that helped.

This participant identified the granting of tenure as an important component of being involved in change. This participant specifically identified their university as being more conservative. Faculty participants also recognized the importance of junior faculty involvement. One participant said "I really commend [untenured] faculty and I'm well aware of the ability that I've had, the freedom I've had because of tenure." It is an important note, however, that one faculty member felt that faculty voices did not mean as much as student voices in this process.

Individual Administrators/Staff

Staff and administrators also operated as key change agents. Six participants were either staff or administrators in residence life and played a key role in change. One participant identified nuanced changes these staff members made that contributed to the larger change of the university's culture or climate around issues of gender:

> The Residence Director and the Assistant Residence Director and RAs—they've done some of their own educational initiative, more passive programming around, I think, the first year with gender 101 as a theme and they had this poster series and so for doing

more passive programming and then community dialogues within the community from the RAs.

It was not uncommon for staff members to begin creating change at a student-service level, rather than starting at the institutional level.

Administrator participants discussed their role as changemaker often with more security than staff members. Staff members recognized that they could get fired for doing this work, while administrators seemed to express more power over the institutional culture and less fear of termination.

Various Offices

After the principal changemakers, the second group supportive in the change process were various supporting offices. Most frequently mentioned were the offices of residence life and student life. Other offices discussed as helpful included the office of mission and ministry, campus ministry, the counseling center, and the theology or religious studies department.

Residence/Student Life

The offices of residence life and student life often played roles on the forefront of change around issues of sexuality. Residence life often dealt with issues of gender inclusivity in on-campus housing and bathrooms, while student life frequently dealt with student organizations and making change possible from the student level into the organization structure. Directors, associate directors, student affairs, and student development personnel were all mentioned as being critical components to change for students and the university environment. When asked why resident assistants played such a key role in change around gender diversity, one participant replied:

> They understood the need. They saw it within their communities ahead of time, whether prior to being a resident ... or just living in the campus communities, they understood that there was a need. That they had friends who identified themselves within certain orientations or sexualities and they knew that there was not a good support system for them, especially understanding how other universities had that support.

The residence life office was seen as particularly close to the student experience, giving them a relationship from which to advocate for change. A participant identified the residence life office as:

One of the more, like, forward thinking offices on a lot of our campuses. They are more quick to, at least it's my experience in general, we're more quick to champion—to act on diversity and celebrate diversity in all aspects and forms, we're more quick to do that because it's often a more positive reaction around that.

The same was said about student life or student affairs. One participant identified this office as "such a ripe environment for doing these kinds of things. It's so obvious, how to do that and it's fun." When describing how the office was helpful to change, another participant said:

> A lot of folks [in student life] tend to be doing a lot of work around identity development. So it was easy just to have a buy-in from really the whole division of student life and then I think a lot of the folks that were in student life then also had partnerships and relationships that they were developing with some faculty across campus.

Other Offices

Mentioned with less frequency but great importance to each of these campuses were the offices of mission and ministry, campus ministry, the counseling center, or the theology and/or religious studies department.

The office of mission and ministry (or university ministry) is often an administrative office at some Catholic colleges and universities designed to oversee the university's ministry efforts and how various facets of the university are living out the institutional mission—or more broadly, to ensure the integrity of the institution's Catholic identity (Wilcox, 2013). This office was identified as helpful support when the administrators collaborated on change efforts. Identifying the role of this office in the nature of change, one participant said,

> The Vice President of mission and ministry ... she's been always great, and always is supportive and has our back. I think a lot of people view her as a little bit of a "Catholic nark" so then when she's so supportive of us, that's really very powerful.

The intersection of the Catholic nature of this office and support for a change around sexuality was often identified as powerful for many participants' change efforts.

Campus ministry, an office with direct relation to students around matters of faith, was also at times cited as a support for change efforts. When asked about supportive components, one administrator remarked, "Our Campus Ministry ... the staff was very Catholic and supportive of the change and actually spearheaded a couple of the group engagement programs." Participants at other universities discussed similar experiences of campus ministry being a place to originate LGBTQ student groups, often seen as a place for confidentiality and counsel. One administrator discussed some difficulty in getting the campus minister "on board" but that it was useful to the university climate once they joined the change efforts. Similarly, during change efforts, the counseling center (though not mentioned as often as one would think) was cited as a helpful support for change around sexuality topics on campus. One participant recalled: "I think the counseling center was seeing a lot of students who needed that support [around issues of sexuality] and luckily our counseling center had that support [for the students]."

The departments of theology and/or religious studies were mentioned as helpful in both curricular changes as well as the overall climate around sexuality. When incorporating sexuality into the curriculum, one faculty member said,

> When the president met with us, the only thing that he wanted was the assurance that we wouldn't entirely ignore Catholic teaching. And that was not a problem. One of the members of the committee that put the proposal together was a Catholic priest who at the time was the Chair of the Religious Studies Department.

The expertise in understanding Catholic theology and identity appeared to be a critical component for including topics of sexuality in the curriculum. This department's involvement was, at times, seen as legitimizing to the conversation around sexuality, often specifically sexual ethics, at Catholic colleges and universities in this study.

Supportive University Leaders/Constituents

The third group, different university leaders/constituents, was often mentioned in the change process as being particularly important in effecting change. When leaders supported the changes or student efforts, change was much more likely to be successful. Most often discussed were various vice provosts or deans of different offices as well as getting the president's approval and participation. In addition to provosts, deans, and presidents, the presence and participation of religious individuals (priests, nuns, friars, etc.), board of trustee members, and donors/alums were helpful in effecting change. This theme differs from the individual administrators as principal changemakers theme because these supportive constituents were not the source of the change, but their support was instrumental in the success of the change efforts.

Higher Administration Buy-in

A theme consistently cited as helpful for change efforts involved vice provosts, deans, and the president siding with the change efforts. Different than the people driving the change, participants cited leadership support as a crucial component backing student efforts. One participant recounted: "We have a VP of Student life [and] that helped. Because she was the person who then [supported students] when it came time for [them] to take on more of an activist role." Other lower-level changemakers also said administrators were helpful: "I think the most helpful was having the administrators on our side…, Dean of students, our VP of student affairs so we had upper lever administration who was on our side."

Other participants sought solace in the president's support. Whether they sought out the president and set up meetings, the proposed change was presented to the president, or an issue about the change was brought to the president, changemakers held presidential support in high esteem and, with it, expressed security. One university held LGBTQ student liturgies on campus to support sexual and gender minority students. When people complained about this practice, the participant recalled: "[Support] even from the President of the university, saying that we offer Masses for a whole range of student groups and we treat the students exactly the same as we would do with any other, was very supportive." Another participant discussed their president's skill in dealing with external pressure about a curricular change around sexuality:

> But it was the president of the university that dealt with the institution, dealt with the larger structure of the church and he fortunately was very supportive of us and he was very adept at dealing with the authorities to sort of deflect any kind of pressure or what not.

Other University Constituents

Helpful to the change were also religious nuns, priests, friars, and deacons; financial donors or alumni of the university; and board of trustee members.

Religious individuals who supported the change around sexuality by either actively changing policies or being present for guidance and support were said to be helpful in the change process. One participant even described this kind of support as a shock:

> Amazingly enough, I mean, we had on campus some clergy, well one priest, a chaplain as well as, I think at the time we had about three sisters ... who were on campus and all were very positive, supportive, so when the idea spreads ... some folks felt that maybe, you know, these folks wouldn't be supportive, because of teachings and what their focus is on campus. But they were very supportive, very influential, involved, engaging with the changes, which was nice.

About five different participants from five different universities said similarly: "We would have a [priest] present and that just helps I think with showing that we can talk about sex, sexuality, gender at religious institutions."

Alumni were occasionally identified as areas of support to change on campuses, often through donations. Whether donating materials to events or financial support for students, alums were seen as helpful in various ways. One faculty member recalled a time when a group of alums spoke out in resistance to a change, and another group of alums responded:

> What was lovely though was a counter group of alumni ... [who] also started a social media campaign to flood the university's emails and phone calls with [support], so there were another about eleven hundred younger alums for the most part who were part of [that effort].

As one might expect, board of trustees' support was one of the most powerful influencing factors of change around issues sensitive to the university. A faculty member who helped form a task force recalls the usefulness of a board member on their team:

> But we also had a board member—a member of the Board of Trustees [on the task force]. So I think that was helpful too, because then the president—like if you're inviting him to come hear the results [of a climate survey], he's going to show up because there is a board member on the committee. So I think getting some connection that way was helpful.

Garnering support from board members was easier when the law required these changes or when a board member could relate to the change from their own personal experience such as owning a business.

Organizational Characteristics

Lastly, many organizational elements also proved to be helpful in the process of effecting change around sexuality. Participants identified the mission, history, and/or heritage as important for change, the university's open or geographic environment, and what I call "good organization," or effective changemaking logistics.

Mission/History/Heritage

Most frequently mentioned was addressing the mission, history, or heritage of the university. Change was more likely to occur when it could be articulated as in-line with the mission and identity of that particular school. It was clear that making a connection between the change around sexuality and the university mission increased the likelihood of a positive outcome. One participant described the founding religious order's mission: "[Our university] comes from this very strong social justice position and ... values ... that's very much [the university's] identity and its brand and so it is kind of a natural for, you know, a more open attitude." While other participants identified change around sexuality as a part of the Catholic faith: "I want very much for students at a Catholic ... university to see that this is part of our Catholicism, is being able to dialogue and questions and discern in responsible ways, in ways that engage our critical thinking."

Some participants also mentioned that mission-related articulation of the change was part of the process necessary for university review and approval, but no one reported difficulty with this particular task. Connection to the religious order's mission, the Catholic theological foundation, or the specific university history (i.e., the founder's vision or life work), whether the school was founded by sisters, religious order priests, or the diocese, participants identified employing the institution's Catholic identity as helpful to the change process. One participant succinctly identified their university mission's usefulness:

> Our value proposition in higher education is our strong sense of community here, it's part of our core mission and values and that's only as good as you're really seeing that through. And so there's been a really easy in-road to kind of working for these kinds of things because we claim to be very community-focused and that everyone is welcome in this community.

University's Open/Geo-political Environment

Another frequently mentioned organizational theme that participants viewed as a fortuitous circumstance—the university's open and accepting, or geographic/local political environment. Some participants discussed the university's general open and accepting environment as helpful in that "it's just a liberal environment," or "we had very little opposition," etc. This component involved the general culture of acceptance to new ideas and change at the university. Participants viewed this as a helpful starting point, rather than the other "less fortunate" (participant language) universities whose changemaking efforts occurred in a more restrictive climate.

The other environmental factor often mentioned involved the geographic/local political environment—when the surrounding area is seen as "progressive" or accepting of diversity in ways that other places (i.e., universities in other cities or surrounding neighborhoods) are not. Components mentioned here involved the local community being more urban, surrounded by a supportive LGBTQ community, or when the civil community actively engages LGBTQ issues. One participant recalled being told that the type of change for which they were advocating would be more acceptable if they were "in California, or on the East Coast" but not where they were located.

Good Organization

The last theme, "good organization," were matters of help and support largely reported as the system working effectively. Participants identified a team of people who worked well together—communicated and collaborated effectively—as effective in making change. About forming a task force, one participant said, "You have to have really good people ... who are going to work, and who aren't just going to show up and [complain] or show up and not do anything."

Along with good people who work well together, some participants identified having a network of well-connected people, submitting information to the proper channels, or working "through the system to make things happen." One participant discussed several LGBTQ student events: "[The events] were seen as controversial events and as controversial events they had to go through a set protocol, they had to follow certain parameters that had been here before." The participant goes on to add that "one of the big changes that happened recently is those three events are no longer controversial events."

The changemaker may also have a particular network of people that they contact for swift, effective change. One long-time faculty member explained:

> There is this network all over campus and—for good or ill—I am the lightning rod for that or a common nexus for much of it but the fact that it exists and that I know who to call ... I can pretty

much get what I need, usually ... under the radar, under the table, for whatever a student needs or sort of how I wanna go.

As part of "good organization," I coded good internal communication as important to effective change. While this is a general component of effective organization, it was still an important component for change around sexuality at these institutions in contrast to the barriers of poor organization above. For example, participants consistently praised the groups of people who really made effective, logistical contributions to the change, or staff members who work in IT who can research and effectively change the cataloguing system to insert a preferred name field. When recounting the process of getting a preferred name field in the university databases, one participant said:

> So like, the IT people, the registrar people, the [technical systems] people ... all have to do something every semester just because it's not an automated process by which the course management system just plucks the name out of the database system. Somebody's got to tell it to point to the right place and then they got to check to make sure that it happens.

In reflecting on this change, the participant appreciated the efforts of all involved who made this a relatively easy change.

Discussion

Supportive Components

Drivers of Change

The themes identified as helpful for change often resonated with the current literature, with a frequently mentioned component for future research direction. The principal change agents or the people driving the change were most often described as students or faculty members. The tenured faculty component has been prevalent in other research about changing around issues of LGB student organizations (Getz & Kirkley, 2006; Hughes, 2015; McEntarfer, 2011), but did not seem to capture the magnitude with which it was prevalent in this study. This may be due to the population selection, as many seed informants were involved in professional faculty and scholarly organizations. The participants in this study helped give context to the relief they felt when tenured faculty spoke up about issues of sexuality, adding to the literature about why tenured faculty involvement is important (Getz & Kirkley, 2006; Hughes, 2015; McEntarfer, 2011).

Students were mentioned by many participants as being even more influential than tenured faculty. Most frequently, it seemed that a student force for change was needed to create change. Most previous research focused on the experience of LGB students in Catholic higher education (Getz & Kirkley, 2006; Hughes, 2015; Love, 1998; Maher & Sever, 2007; McEntarfer, 2011; Miceli, 2009) but did not often focus on other areas of sexuality. Students were instrumental in change around gender diversity issues, obtaining sexuality-related resources, and feedback about how sexual assault education can be most useful.

Supporting Offices

The supporting offices described in this study included student and residence life, ministry offices, and the department of theology/religious studies. Love (1997) discussed what he called "paradoxes" in the change process around LGBT student groups—or components that one would "not assume" would be helpful in the change process for issues of sexual minority students. He identified having campus ministry and theology departments support changes around LGB identities as one such paradox. Data from the current study supports Love's previous findings while also adding some depth to how these offices were most useful. Theology and religious studies (TRS) departments often acted counter to the supposed narrative that they would be conservative and/or were instrumental in connecting the university or Catholic mission to the change efforts. Hughes (2015), however, reported an instance of an LGB student organization being forced to work with campus ministry as a sort of Catholic overseer. The consistency of these themes coming up across studies (TRS departments and campus ministry involvement) identifies a direction for more contextual study into the relationship between campus ministry, theology and religious study departments, and issues of sexuality on campus.

Less mentioned in the literature are the offices of residence and student life. These offices were most commonly mentioned because of their proximity to the student experience as well as the way the offices function as a resource for student activity. Hughes (2015) explicitly mentioned student affairs staff and their experience of discrimination in his study examining support for LGBT students. The present study further contextualizes how these staff members operate around effecting change and acquiring resources for students on these campuses. Data from student affairs members from diverse types of Catholic institutions in the present study—by religious heritage, geographic location, etc.—identifies themes of how these employees created change and how they were included as helpful constituents in changemakers' social networks.

Organizational Characteristics

The organizational characteristics of the mission/history of the university and good organization (effective internal communication, efficient networks of people, hard workers, smooth logistics, etc.) seemed to be most prevalent in the literature, while university openness and geographic environment seemed to be less apparent. Hughes (2015) stresses the importance of incorporating the mission into work around changing LGBT student support. Hughes' study involved only a single Jesuit university, offering suggestions which may help with that particular order. The breadth of the present study offers support for the claim that incorporating the mission is an important and supportive practice across Catholic institutions. This data also suggests that other organizational characteristics such as the university's geographic location/local political environment and general openness as a university culture may also influence change around sexuality.

Morey and Piderit (2006) identified various Catholic universities as liberal or conservative. Participants in my study largely identified universities in the same way. Some participants identified that certain orders were more liberal or conservative than others. However, it was apparent that the liberal or conservative nature of the university had a stronger connection to its geographic location and surrounding political environment. If the surrounding community was more open to discussing sexuality, the university was likely to have an easier time addressing matters of sexuality as well. An order that might be generally identified by others as "liberal" may be less open to discussing issues of sexuality if their surrounding civil community were restrictive on these topics. Albeit only preliminary data, there appeared to be differences based in liberal or conservative metropolitan, suburban, or rural areas. This may be connected to the fear of external protestors, but requires further study on a broader scale (for a closer look at a case study of blue state/red state dynamics and two Catholic universities, see Coley, 2018).

Barriers/Challenges

Fear

Previous studies about change around LGBT student support cited fear as a common theme (Hughes, 2015; Love, 1998; Maher & Sever, 2007; McEntarfer, 2011). Given the Catholic environment, the presence of fear around sexuality was an expected barrier (Morey & Piderit, 2006). It is no surprise that fear is a barrier to how people might respond to changes about sexuality. Love (1998) identified the fear of specific barriers present in our data—donors, alumni, parents, etc. Maher and Sever (2007) talk about fear as the reason for administration's lack of support—particularly fear of the community's reaction. Hughes (2015) discussed these barriers as "power dynamics" and "oppressive reactions" in the relationship the changemaker has with the university (including what I call "conservative constituents") but omitting fear as a dynamic itself.

I have left fear as independent of these other barriers because, at times, fear was undefined, unspecified, or ambiguous with regard to where the fear was placed or of whom (or what) the participant was afraid. For example, a participant could be afraid of their own commitment or public speaking abilities, fear of job termination, fear of being targeted by specified or unspecified groups, or a fear of conservative constituents or colleagues. The fact that fear was present in so many different ways indicates the need for further study into how fear has been operating in this cultural context and how people can best overcome it. Fear was not a main focus of this study, but there seems to be much to study here. Without asking specifically about fear in the interviews, my data was not too specific about the dynamics around fear. With the information I had, I attempted to get a clearer picture of fear present in this process (see Table 5.2), though more attention and research is necessary.

Conservative Constituents

Conservative constituents—administrators, faculty, student groups, donors, parents, and self-appointed defenders of Catholic orthodoxy—were identified as barriers to participants' change efforts. Both Love (1998) and Maher and Sever (2007) discussed various conservative constituents preventing change or inciting fear in the change process. For Maher and Sever (2007), donors and funding were a big concern. Love (1998) also mentioned a fear of what he called "external and peripheral constituents," in which he included bishops, donors, board of trustee members, alumni, parents, and students. The results of the present study add to this data by showing an explicit concern of conservative external constituents such as bloggers and whistleblowers who will call the bishop to complain about a concept they feel is contrary to the Catholic faith.

Administrative Resistance

Resistant administration had been discussed in various studies as well (Hughes, 2015; Love, 1997; Maher & Sever, 2007; McEntarfer, 2011). The vagueness with which participants would discuss this resistant administration indicates that the source of the resistance remains ambiguous. This is likely a result of what Morey and Piderit (2006) call the "shadow culture"—or where the structures of an unspoken culture drive behavior, different from what is publicly endorsed. When this barrier exists, there appears to be a cultural overtone of resistance

Table 5.2 Themes of fear related to change around issues of sexuality in Catholic higher education

Group Experiencing Fear	Fear of…	Related Quote
"The University"	• Making a change seen as not congruent with a Catholic mission • Other undefined*	"… the university was scared to bring that to fruition, because of their affiliation with Catholicism."
Members of the university community	• General fear of the change • Fear of being outed/identified as a sexual/gender minority • Other undefined*	"A lot of our students were afraid to come out to voice their opinion, to identify themselves in certain ways [regarding sexual orientation or gender identity] …"
Faculty	• Reprimanding by administration or negative career ramifications (e.g., not getting tenure)	"… not everybody has tenure, people hopefully wrongly, but you know, some people are just afraid to sign something like that"
Changemaker	• The administration's reaction • Job termination • Being targeted • Their own efficacy (imposter syndrome)	"There were people coming from institutions where they were afraid to tell their institutions they were even attending [a conference about LGBTQ topics in Catholic higher education], and they didn't."
Administration	• The local bishop • Negative public attention • Being "the first" to make such a change	"And it just takes somebody who doesn't get it, a couple of phone calls, either to the religious order or the bishop and now all of a sudden you got a problem on your hands."

* - indicates that more specific fear existed but was not further explained by participants. There is likely more to be expounded on here in future studies. Groups are not mutually exclusive.

expressed by the administration. This component of the results are congruent with previous studies in the area of change around LGBT student groups, and can be expanded to be seen as a barrier to general changes around sexuality.

Organizational Challenges

The various other organizational challenges—language sensitivity and poor organization—appeared briefly in other research with less context. McEntarfer (2011) identified language sensitivity in terms of words rejected by administration for change around a gay-straight alliance. In her study, the concept of language sensitivity was present about when or when not to concede, such as accept not using a term in order to continue with the change though not explicitly mentioned as a theme. Hughes (2015) also discussed a participant being told not to use direct language (i.e., students have sex, rather than students *may* have sex). This may be a desirable way of operating for some, but for others, changing a word may contribute to a larger problem (e.g., erasure) impacting the campus culture. Each study identified language being a point of discussion in the change process and the current research affirms this experience but also particularly identifies language sensitivity as a barrier when effecting change.

The theme of poor organization has also been prevalent in previous research. Pertaining to university leaders specifically, Love (1997) identified this as a paradox—that the "university leaders could not lead"—when describing contradictions and paradoxes around an LGBT student group at one university. At one Jesuit university, Hughes (2015) identified the experience of stalling changes in the process. The current research, however, gives a breadth of ways this may occur across Catholic higher education. It may be administrators that stall a change, but it may also be stalled by a single staff member in human resources, IT, or registration because they may not personally agree with the desired change.

A theme of particular importance involved the perceived barrier or assumptions made about what can and cannot be done at a Catholic college. In Miceli's (2009) study comparing coming out lesbian, gay, or bisexual on Catholic and non-Catholic campuses, the author identified that there was a higher perceived limitation at Catholic universities. Data from the current study supports Miceli's quantitative finding of perceived limitation and offers some qualitative data—evident in participants' recounting of what "could or could not happen on a Catholic campus." Further research can be done about the dynamics of these assumptions and how often they are founded or imagined concerns.

Theological Insights: Confronting Fear, Right-Relationship, and Solidarity

Many of these supports and barriers to change can be theologized about in great detail. For this book, I find it important to focus on two theological components from this chapter: (1) the fear that permeates Catholic culture when dealing with matters of sexuality and (2) the emphasis on forming relationships when working toward the common good of a community.

What of Fear?

Fear was so common throughout the interviews, I feel like it deserves its own theological discussion. Fear is generally a common theme around sexual morality in Catholic thought, but I want to look at it specifically in the face of change and dealing directly with matters of sexuality. Arguably, dealing with matters of sexuality at an institutional level like this is related to sexual morality which is also a worthy topic to explore (as many moral theologians would agree). But I want to focus this discussion on the fear about organizational change related to these topics.

Fear is a common theme throughout Christian scripture. In both Jewish and Christian texts, we hear some version of the message "do not be afraid" time and time again. Of course the object of fear is pertinent to this message—afraid of what? I'm fairly certain that not once in scripture are people instructed to "not be afraid" of institutional change in Catholic higher education. But we also hear important messages about the nature of fear. In 1 John, we hear that "there is no fear in love. But perfect love drives out fear" (1 Jn 4:18. NIV). We hear the message that fear is contrary to love—contrary to the greatest commandments (cf. Matthew 22:37–39, to love God and love your neighbor). And in the *Catechism*, we read the "law of the Gospel" is considered the "*law of love* because it makes us act out of the love infused by the Holy Spirit, rather than from fear," positioning fear as a reaction opposite to acting out of love (#1972).

Not only in scriptures and the *Catechism* do we hear about the dangers of operating out of fear, but we hear Pope Francis denounce fear in his encyclical *Fratelli Tutti*. When discussing international relations, Francis (2015a) speaks of the harm that comes from basing stability (of country relations) on fear "when it actually increases fear and undermines relationships of trust between peoples" (para. 262). I believe this is also true in our institutional decisions. If we allow fear to guide how we make choices in our institutional relationships, we undermine the trust involved in making beneficial decisions in university life. If we allow fear to dampen our courage to bring about loving change, Francis (2014) cautions in his apostolic exhortation *Evangelii Gaudium*, "we will remain comfortable and make no progress whatsoever. In this case we will not take an active part in historical processes, but become mere onlookers as the Church gradually stagnates" (para. 129). Pope Francis (2015b) encourages Christians to listen to the signs of the times and grow freely, without fear in the truth of faith.

Fear of topics related to sexuality is rampant in Catholic higher education. Fear has caused people to prevent changes crucial to the inclusion and support of others. This avoidance of topics of sexuality in Catholic institutions causes harm to many people for many different reasons. Just as people erroneously conclude that "Catholic institutions can't affirm LGBTQ+ people," we also see people claiming that Catholic institutions cannot educate about components of sexuality. Moral theologian Dr. Karen Ross and I talk about this very phenomenon in an article we wrote about including sexuality education in Catholic institutions (Levand & Ross, 2021). In it, we point out the importance of educating for whole person development (as called for in much of Catholic education, see *Ex Corde Ecclesiae*, John Paul II, 1990, para. 20) and the human right to education (Paul VI, 1965, para. 1). Despite much of the very Catholic support for education about sexuality, many people are still afraid to engage with the topic at these institutions of higher learning. Resistance to and fear of making changes that help people—people often in dire need—is not only harmful to members of the community, but specifically named in our Christian tradition as something to be confronted, calmed, and offered up to God (see Philippians 4:6). Pope Francis (2015a) adds that reparation and reconciliation (discussed as a *communal* act in the last chapter) "will give us new life and set us all free from fear" (para. 78). This concept of communal reconciliation as an antidote to fear is an excellent segue into the next topic I wanted to discuss in this chapter: being in relationship.

Being in Relationship

In the data above, we heard residence life and student life members discuss the concept of being close to the experience of students ("closeness to student experience" theme from Chapter 3), and how that influenced their ability to listen and be present with students in matters pertinent to their lives. We saw that from this social location, these staff members were in a meaningful position to champion change and advocate for students in a system that may otherwise silence or avoid student inquiry on the topic. It is here that a quick theological discussion on the importance of solidarity through relationship may be useful.

The concept of being in relationship is a core theme in Christian theology. Being in relationship with God, with self, with creation, and with other humans is a core tenet of our humanity (Robinson, 1994). Carter Heyward (1984) notes that "the Bible as a whole speaks of justice as 'right relationship' between and among people" (p. 30). The staff members listening to and advocating for students in need are practicing a truly Christian principle of being in relationship with, alongside of, and there for others. In Catholic social teaching (CST), the concept of being in relationship with and caring for a person or group of people is called solidarity.

Being in Solidarity

Catholic theologian Gerald Beyer (2014) discussed three aspects of solidarity: (1) the recognition that human beings are interdependent by nature (and that the good of individuals is related to the development and good of the whole community), (2) the move from recognition to an initial response, and (3) solidarity's institutionalization as policy. People with institutional power must recognize that the needs of students are not only integral to the life of the institution, but that this dynamic plays a part in the whole of human history for the good of the human family. Once initial change occurs, solidarity demands that we move beyond single-layer or temporary change. It demands we adopt a principle of solidarity that guides policy on matters related to sexuality at the institution. In order to most effectively be in relationship with students—to hear and tend to their needs—it is important to orient oneself toward solidarity. The above data suggests that those in positions of institutional power in Catholic higher education who are not intent on being *in relationship* with students, may be unable to hear or understand these concerns. When we are disconnected from the concerns of those who are most deeply affected by institutional policy or selective silence/avoidance on matters needing change, we are failing to confront the fear which prevents justice in relationship. When changemakers name the fear present in the process, those who hold power have the opportunity to act in solidarity for change, becoming a supportive participant in changes that can bring about growth of the university community and of the global human family.

Conclusions

The experience of effecting change around human sexuality in Catholic higher education can look differently depending on the university culture, the political climate of the surrounding area, the people involved in the change process, the relationship to the bishop, mission of the school, and fear involved in the process. I have been told that themes in this chapter are among the most helpful for people embarking on change at their institutions. Fear can play a big role as a barrier to change, but there is great Catholic wisdom about how to deal with this fear when growing and changing as a community. The data in this chapter helped us draw out some important theological concepts about being *in relationship* with others and their needs while practicing solidarity at both the personal and institutional levels. Let's turn our attention now to how changemakers attempted to navigate the barriers to change named above.

References

Beyer, G. J. (2014). The meaning of solidarity in Catholic social teaching. *Political Theology*, *15*(1), 7–25. https://doi.org/10.1179/1462317X13Z.00000000059

Coley, J. S. (2018). *Gay on god's campus: Mobilizing for LGBT equality at Christian colleges and universities*. University of North Carolina Press.

Francis I. (2014). *Apostolic exhortation: Evangelii gaudium*. http://w2.vatican.va/content/francesco/en/apost_exhortations/documents/papa-francesco_esortazione-ap_20131124_evangelii-gaudium.html

Francis I. 2015a). *Fratelli tutti*. https://www.vatican.va/content/francesco/en/encyclicals/documents/papa-francesco_20201003_enciclica-fratelli-tutti.html

Francis I. (2015b, November 10). *Times change: Morning meditation in the chapel of the Domus Sanctae Marthae*. https://www.vatican.va/content/francesco/en/cotidie/2015/documents/papa-francesco-cotidie_20151023_times-change.html

Getz, C., & Kirkley, E. (2006). Shaking up the status quo: Challenging intolerance of the lesbian, gay and bisexual community at a private Roman Catholic university. *College Student Journal*, *40*(4), 857–869.

Heyward, C. (1984). *Our passion for justice: Images of power, sexuality, and liberation*. Pilgrim Press.

Hughes, B. E. (2015). *"Who am I to judge?": How a Jesuit university addresses LGBT issues on campus* (Publication No. 3706207) [Doctoral Dissertation, University of California, Los Angeles]. ProQuest Dissertations & Theses A&I.

John Paul II. (1990). *Ex corde ecclesiae*. http://w2.vatican.va/content/john-paul-ii/en/apost_constitutions/documents/hf_jp-ii_apc_15081990_ex-corde-ecclesiae.html

Levand, M. A., & Ross, K. (2021). Sexuality education as a moral good: Catholic support for accurate, holistic sexuality information. *Theology & Sexuality*, *27*(2–3), 169–187. https://doi.org/10.1080/13558358.2021.1872827

Love, P. G. (1997). Contradiction and paradox: Attempting to change the culture of sexual orientation at a small Catholic college. *Review of Higher Education*, *20*(4), 381–398. https://muse.jhu.edu/article/30031

Love, P. G. (1998). Cultural barriers facing lesbian, gay and bisexual students at a Catholic college. *Journal of Higher Education, 69*(3), 298–323. https://doi.org/10.2307/2649190

Maher, M. J., & Sever, L. M. (2007). What educators in Catholic schools might expect when addressing gay and lesbian issues: A study of needs and barriers. *Journal of Gay & Lesbian Issues In Education, 4*(3), 79–111.

McEntarfer, H. K. (2011). "Not going away": Approaches used by students, faculty, and staff members to create gay–straight alliances at three religiously affiliated universities. *Journal of LGBT Youth, 8*(4), 309–331. https://doi.org/10.1080/19361653.2011.607623

Miceli, M. J. (2009). *Coming-out at Catholic and non-Catholic colleges and universities* (Publication No. 3355077) [Doctoral Dissertation, Johnson & Wales University]. ProQuest Dissertations & Theses A&I.

Morey, M. M., & Piderit, J. J. (2006). *Catholic higher education: A culture in crisis*. Oxford University Press.

Paul VI. (1965). *Gravissimum educationis.* http://www.vatican.va/archive/hist_councils/ii_vatican_council/documents/vat-ii_decl_19651028_gravissimum-educationis_en.html

Robinson, G. (1994). Christian theology and development. *The Ecumenical Review, 46*(3), 316–321.

Wilcox, J. R. (2013). *Higher learning: Catholic colleges and universities on a mission.* https://www.americamagazine.org/issue/article/higher-learning

Material from this chapter is reprinted with permission from the following source:

Levand, M. A., & Dyson, D. A. (2021). Areas of support and barriers to change around issues of sexuality in Catholic higher education. *Sexuality Research and Social Policy, 18*, 170–183. https://doi.org/10.1007/s13178-020-00447-9

Chapter 6

Over, Under, Around, or Through?
How Changemakers Navigated the System

When people encountered barriers, how did they respond? What communication strategies did people employ to effectively navigate the change process?

Of the studies I discussed in Chapter 2, two stand out as important for the content of this chapter: McEntarfer's (2011) study that included two Catholic universities, and Coley's (2018) book *Gay on God's Campus*. In short, McEntarfer categorized changemakers' communication in four ways: collaborative, conciliatory, assertive, and underground/subversive. Coley identified tactics students used in effecting change for these groups. Coley defined tactics either by their communicative type (direct confrontational tactics, conscious-raising tactics), and/or institutional relation (extra institutional, institutional), at times using them together with no clear definition or distinction. This lack of distinction acts as a limitation for those curious about the specific communicative methods (or strategies) people used alongside the nuanced responses they received. While students are important to the change process, institutional change requires action from a number of agents. Employees are often in meetings that students may never attend or aware of institutional history inaccessible to the student experience. The present study differs in that it offers (1) an in-depth description of the tactics or methods of communication employed (2) largely by employees of these institutions rather than students.

Given the sensitive nature of sexuality in Catholic higher education, and the methods of communication described by McEntarfer (2011), I analyzed the methods of communication by changemakers around any issue of sexuality on Catholic campuses—sexual orientation as well as sexual assault, transgender students' living accommodations, sexual health and reproduction, incorporating sexuality into the curriculum, obtaining same-sex partner benefits, etc. Because this scope included more than changes around sexual orientation groups and included more than three Catholic institutions, I have broadened the

DOI: 10.4324/9781003218159-6

themes of communication while examining specific communication methods more in-depth than McEntarfer. The present data builds on past studies by including a broader sample size of institutions as well as a contextual look at effective methods of communication offering more verbiage and situational context than past studies. These communication strategies were often used in relation to the reactions changemakers encountered discussed in Chapter 4. I will discuss the process of paring effective strategies with reactions in Chapter 8. In this chapter, I will describe in-depth the strategies changemakers used in the change process. Themes can be found in brief on Table 6.1.

Effective Change Strategies

Where McEntarfer (2011) coded these types of navigation regarding the relational factors between the LGBTQ group efforts and the university, I have coded methods of communication as unilateral, in relation to what the changemakers actually did to create effective change. For example, I have omitted instances of concession (i.e., McEntarfer's conciliatory navigation in which groups needed to concede to university limitations) and only included helpful initiatives employed by those effecting change. I have organized these 12 themes into 3 major groups: preemptive, active educational, and policy/institutional.

Preemptive

Preemptive methods of effecting change involved actions or mindsets taken by changemakers prior to moving forward with larger, institutional change. These methods involved data gathering, increased visibility, and taking a student focus.

Data Gathering

Participants occasionally mentioned gathering data before moving forward with change efforts. This took the form of seeking out what other universities had done regarding their primary issue of concern. For curricular changes, participants identified doing readings in gay studies to prepare for a new set of courses:

> So the group of us that wanted to develop this program had to educate ourselves and each other.... We read our way through [an anthology on gay studies]. ...we had to ground ourselves enough in the literature to be able to say with any kind of authority, this is what should be done.

Table 6.1 Communication strategies employed to effect change around issues of sexuality in Catholic higher education

Theme	Definition	Example
1. Preemptive		
Data Gathering	Gathering information about the topic or what other institutions had done with similar changes.	Researching content about sexual assault awareness training to create a new program; asking how surrounding universities made a similar change.
Increased Visibility	Communications, presence, visual representation about the issue on campus.	Flyers about an event; a series of events on a particular sexuality topic; the presence and centering of out university members.
Student-Focus	Focusing on the welfare and/or involvement of students in framing change efforts.	Identifying sexual health risk if students are not informed about sexuality; correlating student emotional and spiritual health to having identity-based community.
2. Active Educational		
Public Conversation	Generating conversation throughout the university about the sexuality topic(s) of change.	Holding a conference about LGBTQ health at the university; circulating a petition for signatures; holding a prayer service for Transgender Day of Remembrance; pamphlets, handouts, presentations on drag culture.
Trainings	Holding formal trainings for students, faculty, or staff related to the desired change.	Conducting ally trainings for university staff; training residence life members on transgender experiences of living on campus; training administrators on language related to sexuality for a campus culture change.
Outside Resources	Referral to external/local resources or inviting external speakers/trainers onto campus.	Inviting a scholar or activist to discuss their topic of expertise; have an external company train university members on gender identity or handling sexual assault; seeking a grant to fund a university change.
One-to-One Education	Having conversations with key members of the community resistant to the change, helping them navigate their feelings and knowledge on the matter.	Helping an administrator see the need for student groups based on sexual identity; talking to individual parents who were upset about a particular change.

Task Forces	Forming groups (often with representation of those most affected by the change) to discuss how a change can be institutionalized.	People of diverse gender identities on a committee to discuss a university's policy change related to gender; a group of administrators across campus on a task force to coordinate a name-change system update on campus.
Student Protest	Students organizing and facilitating an institutionally visible protest related to the change.	Students gathering in a public place to raise awareness about including sexual orientation and gender identity in the university's non-discrimination clause.
3. Policy/ Institutional		
Engaging Tradition	Tying the mission, history, or heritage of the university and/or Catholicism to the need for change.	Discussing Christ's inclusive love and human dignity relating to LGBTQ student group creation; explaining how theological concepts related to the university's founding religious order are related to the change.
Language Sensitivity	Intentionally using or avoiding certain words or phrases to make a change more palatable for those uncomfortable with the change.	Using "family restroom" instead of "gender-neutral;" not using the words "recruitment" or "activism" in educational material about a LGBTQ student group.
Discreet Methods	Making changes without explicit permission, as to "fly under the radar" of changemaking.	Updating a form to be more inclusive without asking a supervisor; operating on an inclusive policy that is not publicly espoused by the university or department.

Participants working in several areas around sexuality reported similar experiences. One administrator working to enhance sexual assault awareness training recalled:

> The way we approached [the change] was we spent a full year in my office evaluating the different existing Bystander Intervention training programs that were already out there, and we did not settle on just taking an existing program and implementing it here. We actually created a hybrid [training].

Participants working in gender-inclusive housing and restrooms, gender diversity in leadership, and campus climate around LGBTQ discrimination all reported gathering data from their own university population and/or other universities' efforts.

Increased Visibility

An observation by many participants, especially when changing campus climate, involved a need to increase visibility for their particular issue of change. The presence or absence of visibility impacted the environment. Some participants recognized this and increased visibility as a way of changing the conversation on their campus. One participant said, "We even had administration on campus who identified themselves with specific orientations," which they noted was not commonplace at their university but started to come out more once the university seemed to support it. Participants used employee sexual identity visibility to influence the way that the student body and broader university talked about LGBTQ identities in a more accepting way. One participant recalled a program on LGBTQ community issues they moderated at their university. Students could and would use this platform to come out publicly at which allies and friends would support them, engaging in a conversation about the appreciation for diversity. The participant identified this as

> one of the most heartfelt experiences that you ever can have because people were leaving, I mean there's not a dry eye in the house, ... students were feeling like a weight had been lifted off of them—that they are finally able to, you know, publicly identify themselves and [the] connection between the administrators and faculty and the students had become so significant because now students are looking in the audience and they are seeing their professors.

Student-Focus

Particularly helpful to change was adopting a student-focused mindset or frame for the change, or explicitly employing the welfare of students. Recalling how they began change around an already existing LGBTQ educational initiative on campus, one residence life staff member said, "We could [still] have [this program], but just tailor the events towards our students like, at night time, and like, with a panel about what it is like to navigate certain spaces" or have a student panel or someone from the community "speak on personal experiences, talking about culturally sensitive issues, that we are a university that focuses on social justice." This participant outlined the need to make a program about LGBTQ information on campus more student-focused, which ultimately led to more student involvement.

Another participant described bringing conversations on healthy sexuality to campus by highlighting the disservice to students:

> And there was some question about what happens when students want to have conversations around sexuality and so basically the message that I was given was, "oh, you know, we don't talk about that, we don't talk about contraceptives, we don't talk about this, we don't talk about that." And so I had to make the case to say ... we are doing a disservice to students ... this is probably the only arena that they have to have those types of conversations.

Active Educational

Active educational methods of effecting change included what the changemakers did to create interpersonal or institutional movement around their issue. This theme involved public conversation (including prayer services, forums, and public letters/petitions), trainings, outside resources, one-to-one education, task forces, and student protests.

Public Conversation

More than half of the participants described the active education method of having the conversation in some public format. Whether the university held a conference about LGBTQ people's experience in Catholic higher education, held a prayer service, held a public forum, or used a public letter or petition, participants described strategies placing the conversation in the broader university environment as useful for change. One faculty member drafted a letter that garnered signatures to support adding sexual orientation and gender identity to the university's non-discrimination policy. He gathered signatures, money, and contacted the newspaper. Recalling that many people were lending support, he noted, "I want to say the students [had] their own letter and that had maybe like 2,000 signatures. So there was lobbying going on all around."

When describing materials for a drag show sponsored by the LGBTQ student organization, one residence life staff member listed the types of visible education involved:

> Like pamphlets, handouts, presentations—that were constantly going on in the room, like there were TVs set around the space and there was a constant presentation PowerPoint loop of just what drag is, and how the trans community is at high risk violence ... according to research and just statistics.... and just resources that we don't normally offer here.

Other participants identified forums were helpful in educating the university. One faculty member cited the forum they held on campus climate data around gender representation in leadership saying, "We had a public forum where we told everybody what we had done and what our results were, and then we had recommendations that went to the president. I think that that, even in and of itself, was helpful." These types of conversations made accessing information about the topic or change easy and made digestible information about it readily available.

Trainings

Holding formal trainings for students or staff members was another method commonly employed by changemakers. Whether these trainings were in-house safe space trainings or inviting an outside entity to educate the university community about topics, many participants identified trainings as helpful for getting the information about sexuality to the university community. Residence life members talked about training key staff:

> We worked very closely with resident assistants to help train them to understand the reasoning and the needs when students are putting themselves out there about their sexuality and their change, how to embrace that ... how to support them and how to ... [help] the other students within the community to understand that more.

Another administrator described training campus safety around managing cases of sexual assault as well. They described, among other things, campus safety because they would be first responders to incidents and should be included in trainings on sexual assault and diversity—trainings in which they were not previously included. Trainings happened around many types of issues of sexuality, often from on-campus departments, but at times, called in outside resources.

Outside Resources

Participants also identified referring to outside community resources or inviting community resources to campus as a helpful strategy. Some participants might have had the funds to invite an outside source to conduct a training or invite speakers to campus. An administrator recalled inviting a civil rights lawyer to speak on campus. They discussed how the conversation that followed about the law and the Catholic identity of the institution was helpful, citing specifically the student benefit and involvement in deciding the message that they wanted to send as an institution.

One faculty member looked to outside resources for funding and when identifying a grant opportunity said, "we received a call for proposals for an external foundation [that] wanted to give grants for the multiculturalization of the university." Outside resources could have also consisted of connecting students to various LGBTQ resources provided in the surrounding communities, organizations to help with events, or references on where to get birth control or condoms.

One-to-One Education

It was with great importance that participants described the impact of talking with people individually to help educate about a cause. One participant discussed creating a team of administrators to create a safe space training on campus; when recalling difficulty persuading one member for help, the participant said:

> He had some value conflicts with it but we had coffee many, many times. I showed him different small Catholic campuses that have safe zone training programs and then also did some YouTube videos with him that they talked about that what type of conflict it is or is not with the faith, so it was the first beginning piece.

Another administrator described using this strategy particularly with parents: "But generally it would be parents. A parent who would call to say, 'why do you have a group like this on your campus?' And sometimes, through a conversation, they really kind of got it."

Task Forces

An initial effort of several universities involved creating task forces to work on particular issues related to sexuality. Some task forces were formed around issues of gender or orientation in order to best address the needs of those with similar identities at the institution by incorporating voices of those with these identities in the change process.

One participant recalled a new president's initiative to "put together this inclusivity committee to identify these areas and then to put into practice these policies and procedures to help support the students." Another administrator described the constituents of the task force he formed:

> So I had a newly established college ombudsman who is a student advocate so that was huge. I had those two folks that served on president's council ... I had the mission officer ... that was a tough one, I'm not going to lie to you there. The campus minister, director of residence life, three full-time professors...and then I actually had two people from the finance office and obviously my direct supervisor [VP of Student Affairs].

It is important to note, however, that one participant felt like the task force, though formed, had little effect towards change.

Student Protest

Almost seemingly as a last resort, participants described how student protest was an effective method of persuading the university to change policies. One faculty member attributed a policy change at their college to student influence and recalled that "students had successfully protested and lobbied and used their leverage to get the College to modify its statement on non-discrimination to include gender identity and sexual identity." This was not a very prevalent theme in the interviews, but when it occurred, participants identified its strong impact.

One participant, however, identified a situation about including transgender healthcare in the medical insurance in which protests seemed to have lost impact due to their general frequency on campus. This participant said that rather than a protest, students should work through the network of connections the participant had formed which eventually led to effective change with minimal public attention.

Policy/Institutional

Various policy or institutional methods of navigation involved how the changemakers either used or avoided various institutional components to effect change. These themes include engaging tradition, language sensitivity, and discreet methods.

Engaging Tradition

Engaging the tradition (mission, history, heritage) of the university or Catholicism proved to be a useful method of effecting change in

Catholic universities for over two thirds of participants. One administrator recalled hosting an event supporting LGBTQ students on campus and navigating some backlash from student groups, mentioning:

> We just kept pushing that Christ taught us to love all individuals regardless. So love one another as you love your neighbor. So that was pretty much our purpose, regardless of the Catholic teaching or what not, that was our focus—to support everyone.

In getting a safe space training on campus, one participant recalled personalizing the training, making it more applicable to their Catholic environment, saying, "We had tried to make some amendments that would make it more mission-focused or mission-oriented and how people understand, that actually, commitment to human dignity and diversity is part of the Catholic social teaching of the church."

An important note, however, was a contradiction that appeared in a couple interviews. Some participants echoed similar viewpoints around the Catholic pastoral approach and dogmatic approach, sating "I think that fundamental contradiction between the dogma of the church and the reality of people's lives is something that those of us who are concerned with education around sexuality and the Catholic institutions have to push to resolve."

Language Sensitivity

Language sensitivity could have been a source for dispute or resistance, but was also used as a method of creating successful change. As a resolution to the language issues discussed in Chapter 5, participants recounted ways in which they avoided certain words or clarified words/misunderstandings because of social connotations. One participant recalled the creation of their LGBTQ student group: "We definitely had some pushback, but we were very careful with how we framed it. We had to avoid all words like activism, advocacy, recruitment; it was all about raising awareness and doing education." Changes in partner benefit plans underwent similar scrutiny:

> [The university] really tried to finesse it, so nowhere does it say that they provided same-sex benefits instead they did a plus-one system so that you could add one person to your...health insurance coverage.

Discreet Methods

Similar to McEntarfer's (2011) underground/subversive description of navigation, I have coded some participants' methods of navigation as discreet. These are instances when participants described making changes, often institutional, without asking permission. One participant described a practical change in dealing with transgender student housing as "not an outspoken one, not anything you're going to find in policy but just in practice."

Another housing director described adding components to a document that recognized more than two genders:

> So, it was pretty simple. Like, I didn't actually ask for permission. I had mentioned it to my supervisor, but my supervisor is responsible for way too many things that one person does.... I know I mentioned it but now that form has actually changed [to reflect more than two genders].

On the topic of communication, this participant added, "I didn't get any emails back from the Vice President or the dean of students, though. So I guess I never followed up and I just went ahead and made the changes." This particular participant identified supervisors avoiding answering the question and felt that making the change was more helpful to students than waiting for explicit permission.

Though participants might have been doing these changes without permission, it was not often out of being told directly they should not make a change, but they rather used it as a way of avoiding confrontation until the change was already in effect (i.e., on a housing form, or conducting an event using external funding).

Discussion

McEntarfer (2011) examined the ways in which changemakers communicated to effect change at three different religiously affiliated universities. She identified these ways of communicating as collaborative, conciliatory, assertive, or underground/subversive. This categorization may be useful in describing the communication between changemakers and the university leadership to navigate the power dynamic. I have expanded my scope beyond this power dynamic and coded these methods of communication by operational effectiveness—or where these types of communication were most appropriate. This analysis places emphasis on the method's contextual usefulness in the change process for those planning to implement change. In short, my analysis broadens the scope of what constitutes "communication" in how people effect change around issues of sexuality, broadens what constitutes "sexuality" beyond sexual orientation student groups, and examines 17 universities from a variety of Catholic backgrounds, increasing the environmental scope of the change.

The ways employees have communicated here are components of organizational change. Organizational change theories often take into account the uniqueness of the environment and situational analysis which may take much trial and error (Batras et al., 2016). Many of these changes require a number of what Rogers (2003) calls "champions"—or what I term "changemakers—people leading the change. Rogers" institutional stages of change have three main parts: initiation, decision, and implementation (Batras et al., 2016). The initiation activities of the process include agenda setting (identifying the problem or need for a change) and matching (trial of solutions to the problem). The initiation and implementation activities are separated by the decision to adopt a given change. After organizational leaders decide to adopt a change, the implementation activities can happen: redefining/restructuring (the re-making of an innovation to fit the specific institution), clarifying (slowly implementing the change across the organization, helping to clarify misunderstandings or addressing adverse side effects of an implemented change), and routinizing (when the change has become embedded in the organizational culture).

The various tactics employees used to communicate in effecting change often fall before or after the leadership's decision to implement such a change. The way I have coded the preemptive, active educational, and policy/institutional communications do not fit neatly into the stages of change in a linear process. Rather, depending on the institutional environment, the communication tactics used can appear at any of the stages in Rogers' model. Leadership (i.e., administrators) may also be fragmented, where some leaders want to adopt a change and others are disinterested or resistant. These will be important situational factors to consider when implementing change on a campus.

1. Preemptive: What Needs to Happen First?

The preemptive strategies identified in the data include the behind-the-scenes work—gathering data, increasing visibility, and focusing on students.

Gathering data about what other universities are doing or what one's own university has done in the past has been reported as a useful step. Hughes (2015) identified communication tactics such as using research to build a case as an important component of effecting change. Along with many other tactics, Hughes noted these tactics as stemming from the organizational change literature (Kezar & Lester, 2011; Meyerson, 2003, 2008). From the above data, an important part of this process is examining other Catholic universities in similar geographic and social/political environments more so than just schools within a similar religious order. A key insight from this study is that participants at universities of the same religious order identified vastly different environments around LGBTQ attitudes, largely because of their geographic environment and its social/political location (see Chapter 5).

Increasing visibility of LGBTQ employees on campus was an important tactic used in creating change. Hughes (2015) identified intellectual discourse and demonstrating allyship as useful tools for change. The particular method of employee visibility as a mode of communicating safety, allyship, or bravery can provide support for students in ways that public discussion or other forms of allyship cannot.

Part of the preemptive communication strategies included adopting a mindset that involved a student-focused philosophy about the change. Hughes (2015) stresses the importance of framing the message within the mission of the school. While I also found religious mission incorporation to be an important method of communication (and coded it under *policy and institutional* forms of communication), if participants discussed how this change benefits students, change was much more likely to happen. The philosophy of student-focused concern seemed to be driving many of the changemakers not only in my study, but those of other scholars as well (Fox, 2017; Love, 1998; McEntarfer, 2011). This may be helpful because many schools focus on undergraduates for financial stability (Morey & Piderit, 2006).

In Rogers' (2003) stages, data gathering almost always falls in the initiation stage. If employees are gathering data about how other universities handled a similar situation, they have likely identified a problem they are trying to address. In the early stages of a larger cultural change, increasing visibility and a student-focused philosophy can increase awareness of the issue which requires a larger systemic change. Bringing this awareness and frame can help constituents of a campus culture begin to understand the problem, increasing the chances of adopting a solution.

2. Active Educational: How to Keep the Conversation Going

Consistent with other types of organizational change models is the concept of good education or training. In discussing eight factors of effective organizational change, Fernandez and Rainey (2006) identified this process as providing resources, often seen in the present study as making educational resources available to the community. Many participants did this by engaging in public conversations with forums or inviting speakers. Safe space trainings proved to be a useful tactic for participants in this study, congruent with that of others (Getz & Kirkley, 2006; Hughes, 2015). Some campuses had the finances to invite outside resources like professionals and trainers about a specific change around sexuality. Forming task forces or other groups that are in charge of motivating the public dialogue also helped keep the issue in the public sphere. Hughes (2015) identified one-on-one interactions as a helpful method of active education, a finding supported by the present study. As suggested by McEntarfer (2011) and supported by this study, if the resistance was high, student protest appeared be a useful tool in the conversation. A unique insight from this study, however, indicates that the administration on campuses that protest too often may not take the protest seriously enough to effect change and that other methods of navigating change may be more useful.

Most of the active educational methods had been documented as useful in previous research (Getz & Kirkley, 2006; Hughes, 2015; McEntarfer, 2011). A method less mentioned in the literature that appeared in the present study was keeping the university informed by inviting outside speakers to speak on a topic. In the Catholic context, having speakers seemed to be a useful educational practice because of the protection of academic freedom and its connection to the Catholic intellectual tradition. Though speakers were disinvited at times, several participants saw speakers as useful in keeping the conversation about a particular sexual topic active on campus.

Active educational methods of communication are often used either to raise awareness about an issue prior to big decisions or as part of the implementation activities. Trainings may happen because of a campus-wide initiative to increase an understanding about a topic in sexuality, or a training may be one department's attempt to educate the entire campus about a particular issue. As part of organizational change, it is apparent that group experience plays a significant role in determining organizational culture (Batras et al., 2016). If a group engages enough of the campus in discourse about the issue, it may influence the experience of enough members of the institution to effect change. Another important insight from organizational change is that an organization's access to experts in the topic can further assist in effective change (Rogers, 2003). Task forces, for example, may work at universities who have access to experts on staff, while another university may not have the necessary expertise to from an effective task force.

3. Policy/Institutional: Steps to Institutionalize

While the methods of engaging the tradition, language sensitivity, and discreet methods are all present in prior research (Hughes, 2015; McEntarfer, 2011), the current study yields more situational context for these communications. I have coded them under policy or intuitional method because of the ways in which changemakers employed them. Changemakers used discreet methods or being aware/sensitive to the language when they were encountering institutional university barriers. The discreet methods were not necessarily subversive or underground as McEntarfer (2011) may indicate, but may also be employed as a conflict avoidant strategy or as part of a cultural norm. Hughes (2015), Kirkley and Getz (2007), Perlis and Shapiro (2001), and Yoakam (2006) all stressed the importance of engaging the institutional tradition in change around LGBTQ student services. This strategy was also particularly helpful in the present study when discussing issues like sexual decision-making, incorporating sexuality into the curriculum, addressing sexual assault, and partner benefits. Engaging the Catholic and/or order tradition for any topic of sexuality seemed important for further institutional dialogue.

Schein (2017) discusses the underlying basic assumptions of an organizational culture as assumptions of operation that have had repeated success in implementing certain beliefs and values. People in Catholic institutions may find that operating discreetly about issues of sexuality may be one of these underlying assumptions. Depending on the university environment, this may be a preferred norm for dealing with topics of sexuality, while discussing the issue aloud may go against cultural norms in a way that is not conducive to change (until these underlying assumptions are questioned and worked out at an institutional level). Many people in Catholic institutions will call this type of communication "flying under the radar" or that administrators will "turn a blind eye" enacting a don't-ask-don't-tell type of communication when implementing change around issues of sexuality.

Theological Insights: Solidarity, the Common Good, and Addressing Structural Sin

The focus of this chapter so far has been about communication—not only of advocating for marginalized identities, but communication used to effect change to ultimately meet the needs of students and bring healthy conversation of matters of sexuality into Catholic higher education. In the last chapter, I discussed solidarity as an aspect of being in relationship with those working for a positive change within an organization toward the common good. Here I will continue that conversation, looking at these communication strategies as changemakers' active participation in that solidarity and how these methods are oriented toward the common good.

Solidarity's Goal: Toward a Common Good, Addressing Structural Sin

In earlier chapters, I discussed how Pope Francis talks about not letting fear stand in the way of progress and how we as Christians are called to change with the times, lest we "become mere onlookers as the Church gradually stagnates" (*Evangelii Gaudium*, 129). Tightly tied to the concept of solidarity is the CST principle of participation. The US Catholic Bishops (1998) discuss participation as a societal duty, "seeking together the common good and well-being of all, especially the poor and vulnerable" (para. 23). While participation is typically discussed in the context of political and economic life, there is certainly a social component to participation. When discussing problem-solving of a local political culture, we hear Pope Francis (2015) discuss in his encyclical *Laudato Si'* that "the complexities of local problems ... demand the active participation of all members of the community" (para. 144). Changemakers are facilitating their own participation and the participation of others through these communication strategies to affect the local (university) culture around any of these given topics of sexuality. When an institution ignores victims of sexual violence, change is needed to lift up the voices of the victimized. When the fear of talking about sexuality prevents sexual health information from being incorporated into students' lives, change is needed to help them make the best-informed sexual decisions. When sexism and gendered assumptions create a hostile environment for people of particular genders on a campus, change is needed to protect people from discrimination, dehumanization, and sexual violence. These changemakers are participating in the life of the university through solidarity working for a change in the university culture toward the common good.

What does participation and solidarity have to do with the common good? We see John Paul II (1987) remind us in *Sollicitudo Rei Socialis* (The Social Concern) that solidarity is not simply a "vague compassion" for others or a "shallow distress at the misfortunes" of others, but rather a "determination to commit oneself to the common good" (para. 38). If solidarity is the determination to commit ourselves to the common good, how can we say that these communication strategies are, in fact, bringing about the common good? Again, from the wisdom of the Second Vatican Council, *Gaudium et Spes* famously describes the common good as "the sum of those conditions of social life which allow social groups and their individual members relatively thorough and ready access to their own fulfillment" (Paul VI, 1965, para. 26). Every single participant in this study saw their work as bringing more voices into the conversation—connecting individuals to groups and information they need to access their own fulfilment. And this was indeed the outcome of these changes: more students became connected to each other; LGBTQ members of the university found community and love in various events and group activities; transgender students were housed in safe and affirming ways; communities became informed about sexual assault and sexual health in ways that fostered a safer and more knowledgeable community. Access to one's own fulfilment can take many forms within the realm of sexuality, but there is also another component in solidarity's relationship to the common good. When we consider the "sum of conditions of social life" we turn our attention to the concept of social or structural sin.

How can we tell exactly what is the common good? When we look at the common good in contrast to social (sometimes called structural) sin, we get a clearer picture of the aspects of our institutions we must address. Continuing with the words of St. John Paul II (1984), social sin is "every sin against justice in interpersonal relationships, committed either by the individual against the community or by the community against the individual" (para. 16). Social sin is the way institutions do harm to justice in relationships and the way we institutionalize those harmful mechanisms into our social structures. What then is social/structural sin with regards to sexuality in Catholic institutions? When the cries of victims go unheard or outright dismissed. When policy excludes or discriminates against people based on matters of sexual and gender identity. When sexuality education is systematically ignored, limiting information people need to make healthy decisions. When organizations protect those who sexually abuse or lack adequate response to abuse in the organization. In these ways and so many more, whenever human dignity is not upheld, we are called to more critically examine the sinfulness of the social structures that allow that injustice to happen. The changemakers in this study all noted an injustice that needed to be addressed at their institution and worked to address it. In the face of structural sin—institutional policy or culture that was leaving individuals and groups disadvantaged, unable to access their own fulfilment, and suffering injustices in their Catholic institutions—these changemakers were working toward the common good by addressing these injustices.

Conclusions

This chapter was a look at how changemakers went about making a change at their university. I looked at the many ways they communicated to create effective change and grouped them into descriptive themes. These strategies have mostly been present throughout the literature, but the present study offered a couple new insights. First, instead of only seeing these at one or two institutions, the larger sample size of 17 institutions indicates that these strategies are in wider use than a single localized university setting. Second, these themes offer more nuance to the previous discussions of communication strategies. Nuances such as the university's relation to its social/political environment and the concept of over-protesting as ineffective are unique insights of this study that add to change efforts at Catholic institutions of higher education.

We also looked further into the meaning of solidarity and participation in the process of change and the social life of the university. We considered the common good (the goal of solidarity) and how structural/social sin is in direct contradiction to the flourishing of humanity. We considered how these changemakers were living examples of acting in solidarity and addressing structural sin for the betterment of the common good related to matters of sexuality.

They were working toward not only the common good of the university but also the common good of the church as a whole in continuing to have these conversations.

These communication strategies were ways participants helped to effect change. In earlier chapters, we considered participants' motivations, the key areas they saw in need of change, the supportive or challenging components in the change process, the reactions they countered along the way, and now the strategies they used to effectively communicate about these changes. Before we weave these all together, let's explore these changemakers' hopes for future change in Catholic higher education in the next chapter.

References

Batras, D., Duff, C., & Smith, B. J. (2016). Organizational change theory: Implications for health promotion practice. *Health Promotion International*, *31*(1), 231–241. https://doi.org/10.1093/heapro/dau098

Coley, J. S. (2018). *Gay on god's campus: Mobilizing for LGBT equality at Christian colleges and universities*. University of North Carolina Press.

Fernandez, S., & Rainey, H. G. (2006). Managing successful organizational change in the public sector. *Public Administration Review*, *66*(2), 168–176. https://doi.org/10.1111/j.1540-6210.2006.00570.x

Fox, D. M. (2017). *That's so gay: An analysis of LGBTQIA+ students and school climate within institutions of higher education* [Master's Projects and Capstones, University of San Francisco]. Repository.USFCA.edu. https://repository.usfca.edu/cgi/viewcontent.cgi?referer=&httpsredir=1&article=1570&context=capstone

Francis I. (2015). *Laudato si'*. http://www.vatican.va/content/francesco/en/encyclicals/documents/papa-francesco_20150524_enciclica-laudato-si.html

Getz, C., & Kirkley, E. (2006). Shaking up the status quo: Challenging intolerance of the lesbian, gay and bisexual community at a private Roman Catholic university. *College Student Journal*, *40*(4), 857–869.

Hughes, B. E. (2015). *"Who am I to judge?": How a Jesuit university addresses LGBT issues on campus* (Publication No. 3706207) [Doctoral Dissertation, University of California, Los Angeles]. ProQuest Dissertations & Theses A&I.

John Paul II. (1984). *Reconciliation and penance*. http://www.vatican.va/content/john-paul-ii/en/apost_exhortations/documents/hf_jp-ii_exh_02121984_reconciliatio-et-paenitentia.html

John Paul II. (1987). *Sollicitudo rei socialis.* http://www.vatican.va/content/john-paul-ii/en/encyclicals/documents/hf_jp-ii_enc_30121987_sollicitudo-rei-socialis.html

Kezar, A., & Lester, J. (2011). *Enhancing campus capacity for leadership: An examination of grassroots leaders in higher education.* Stanford University Press.

Kirkley, E. A., & Getz, C. (2007). A model for sexual orientation education at a religiously affiliated institution. *Journal of Gay & Lesbian Issues In Education, 4*(3), 113–119. https://doi.org/10.1300/J367v04n03_07

Love, P. G. (1998). Cultural barriers facing lesbian, gay and bisexual students at a Catholic college. *Journal of Higher Education, 69*(3), 298–323. https://doi.org/10.2307/2649190

McEntarfer, H. K. (2011). "Not going away": Approaches used by students, faculty, and staff members to create gay–straight alliances at three religiously affiliated universities. *Journal of LGBT Youth, 8*(4), 309–331. https://doi.org/10.1080/19361653.2011.607623

Meyerson, D. E. (2003). *Tempered radicals: How everyday leaders inspire change at work.* Harvard Business Press.

Meyerson, D. E. (2008). *Rocking the boat: How to effect change without making trouble.* Harvard Business Press.

Morey, M. M., & Piderit, J. J. (2006). *Catholic higher education: A culture in crisis.* Oxford University Press.

Paul VI. (1965). *Gaudium et spes: Pastoral constitution on the church in the modern world.* http://www.vatican.va/archive/hist_councils/ii_vatican_council/documents/vat-ii_const_19651207_gaudium-et-spes_en.html

Perlis, S. M., & Shapiro, J. P. (2001). *Understanding interconnections between cultural differences: A social justice imperative for educational administrators* [Conference paper]. Annual Meeting of the University Council for Educational Administration, Cincinnati, OH, United States. https://files.eric.ed.gov/fulltext/ED467730.pdf

Rogers, E. M. (2003). *Diffusion of innovations* (5th ed.). Free Press.

Schein, E. H. (2017). *Organizational culture and leadership* (5th ed.). Wiley.

United States Conference of Catholic Bishops. (1998). *Sharing Catholic social teaching: Challenges and directions.* http://www.usccb.org/beliefs-and-teachings/what-we-believe/catholic-social-teaching/sharing-catholic-social-teaching-challenges-and-directions.cfm

Yoakam, J. R. (2006). Resources for gay and bisexual students in a Catholic college. *Journal of Men's Studies, 14*(3), 311–321. https://doi.org/10.3149/jms.1403.311

Material from this chapter is reprinted with permission from the following source:

Levand, M. A. (2021). Communication strategies and responses to change around issues of sexuality in Catholic higher education. *Profesional de la Información, 30*(5), 1–14. https://doi.org/10.3145/epi.2021.sep.04

Chapter 7

Voices of Change
Hopes for the Future and Suggestions for Improvement

> What do changemakers want to see changed in the church moving forward? How can the church engage with sexuality in the future?

At the end of the interviews, I asked participants about their efforts and hopes for the future: why did they advocate for change? What role did they play? And what did they hope their institution or the Catholic Church might do in the future to more holistically address the topic of sexuality? Most of the participants took a deep breath—to sigh in awe at the enormity of the issue saying, "That's a big question" or to laugh in disbelief that anything could be done. I asked them this question because these participants are experts in the lived experience of addressing issues of sexuality in their Catholic institutions. I figured they may have some insight that I could report on, and they most certainly did.

When I asked what they hope to see change in the church or Catholic higher education, participants often prefaced their answers with concerns about the systemic problems that currently exist. There are three immediate concerns when it comes to changemaker's hopes for future change: (1) college is an incredibly important developmental time for students to be given information about sexuality; (2) discussion around issues of sexuality may be stifled or discouraged in a culturally Catholic setting; and (3) this leaves students unprepared to deal with matters of sexuality in both personal and professional settings. Before we examine changemakers' hopes for the future, I want to address these concerns.

College as Developmentally Appropriate for Sexuality Education

To the first concern, developmental theorists such as Erikson (1968) and Levinson (Levinson et al., 1978; Levinson & Levinson, 1996), and student developmental theorists like Chickering and Reisser (1993) and Arnett's (2000), all support the developmental need to discuss sexuality in Catholic higher education (see Chapter 2). Regardless of religious affiliation, students are curious and feel uninformed about the topics discussed in class. Many students receive their first positive experience of discussions about sexuality in college classes. This is true of both secular and religiously oriented institutions of higher education, but anecdotally seems to be most salient with students from Catholic educational backgrounds. In my experience as a sexuality educator, many students from Catholic institutions appear to have higher rates of fear or shame around sexuality that is not often reflected in the same way in secular populations. Theorists and researchers in the social sciences tell us that social development around sexuality can be a confusing time for many young adults (Moreira et al., 2015).

Culturally Catholic Avoidance of Sexuality Discussion

Regarding changemakers' second concern, policing and fear around sexuality in Catholic higher education is well documented. Richard McCarty (2014), associate professor of religious studies at Mercyhurst University, authored an article chronicling such activities on sexuality scholarship in the Catholic world. He discusses the Catholic hierarchy's censoring of scholars like Todd Salzman, Michael Lawler, and Margaret Farley, and occasions of firing LGBTQ+ people or rescinding job offers in Catholic higher education based on scholarship around sexuality. McCarty was concerned with the way that fear infringes upon academic freedom around sexuality scholarship. McCarty (2014, 28) concludes that "the Roman Catholic hierarchy has created a silence-inducing culture of fear through its own moral and theological anxieties. We can only wonder how many scholars have abandoned projects, whether to spare their college or university embarrassment, to spare their administration 'trouble,' or even to avoid a feared loss of job security." In scholarship over the years, the theme of fear around sexuality and the silencing of that discussion is fairly evident. Not just with LGBTQ+ individuals or censoring scholars, but we also see this "silence-inducing culture of fear" around other issues of sexuality, such as mishandling sexual assault reporting at a number of Catholic institutions and the pressure applied to health centers on Catholic campuses to refuse medical information on contraception, abortion, or trans-affirming medical interventions. Of course, there are some universities that have these conversations well, but they are not the norm for Catholic educational culture.

Students as Unequipped to Address Sexuality

To the final concern, given the student need for this information combined with the Catholic avoidance of sexuality, it may be no surprise that suppressing sexuality information leads to students who are ill-prepared to understand both themselves as sexual persons and how to interact with others around issues of sexuality, in both sexual and non-sexual ways. When we stifle conversations about sexuality, students and others cannot get answers to questions about what to do with their unaddressed shame; how to have conversations with partners about sexual activities with which they are comfortable; how to intelligibly discuss topics like sexual orientation, biological sex, and gender identity; or how power structures impact the sexual media they might consume.

While the systemic moral implications of these three concerns is quite long, I will take a quick sexuality-educator-break to say this: if a Catholic university supports whole person development and cannot have a conversation about an essential aspect of personhood, it violates some of the core tenets of Catholic education, namely the call we see in *Ex Corde Ecclesiae* to "enable students to acquire an organic vision of reality" (John Paul II, 1990, para. 20), or to make them "ready to undertake weighty responsibilities in society" as found in Vatican II's teachings on education, *Gravissimum Educationis* (Paul VI, 1965b, para. 10). In regard to sexuality, weighty responsibilities go beyond the moral gravity of sexual decision-making, expanding into the institutional management of sexual assault reporting; organizational safety of individuals who are diverse in their gender, gender expression, and sexual identity; being well informed about topics of sexuality when engaging in political conversation about sexual and gender identity; sensitivity to others' sexual trauma; and much more.

Given that stifling such conversations leave members of Catholic colleges and universities unprepared, unprotected, and underdeveloped around issues of sexuality in relation to the world around them, asking changemakers about their hopes for the future may offer some projected insight into how things might be different moving forward. I was interested in the space where the Catholic tradition intersected with the hopes of changemakers who had first-hand experience in the institutional process of change around issues of sexuality. What follows are the themes that arose from their responses.

Themes in Changemakers' Hopes for the Future

When asked about how they conceptualize their role in the change-making process, participants discussed giving a voice to the voiceless, protecting others from harm, caring for humanity, and upholding the Catholic tradition. When asked about hopes they have for the future of sexuality in Catholic higher education, their answers often related to the nature of fear around sexual issues as well as the need for ongoing study or dialogue. Participants gave answers that were both explicit, concrete action steps as well as broad, theoretical answers. Themes are listed briefly in Table 7.1.

Concrete Responses

The concrete responses were often administrators suggesting a generalized need of the particular project they were working on at the time: operationalize inclusivity by increasing funding, creating offices, and institutionalizing the change—whichever change they were addressing on their campus, they felt should be applied to all Catholic higher education. It makes sense that administrators would think the change they were working on should take place across all Catholic higher education. If they have been working hard in their leadership roles to navigate these systems, they probably have more reason than most to believe it can be done.

Theoretical Responses

The broader, theoretical responses often came from participants who saw a need in Catholic higher education and tried to articulate the root of this issue. I have grouped these responses into three themes: be not afraid, continue dialogue/study, and be a resource.

Be Not Afraid

In at least a third of the interviews, participants expressed a plea to overcome fear of engaging in discussions of sexuality. One faculty member identified that Catholic higher education "not be afraid of talking about sexuality and I think that's one of the biggest things is that Catholic higher education is oftentimes afraid to open up the conversation, because they don't know where it's going to go." This participant further mentioned the fear of conversation about sexual behavior,

> most of the problems around talking about sexuality ... has everything to do with the sexual behavior of anybody and so the minute you talk about sexuality in Catholic higher education, it is not just focused on one group [i.e., gay students or straight students], but it is on everybody.

Table 7.1 Hopes for future change around issues of sexuality in Catholic higher education

Theme	Definition	Solution Example
Concrete Responses	Hopes for the future included that other universities should be doing what the participant/their university were doing.	Working to create an LGBTQ+ or Sexuality resource office; advocate for insurance to cover other adults in the household; increase funding for climate assessments, or sexuality resources for the university.
Theoretical Responses	Responses that reflected participant beliefs about how to address the root of the issue.	
Be not afraid	A hope that universities overcome the fear of engaging in discussion of sexuality.	Engage in a culture of sexuality knowledge and discussion on campus by: having sexuality education courses; training faculty and staff how to talk about sexuality; publicly acknowledging the need for more dialogue in strategic plans; instituting a speaker series.
Continue dialogue/study	A hope that universities continue the conversations that are happening and encourage further study about all areas of sexuality.	Institutional reflection on how the institution has been dealing with issues of sexuality and commitment to bettering their Catholic institutional relationship with sexuality; recognize most Americans are ill-equipped to deal with matters of sexuality and offer training to all institutional levels; encourage faculty and student to engage in sexuality research across disciplines.
Be a resource	A hope that Catholic colleges and universities can be a resource for the community in learning about sexuality and a resource for the formation of college students.	Act as a community resource by holding sexuality education events open to the public or faith discussions on matters of sexuality; focus on student empowerment by giving them language to navigate their sexual lives and openly dialogue how to integrate their faith and sexuality.

This faculty member discussed the restrictiveness in Catholic dialogue about sexuality around orientation and thought that once the church more honestly begins including the sexual behaviors of all people, there might be growth in understanding.

Another concern shared by participants was the polarizing and excluding rhetoric. One participant discussed the results of a university climate study, identifying students feeling marginalized—both their LGBTQ+ students as well as their more conservative students:

> I think we have a responsibility as a church to engage these conversations. It is one of the kind of pressing and just popular issues of the time and that's what we need to have—engage and not be afraid ... and unfortunately it's turned into a very huge polarized kind of a conversation where people on all sides sometimes don't feel comfortable even in the classroom speaking about it because they don't necessarily think that they will be safe and respected in their opinion.... We've got our LGBT community who feel marginalized, but our traditional Catholic community also came up [as marginalized] in the climate survey.

A select few participants also identified that the Catholic context along with the American context were particularly detrimental to conversations about sexuality with statements like "the whole talk of sexuality needs to be opened up, not just in Catholic higher education, I think in general, we are just afraid of that topic."

Continue Dialogue/Study

Almost unanimously, participants called for an ongoing dialogue on or study of human sexuality. Participants noted the importance of the responsibility of Catholic higher education to both continue and improve conversations around sexuality. Participants suggested three ways to go about this: (1) a "Catholic self-reflection" of the university, defined here as the need for examination of the institution's Catholic identity and how the university is dealing with issues related to sexuality; (2) participants called for universities to have a healthier understanding of sexuality; (3) some of the more radical responses called for leaving Catholic teachings behind and continuing the dialogue in a non-Catholic direction.

The Catholic self-reflection theme was present in statements like, "I think that Catholic universities have to face the fact that it can't be true to their identity as Catholic, as institutions of higher learning, if there's this area of the human experience which is a 'no go area' for them [in] the courses ... they're offering." This theme was similarly present in a request for the institution to reflect on its mission and identity in relation to how it actually deals with issues of sexuality—asking the question, "Is how we are handling this topic reflective of our institution's values?" One administrator said:

> It is really trying to understand what are the values and mission of the institution and how do they respond to these different issues, these different needs of diversity, sexuality and Title IX etcetera, and how these institutions live their values, and if that's something that resonates with them or not. I think that's very critical.

Whether it involved critical analysis of identity or simply the acknowledgement of broader sexual diversity, participants called for an ongoing dialogue. One participant concisely summarized this need by saying, "If it were up to me, there would be an increasingly open discussion on issues of sexuality and acknowledgment of complexity and diversity."

The healthier sexuality theme appeared in participants' call for a more holistic understanding of sexuality. One participant discussed moving the conversation beyond "don't have sex, don't use birth control, don't have an abortion" by saying:

> The real conversation that I think the church invites us to which is: healthy sexuality is very full—it's a wholeness. It's about your relationship to yourself to another and to God. And it is congruent with your thoughts and your behaviors and actions and it requires responsibility and respect ... as well as love and connection and desire and all that other stuff.

Similarly, another participant outlined the issue in terms of its systemic roots.

> I think just talking about sex in a positive way is something that's missing from a lot of Catholic higher education.... If you're only going to talk about [sex] as how you avoid bad occurrences of this [i.e., sexual assault], and you don't offer many examples of what healthy relationships look like or healthy communication or healthy sex looks like, I think that could be just as damaging as failing to teach on what sexual assault is. And a lot of these students that go to Catholic schools many of them come from Catholic K-through-high-school education where sex is also rarely talked about as a sex-positive thing.... [And] if they're coming from more conservative areas and then going to Catholic higher

education—they're really lacking the skill-set to have a ... healthy sexually communicated relationship with partners and so that can only aid to a lack of understanding [about sexuality]. As well as possibly leading to harmful relationships, harmful situations.

Occasionally, participants identified Catholicism as a frame of thought that would never engage in the discussion and that Catholic higher education should leave the institutional Catholic Church behind. "Because it's pretty clear that the church is out of step with the realities of human lives and human experiences," as one participant said. This view of the Catholic Church being obsolete was not a common theme, but was mentioned with strong feelings when it arose in the interviews. Whether viewing the Catholic Church's teaching as having no value or having significant worth, participants expressed a need for Catholicism to re-evaluate its teachings on matters of sexuality more practically.

Be a Resource

Some participants described the seemingly untapped ability of Catholic higher education to be a resource for people on matters of sexuality. One faculty member identified the way Catholic institutions of higher education could act as a "point of better and a more adequate understanding of this faith in relation to human sexuality—that [sexuality is] part of Catholic institutions and Catholic higher education."

Another participant identified the resource Catholic higher education could be for the *formation* of college students—that Catholic institutions can provide a space for allowing students to explore, engage, and understand some of the pieces they are questioning. Acting as a resource for student empowerment was often mentioned, one participant saying, "[We] need to empower our students to be able to identify—to feel proud of their sexual identity really early on and to be able to use that as a way to support them academically." Whether acting as a resource for the Catholic faith itself or for the formation of students, participants said that Catholic higher education must become a resource of useful information about sexuality.

Discussion and Theological Insights: Conscience and the Catholic Erotophobia

When examining this data for theological themes, there are clear issues from the institutions that can be described as a Catholic erotophobia—a fear of or distancing from the topic of sexuality. There are salient themes in Catholic theology and doctrine that support the changes called for by participants. Theological concepts of "bringing into the light what was in the dark," moral obligation, and Catholic social teaching (CST) offer insights into how we can best address sexuality in higher education in a holistic way through the Catholic tradition.

Of the three coded responses, "be not afraid" and "continuing the dialogue" were the most frequently mentioned. When asked *what* in Catholic higher education should change around sexuality, one participant laughed out loud and jokingly responded "everything." He quickly followed this statement with expressing the need for the Catholic Church not to be so afraid of having conversations about sexuality. This sentiment was shared by many other participants. These responses support McCarty's (2014) description of a Catholic silence-inducing culture of fear. The desire to eradicate fear—in this case, from the Catholic discussion of sexuality—is a strong theme in Christianity (see also Chapter 5). There is a scriptural basis for bringing light to hidden topics (Luke 12:2, 8:17; Mark 4:22) and a long tradition of theologians who engage with the topic of sexuality advocating the same. In her book on sexual ethics, moral theologian and Sister of Mercy, Margaret Farley (2006) wisely says about fear: "It is, after all, a good thing to move beyond fear and shame generated by irrational taboos and beyond complacency built on ignorance" (p. 8). The fear of discussing topics of sexuality and the barriers that exist in the shadows of silence should be brought to the light for honest discussion.

In morality, themes of the primacy of conscience and helping form and inform the consciences of others is a root cause for changemaker motivations. Catholic moral theologian William Mattison (2008) describes conscience as "your ability to make judgements about whether a particular act is right or wrong, and the particular judgment you make in a certain circumstance" (p. 106). When participants described what continuing the dialogue looks like, they included the concept of how Catholicism has a *duty*, which I consider here as a moral obligation, to better articulate the human experience of sexuality. These changemakers are acting in accordance with their conscience (afforded a primacy in Catholic thought; see *Dignitatis Humanae*, Paul VI, 1965a, para. 3 and *Catechism of the Catholic Church*, 2000, no. 1800). Participants are following their consciences in a moral obligation to address matters of sexuality that unjustly leave others confused, feeling excluded from the community, or suffering from pain and anxiety. This obligation is, however, not only the responsibility of the administrators, but of the school culture and larger Catholic Church as well.

Tightly tied to this concept of moral obligation are the CST concepts of human dignity, common good, and social sin. The doctrinal position on Catholic education touts the importance of whole person development (*Ex Corde Ecclesiae*, John Paul II, 1990, para. 20) along with the integral nature of sexuality to human personhood (*Persona Humana*, Sacred Congregation for the Doctrine of the Faith, 1975, para. 1). Catholic social teaching has long extolled a value of human dignity—we see this riddled throughout the documents of Vatican II and can be found in any foundational text on Catholic social teaching (see, for example, Thompson, 2010, pp. 58–59). Operating with an incomplete, fragmented, or dissonant understanding of sexuality in this formative environment works against the common good as described in *Gaudium et Spes* (Flannery, 1996, p. 191): the "sum total of social conditions which allow people ... to reach their fulfilment more fully and more easily." If sexuality is addressed in a holistic way, on a surface level, students would be able to intelligibly discuss topics of sexual assault, trauma, and other types of sexuality information. In a deeper sense, discussions on sexuality can help people understand themselves as sexual persons in a more holistic, integrated way. These are essential components of fulfilment with both individual and communal implications. These participants not only saw their work as moral, but there was also a sense of social responsibility. We see through *Gaudium et Spes* and other documents from CST (e.g., *Populorum Progressio*, Paul VI, 1967, para 17) that Catholics are encouraged to have a social role in engaging the human community and forming others around them.

In the last chapter, I discussed the concept of structural sin—the name given to the sinfulness of human social structures. Jesuit Fred Kramer (2004) describes the dynamics of structural sin as, "Human beings structure the sinfulness into a social system or arrangement, and the system or structure coercively shapes the behaviors of individuals" (p. 107). In Chapter 6, I described structural sin in regard to the institutional operation of Catholic universities. Here, I want to look at structural sin in relation to the culture of silence that permeates Catholic discussions of sexuality. The culture of ignorance and avoidance around topics of sexuality can amount to social, structural, or what Dr. Megan McCabe calls "cultural" sin (Ross et al., 2019). The way of discussing moral culpability for large, cultural issues like sex and sexuality is just now being discussed in a new light by scholars like Fr. Bryan Massingale (Massingale, 2010) and McCabe (cited above). For my purposes here, I am less concerned with the culpability of the cultural sin of avoiding issues of sexuality and more concerned with naming this avoidance and ignorance as a sinful injustice according to Catholic thought.

In describing a culture of sin, McCabe focuses the discussion on cultural factors that permit the normalization of sexual violence, which allows a wide range of unjust sexual violence to take place—often called rape culture. Similarly, the omission, avoidance, and disciplinary silencing around topics of sexuality constitute a culture of sin that violates one's "inalienable right to education" (upheld in *Gravissimum Educationis*, Paul VI 1965b, para. 1; see also *Pacem in Terris*, John XXIII 1963, para. 13; *Populorum Progressio*, Paul VI 1967, paras. 1, 6)—an inalienable right that surely extends to education about issues of sexuality. This culture of silence around sexuality is a social sin in that it is difficult to remove, grows stronger, and is a source of other sins by influencing people's behaviors. In the words of John Paul II (1987) in *Sollicitudo Rei Socialis*, structural sin is "always linked to the concrete acts of individuals who introduce these structures, consolidate them and make them difficult to remove. And thus they grow stronger, spread, and become the source of other sins, and so influence people's behavior" (para. 36). Silence around issues of sexuality can create confusion and shame, influencing how people address injustices around these topics.

One suggestion for continuing the dialogue on sexuality consisted of abandoning Catholic identity and dogma altogether. While this may seem detrimental to the Catholic nature of a university, I propose that it is actually an area of insight for how Catholic universities can better serve their constituents. The Congregation for Catholic Education (2019) said in their recent document on gender theory, "the primary outlook needed for anyone who wishes to take part in *dialogue* is *listening*" (para. 8, original emphasis). In listening, we can better hear the unmet needs of others, or in which ways our institutions and communities might be causing unjust harm. Listening is called for as a catalyst for dialogue. Through listening to those who are hurt and ready to leave the Catholic Church, Catholic institutions might find a need that can be addressed through pastoral care and humility that might otherwise be overlooked when holding tightly to less pastoral institutional responses.

Many different models of navigating one's faith and sexual identities have a paradigm for rejecting one of those two identities (Lapinski & McKirnan, 2013; Love et al., 2005; Pitt, 2010; Schuck & Liddle, 2001). Love et al. (2005) used particularly relevant language for this paradigm, "undeveloped spiritual identity," that they defined simply as not being interested in having a spiritual life and thus rejecting one's religious identity. While this language can be considered arguably pejorative to those who choose not to have a spiritual affiliation, I think it draws necessary attention to the way the rejection of a sexual identity can lead to spiritual harm. I find this language pertinent to the participant responses that suggest rejecting the Catholic tradition, seeing it as an immovable barrier to discussions on sexuality insofar as they do not seem interested or invested in the religious identity. A deeper examination of the reasons people see Catholicism as a fixed obstacle warranting rejection may yield theological and pastoral gaps that leave people feeling hurt, alienated, uncared for, ignored, dismissed, or rejected. If people want to leave a Catholic identity behind at an institutional level, perhaps this is a place to begin listening to how administrators and members of the Catholic faith can bring acceptance, love, and dialogue to these discussions of sexuality.

Related to Catholic identity and healthy sexuality, some participants identified the need for Catholic higher education to be a resource for knowledge and intellectual dialogue. Some participants felt the converse was happening with bishop intervention, at times stifling the academic conversation on sexuality. Findings from the present study reinforce the need for Catholic universities to be useful sources for information on sexuality through academic dialogue, rather than avoiding the complexities of the topic.

Conclusion

What can all of this tell us about sexuality in Catholic higher education—and in some respects, Catholicism as a whole? This reflection leaves with the question: if these changemakers see their work as deeply Catholic, how then can people best use their wisdom to inform interventions around sexuality and sexual formation in the context of Catholic higher education? From the above data, it would seem that these individuals are prime examples of following one's conscience, having hope for the future, how to love the Catholic Church with critical diligence, and encouraging further dialogue on a topic some would rather sweep under a rug or ignore. They are living models of Catholic theology in that they are addressing injustices, preventing unjust harm from being done, and in some cases, giving a voice to the voiceless. These individuals are currently bringing about change in a world that is otherwise unfriendly toward that change. Risking their job security in a world where the unethically common rapid descent into perpetual poverty is more salient than it has been in recent US history, these employees are truly acting in accordance with their conscience, in line with the Catholic tradition, to effect change with a hope for a *metanoia* (conversion, change of heart) at an institutional level for the goal of social support as all Christians are called to do.

This chapter considered changemakers' hopes for the future of Catholic higher education around matters of sexuality. Participants hoped universities and the church as a whole would no longer fear engaging with the topic of human sexuality, would continue the discussion and study of sexuality, and act as a resource for communities and student formation around sexuality and faith. We have also come to a point in the book where we heard about the many different components that make up change around sexuality in Catholic higher education. This brings us to the exciting question on the precipice of this enormous topic: what can *you* do at your university in order to address topics of sexuality? The next chapter will be a look into a helpful framework for effecting change around sexuality at your college or university.

References

Arnett, J. J. (2000). Emerging adulthood: A theory of development from the late teens through the twenties. *American Psychologist, 55*(5), 469–480. https://doi.org/10.1037/0003-066X.55.5.469

Catechism of the Catholic Church. (2000). (2nd ed.). Libreria Editrice Vaticana.

Chickering, A. W., & Reisser, L. (1993). *Education and identity* (2nd ed.). Jossey-Bass.

Congregation for Catholic Education. (2019). *"Male and female he created them" towards a path of dialogue on the question of gender theory in education.* http://www.educatio.va/content/dam/cec/Documenti/19_0997_INGLESE.pdf

Erikson, E. H. (1968). *Identity: Youth and crisis.* W. W. Norton & Company Inc.

Farley, M. (2006). *Just love: A framework for Christian sexual ethics.* The Continuum International Publishing Group Inc.

Flannery, A. (Ed.). (1996). *Vatican council II: The basic sixteen documents.* Costello.

John Paul II. (1987). *Sollicitudo rei socialis.* http://www.vatican.va/content/john-paul-ii/en/encyclicals/documents/hf_jp-ii_enc_30121987_sollicitudo-rei-socialis.html

John Paul II. (1990). *Ex corde ecclesiae.* http://w2.vatican.va/content/john-paul-ii/en/apost_constitutions/documents/hf_jp-ii_apc_15081990_ex-corde-ecclesiae.html

John XXIII. (1963). *Pacem in terris.* http://www.vatican.va/content/john-xxiii/en/encyclicals/documents/hf_j-xxiii_enc_11041963_pacem.html

Kramer, F. (2004). *Doing faithjustice: An introduction to Catholic social thought.* Paulist Press.

Lapinski, J., & McKirnan, D. (2013). Forgive me father for I have sinned: The role of a Christian upbringing on lesbian, gay, and bisexual identity development. *Journal of Homosexuality, 60*(6), 853–872. https://doi.org/10.1080/00918369.2013.774844

Levinson, D. J., Darrow, C. N., Klein, E. B., Levinson, M. H., & McKee, B. (1978). *The seasons of a man's life.* Alfred A. Knopf, Inc.

Levinson, D. J., & Levinson, J. D. (1996). *The seasons of a woman's life.* Knopf.

Love, P., Bock, M., Jannarone, A., & Richardson, P. (2005). Identity interaction: Exploring the spiritual experiences of lesbian and gay college students. *Journal of College Student Development, 46*(2), 193–209.

Massingale, B. N. (2010). *Racial justice and the Catholic church.* Orbis Books.

Mattison, W. C. (2008). *Introducing moral theology: True happiness and the virtues.* Brazos Press.

McCarty, R. W. (2014). Objects of the inquisition, or the trials of religion scholars at Catholic institutions who engage with sexuality studies. *Academe, 100*(1), 24–29. www.aaup.org

Moreira, A. D., Halkitis, P. N., & Kapadia, F. (2015). Sexual identity development of a new generation of emerging adult men: The p18 cohort study. *Psychology of Sexual Orientation and Gender Diversity, 2*(2), 159–167. https://doi.org/10.1037/sgd0000099

Paul VI. (1965a). *Dignitatis humanae.* http://www.vatican.va/archive/hist_councils/ii_vatican_council/documents/vat-ii_decl_19651207_dignitatis-humanae_en.html

Paul VI. (1965b). *Gravissimum educationis.* http://www.vatican.va/archive/hist_councils/ii_vatican_council/documents/vat-ii_decl_19651028_gravissimum-educationis_en.html

Paul VI. (1967). *Populorum progressio.* http://w2.vatican.va/content/paul-vi/en/encyclicals/documents/hf_p-vi_enc_26031967_populorum.html

Pitt, R. N. (2010). "Still looking for my jonathan": Gay black men's management of religious and sexual identity conflicts. *Journal of Homosexuality, 57*(1), 39–53. https://doi.org/10.1080/00918360903285566

Ross, K., McCabe, M. K., & Wilhelm Garbers, S. (2019). Christian sexual ethics and the #metoo movement: Three moments of reflection on sexual violence and women's bodies. *Journal for the Society of Christian Ethics, 39*(2), 339–356. https://doi.org/10.5840/jsce201939238

Sacred Congregation for the Doctrine of the Faith. (1975). *Persona humana: Declaration on certain questions concerning sexual ethics.* http://www.vatican.va/roman_curia/congregations/cfaith/documents/rc_con_cfaith_doc_19751229_persona-humana_en.html

Schuck, K. D., & Liddle, B. J. (2001). Religious conflicts experienced by lesbian, gay and bisexual individuals. *Journal of Gay & Lesbian Psychotherapy, 5*(2), 63–82.

Thompson, J. M. (2010). *Introducing Catholic social thought.* Orbis Books.

Material from this chapter is reprinted with permission from the following source:

Levand, M. A. (2021). Addressing the unaddressed: Changemakers' hopes for the future around issues of sexuality in Catholic higher education—theological insights. *Journal of Religion & Society, 23*, 1–16. http://moses.creighton.edu/JRS/toc/2021.html

Chapter 8

A Framework for Change

How do I become a changemaker at my Catholic institution?

Over the course of this book, we looked at the relevant literature and studies about change around sexuality in Catholic higher education (Chapter 2), and we examined the themes that arose from this study, including:

- general themes in the change process (Chapter 3)
- key areas of change for changemakers and the reactions they encountered (Chapter 4)
- supportive factors in and barriers to the change process (Chapter 5)
- communication strategies used by changemakers (Chapter 6)
- the hopes and suggestions changemakers had for future change (Chapter 7)

We now come to the point in the book where we tie the themes together in a cohesive, dynamic model for people to have as a framework for navigating change at their own institutions. I want to preface this chapter with a few disclaimers. First, the change process is unique with lots of moving parts. What this study has named clearly is the nature of individual actors in the process. Just as one person can be the catalyst for massive institutional change, there can also be a single person who stands in the way of an institutional change around sexuality. Much of the change dynamic will have to do with personal relations, networking, and collaboration. Second, while the framework below was created from how the changemakers in the study have navigated change, this is not the *only* way to navigate change. There are many ways people can go about institutional change, some ways remain to be discovered or publicized. We each own creative power in this respect—try new things that fit with your gifts. Third, this is not a guide that will work for effective change in 100% of situations across

DOI: 10.4324/9781003218159-8

institutions. This process takes fineness, a thorough understanding, and may take years to come to fruition with the combination of people, cultures, and beliefs at a given institution. This chapter is based on what changemakers did and did not find helpful. From these insights, this chapter will include places to start and questions you can ask yourself and your institution. We will start by identifying the contextual dynamics of this organizational change followed by looking at a resource for creating change at your institution.

Overview of Change Dynamics

Change around sexuality in Catholic higher education is complex and has many avenues for research. The Catholic culture is a notable context in which these changes take place that differentiates it from other organizational change models. Some Catholic colleges or universities are more accepting of change than others, some are more open to talking about sexuality than others, and some articulate their Catholic identity in terms of openness and acceptance while others articulate more exclusion or silence in areas of sexuality. McLeroy et al. (1988) discussed a model of influence specific to health behavior when creating change around sexuality in institutions of higher education. The authors' model had four main components: intrapersonal, interpersonal, organizational/institutional, and community/public policy. The Catholic context of the present study permeated every level of McLeroy et al.'s model of influence. Changes initiated by employees depended on a variety of these components (interpersonal communication, organizational operations, external community components, etc.) but all of these factors took place in a Catholic setting, necessitating sensitivity to a culture in which change was taking place. When considering the data from this study as a whole, we get a picture of the dynamics participants navigated for effective change. Participants seemed to operate by adopting preemptive mindsets or planning, active educational strategies, and assessing next steps, based on the types of reactions they encountered throughout the change process. Figure 8.1 is a simple visual representation of this process in the Catholic context.

Like other forms of institutional change, planning, executing, and assessing are necessary steps. While longer, more detailed models of general organizational change exist, I have distilled this process for the context of Catholic higher education and for a broader audience to begin effecting change. Of the three steps that I describe below—planning, education, and assessing—it is important to note that the Catholic context will influence each of these in nuanced ways that may be different in other organizations (indicated by dotted lines in Figure 8.1). Organizational change scholars like Adrianna Kezar (2014)

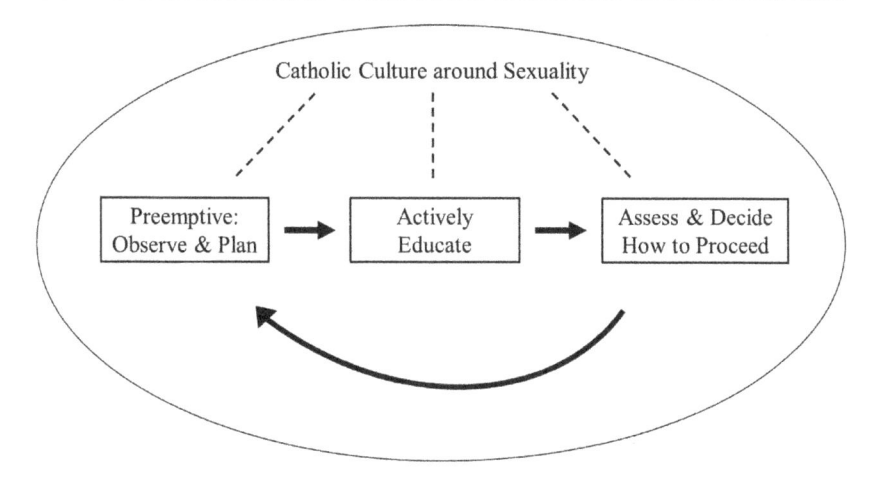

Figure 8.1 The Process of Change Around Sexuality in Catholic Higher Education.

Diagram: An oval labeled "Catholic Culture around Sexuality" containing three boxes connected by arrows: "Preemptive: Observe & Plan" → "Actively Educate" → "Assess & Decide How to Proceed", with a curved arrow looping back from the last box to the first.

talk specifically about the external or environmental components that impact the change process. In her book *How Colleges Change*, Kezar (2014) describes the layers of context that shape institutional change—institutional culture at the center; higher education as an institutional context; external stakeholders; and social, political, and economic factors on the broadest level. Kezar stresses that the social, political, and economic factors must be understood by changemakers effecting change. The Catholic context, however, operates uniquely at each of the levels described in Kezar's model. In other words, whenever making change at a Catholic institution, each layer or factor of change may be influenced by the Catholic context in ways secular change is not. I would add that changemakers must understand the nuances of what works within a Catholic setting and navigating how reactions can determine next steps.

An example of how the Catholic context might influence this process may be of use here. Take, for instance, the topic of creating an LGBTQ student group or Employee Resource Group (ERG). At a secular institution, the process may be relatively easy—identify the structure and focus of the group and go through the necessary channels for its creation (Campuspride.org, 2021). In a Catholic context, however, not only can there be individual actors or community members who would like to prevent a change from happening based on their faith convictions, there are also institutional protections such as religious exemptions from adhering to Title IX requirements or bishops erroneously claiming that this type of organization is contrary to Catholic teaching. There might be protesters from the surrounding communities on campus with signs or speakers condemning such a group from a Catholic perspective. There may be assumptions about these types of groups built into the institutional policy or culture. As such, there may be particular questions to ask, networks to form, and avenues to explore when attempting to make such a change that you may not otherwise need to consider at a secular college or university.

Kirkley and Getz (2007) gave recommendations for creating a training around sexual orientation they called the Rainbow Educators Program in religiously affiliated universities. Their recommendations were "balance critique ... with respect for the institution, work closely with university administration, and start where the institution is" (p. 116). The authors go on to describe the story of how this process worked at their university. While this information can be useful for some institutions, the process of respecting the institution, working with administration, and finding the university's starting point may vary greatly depending on the level of resistance or methods of communication previously used at an institution. For example, if an institution had a bad relationship with a former changemaker working toward the same or a similar change, you may experience added resistance. Knowing about that institutional change history may be helpful in deciding next steps. Kirkley and Getz's recommendations are also specifically referring to an orientation education program. While I feel these recommendations can also work for other areas of change around sexuality, it is possible that different (and very important!) contextual considerations may be overlooked by potential changemakers. Below is a resource to help guide change around issues of sexuality in Catholic higher education.

Creating a Resource: How to Go About Change

From the above stages, I have compiled a resource for change around sexuality in Catholic institutions by combining the methods of communication used by participants in the present study and the organizational change literature. I will describe each area below, as well as offer a helpful guide to operationalize these areas (see Figure 8.2).

Preemptive: Observe and Plan

The preemptive strategies identified in the data include the behind-the-scenes work—adopting a mindset, gathering data, setting up useful/supportive relationships, and planning how to address the issue. Many participants discussed adopting a mindset that used the language of their university. If the university is very student oriented or focused on retention, perhaps a message of how this change is beneficial to students may help. If the university's mission uses language of

Facilitating Change Around Sexuality in Catholic Higher Education

Step 1: Adopt a Mindset, Observe, and Plan

What is the goal of this change? Does your university respond to student focus? Does your university have a mission/heritage that specifically addresses issues of justice? What other universities in your similar geographic situation doing? Is the culture open and accepting, resistant, or somewhere in between? Have people already attempted change? How did it go? If it failed, why? What barriers currently exist on campus? What allies can you make on campus to most effectively bring about this change? What type of language are people sensitive to regarding this change?

Take a mindset using language familiar to the university, create a network of people, make connections, and plan together.

Step 2: Do Education

Do education, even at smaller levels. Is the university engaging in education, educating staff, faculty, or members of the university on the issue of change? Is information readily available? Can you make it available and distribute the information? Can you talk to key offices to begin training at smaller, student-focused levels (i.e., residence life)? Is there a campus-wide training you can initiate or join with? Is there funding for outside speakers? (If not offered by the institution, there may be grants your department is eligible for that can help subsidize.) If you encounter resistance, don't underestimate individual, one-to-one education.

Offer the education needed to make the change make sense to key stakeholders.

Step 3: Assess Reactions & Decide How to Proceed

Assess the reactions of others and the educational interventions. How are people responding? What barriers are arising in this process? Are other areas of sexuality already talked about on your campus? How does it go? When encountering barriers, which methods of communication are the best fit for your university setting? If the culture is open to certain changes but not others, note why that is, and examine the type of language you may be using. Is changing the language an option or does it undermine the change efforts? Examine your communication strategies, the responses/reactions, and attempt to address the reasons for resistant reactions.

Examine what worked and share it with others. Note what has not worked and begin planning a new strategy.

Other Considerations:

Is my institution prepared to deal with external criticism from bishops or other Catholic groups? Will your supervisor support you, and do they have the tools they need to support you? Are there people in the university who will be sensitive to the language you use? How can you use the Catholic mission (or the mission of the school) to support the change you are making? Where in the Catholic tradition do scholars and the magisterium discuss this particular change? Do we have theologians with whom we can collaborate? Note the political climate and the assumptions that prevent people from effecting change.

Figure 8.2 Resource for Facilitating Change Around Sexuality in Catholic Higher Education.

inclusion and supports inclusive initiatives, use this language to discuss your proposed change. At this stage, it is important to be aware of the *language sensitivity* theme within your university: What words and language do they already use to discuss this topic? What language is considered taboo or otherwise should be avoided? How does attentiveness to this impact the people affected by the change (re: erasure)?

Gathering data about what other universities are doing or what your university has done in the past is another useful beginning step. Kezar (2014) discussed valuing mistakes in learning how to effect change. These mistakes can also be made by others who came before you. Learn what has worked and what has not (both at your university and other similar or local Catholic institutions). An important aspect that arose from the data is that it may be most helpful to examine other Catholic universities in similar geographic and social/political environments more so than schools rooted a similar religious order.

Hughes (2015) discussed the importance of creating allies in a change process. He advocated for seeking allies on campus, stressing the importance of those in religious life (priests, friars, nuns) if you have them on campus. Those in religious life most certainly can support the change, but it is also important to look in many other places on campus (deans, VPs of mission and ministry, student affairs, etc.), enhancing your communication with these offices as you begin the process. This can help bring about the *good organization* component in the change process, establishing channels for clear and swift communication.

At this stage, it is possible that change deemed important by a changemaker has not yet occurred at the university. In this case, it is possible for a changemaker to become cynical, which can have a negative impact on motivation (Reichers et al., 1997). There are many things that can motivate a changemaker (e.g., need for student care, justice, one's personal faith), but it is important to identify and hold onto it throughout the process. Hughes (2015) found that a person's commitment to the Catholic faith could act as a positive motivator for change agents—a finding supported in this study. Whether it is compassion for students or a commitment to faith, be sure to assess your motivation and how to maintain that drive and support. This mindset, planning, and preparatory work can ensure a solid foundation and network for beginning change.

Actively Educate

Again consistent with other types of organizational change models is the concept of good education or training. In discussing eight factors of effective organizational change, Fernandez and Rainey (2006) identified this process as "providing resources." Make available to your community the things you want them to know. Many participants did this by engaging in public conversations with forums or inviting speakers. Safe space trainings proved to be a useful tactic for participants in this study, congruent with that of others (Getz & Kirkley, 2006; Hughes, 2015). If your campus has the finances, invite outside resources like professional trainers about that specific change around sexuality. Forming task forces or other groups that are in charge of motivating the public dialogue can help keep the issue in the public sphere. If someone has a difficult time understanding, perhaps a more personal, one-to-one conversation can be helpful. As suggested by McEntarfer (2011) and supported by this study, if the resistance is high, student protest may be a useful tool in the conversation.

Assess and Decide How to Proceed

Implementation and assessment are key components of organizational change. Anderson and Anderson (2010) describe this stage as "learning and course correcting." While assessing the effectiveness of the change is important (e.g., if students feel good about the organization that was created, if the sexuality information is accomplishing its goal of informing the community, if the sexual assault prevention response allows victims autonomy and fills the need to be heard, etc.), this particular step involves assessing the *effectiveness of your strategies*. Assess what has worked and what has not. Encountering excessive barriers or completing a successful change are good times to assess how your process has worked. If you have encountered barriers of administrative resistance or personal resistance, examine which methods of communication you have tried and what might work better. Understand the effects of this change on the university's culture around sexuality. Identify the dynamics of the culture as it relates to the desired change. If the change was successful, assess next steps to address the institutionalization of the change or where you'd like to go from here.

Remember, you are in a Catholic context. While some people may feel that the Catholic setting is a barrier, others feel that it is a great resource and a source for change, love, and compassion. This also means that your environmental factors are not limited to the local community or geographical environment, but you also have religious constituents watching too. Will your supervisor support you if the bishop or public voices get involved (and do they have the tools *they* need to support you)? Are there people in the university who will be sensitive to the language you use? How can you use the Catholic mission (or the mission of the school) to support the change you are making? Where in the Catholic tradition do scholars and the magisterium discuss this particular change? The Catholic context, whether it is open to talking about sexuality or not, effects every level of the change process from the organizational mission and offices, down to the individuals who control those offices, partners on campus, and individual, personal faith and bias. People might be very afraid of this kind of change or avoid engaging in more conversations. In these instances, it might be helpful to offer a meditation on the words of Pope Francis, that the church "has a face that isn't rigid, a body that moves and develops, it has tender flesh: that of Jesus Christ" (San Martín, 2015).

Theological Insights: Vocation

I think an important theological concept that stands to be examined more closely in this process is the theology of vocation. Theologian Edward Hahnenberg (2010) writes in the opening pages of his book *Awakening Vocation: A Theology of Christian Call* that earlier Catholic definitions of vocation focused narrowly on discussions surrounding religious life. Throughout the text, Hahnenberg explores the meaningful nature of vocation beyond this narrow interpretation into a thoughtful theological discussion rooted in a fuller understanding of grace and God's presence in the world named in the Second Vatican Council. He walks the reader through the historical theological developments of vocation from medieval and contemporary Christian theologians through various Catholic Church councils. What I want to name here is Hahnenberg's rich description of vocation as "God drawing us toward the meaning of our lives" (p. 120). We saw that changemakers may have seen their Catholic faith as a source of motivation in effecting a change. For some, seeing an injustice at their institution or an opportunity for love, support, or community that does not yet exist can evoke a compelling motivation to make a change at their institution.

I am not suggesting that any one person's vocation is to make a single change at a college or university. Rather, I am naming the reality that one's response to seeing hurt, isolation, or affronts to human dignity at an institution can be part of their vocation—or God drawing them toward a deeper meaning in their life. In his book, Hahnenberg titles each of the chapters from 3 to 6 a segment of this theology of vocation: God calls ... me ... through others ... for others. He describes God (with an active presence in the world) calling me (a person with free choice to respond) through others (as interdependent, interconnected with the human family, called by our interaction within community) for others (in solidarity with those suffering). Hahnenberg names vocation as an opening toward and growth in the practices that defined Jesus' life. He notes, "The most important of these practices (both in the Gospel and in our own time) are those that open us up to the other in need" (p. 181). For the participants in this study, their motivation for this change, whether grounded in faith or not, was certainly an opening to others in need. The queer student without a community or who is being bullied, the sexual assault survivor tired of being revictimized by the university, the students without accurate sexual health information, the employee with no health coverage for their same-sex partner—all people in need, and constituents of a communal experience that helps call changemakers to name and effect needed change.

Hahnenberg notes succinctly, "Within this world of grace, God's call—my vocation—cannot be reduced to some static state of life or secret voice. My vocation is *me*" (original emphasis, p. 216). To the changemakers or would-be changemakers on campus, listen to and trust yourself. I believe these changemakers looked into their experience of life and the suffering of those around them and acted to effect change in response. These changemakers chose to be present for others in an institution that needed help listening to and caring for those being overlooked, ignored, or injured. The participants in this study spoke with great conviction that they were working toward a change to help stop the pain and isolation others were feeling. To those of you thinking about doing this work, reflect on your social position, the needs of those around you, and respond in ways that feel the most "you" on an authentic level. Another description of vocation Hahnenberg gives is "my life lived out in harmony with the gift of grace" (p. 213). Many changemakers discussed their agency in the change process very much in line with the grace and inclusive love of God in the world. Reflect on your own agency in this process, listening to the voices of those marginalized around you, and see what gifts you can personally bring to the change process to help bring about change for the common good.

Conclusion

Sexuality topics within Catholic colleges and universities can be sensitive issues because (1) sexuality is a sensitive issue in the general population and (2) there are many Catholics who hold harmful views about sexuality that facilitate a culture of Catholic erotophobia. Effecting change at the intersection of sexuality and Catholic institutions is hard work with many barriers, moving parts, and unspoken messages and narratives that drive the values and behaviors of others. It can be a scary process—scary for the changemaker in trying to understand the next best move and scary for those members of the university who have only known sexuality (and all the topics therein) to lead to discomfort, awkwardness, or even pain and anguish. As changemakers, it is crucial to develop an understanding of how sexuality (in the broadest sense and specific ways: sexual orientation, gender identity, sexual trauma, emotional intimacy) can be a sensitive topic for others. Coming to the change process with a comprehensive understanding of how and why people operate the ways that they do around sexuality not only can help facilitate an institutional change but may even be a catalyst for a cultural shift around the topic at your institution. Changemakers and all members of an institution may be in need of resources for seeking assistance in understanding sexuality, developing one's own ideas and feelings about sexuality, and/or having experts to talk to about sexuality. Do what you can to connect people at your institution with resources. If effecting a change is too big of a task at the moment, connecting people with a resource list of local or national sexuality professionals can be a meaningful step. In the theology of vocation, responding to the suffering of others by effecting change can be good, but there are also smaller ways to begin a culture shift and support those in need.

In this chapter, we looked at the dynamics of organizational change in the context of Catholic higher education. We looked at the three key stages in the change process and a resource to help you navigate change at your institution. We explored a Catholic theology of vocation in how God calls us through others for others and how being a changemaker can be part of that vocation. In the next chapter, we will explore what the future of sexuality can look like in Catholic higher education with some guidelines on how colleges and universities can be better equipped to address matters of sexuality.

References

Anderson, L. A., & Anderson, D. (2010). *The change leader's roadmap: How to navigate your organization's transformation* (2nd ed.). Pfeiffer.

Campuspride.org. (2021). *Starting a LGBTQ resource center or student group*. https://www.campuspride.org/resources/starting-an-lgbt-resource-center/

Fernandez, S., & Rainey, H. G. (2006). Managing successful organizational change in the public sector. *Public Administration Review, 66*(2), 168–176. https://doi.org/10.1111/j.1540-6210.2006.00570.x

Getz, C., & Kirkley, E. (2006). Shaking up the status quo: Challenging intolerance of the lesbian, gay and bisexual community at a private Roman Catholic university. *College Student Journal, 40*(4), 857–869.

Hahnenberg, E. P. (2010). *Awakening vocation: A theology of Christian call*. Liturgical Press.

Hughes, B. E. (2015). *"Who am I to judge?": How a Jesuit university addresses LGBT issues on campus* (Publication No. 3706207) [Doctoral Dissertation, University of California, Los Angeles]. ProQuest Dissertations & Theses A&I.

Kezar, A. J. (2014). *How colleges change: Understanding, leading, and enacting change*. Routledge.

Kirkley, E. A., & Getz, C. (2007). A model for sexual orientation education at a religiously affiliated institution. *Journal of Gay & Lesbian Issues in Education, 4*(3), 113–119. https://doi.org/10.1300/J367v04n03_07

McEntarfer, H. K. (2011). "Not going away": Approaches used by students, faculty, and staff members to create gay–straight alliances at three religiously affiliated universities. *Journal of LGBT Youth, 8*(4), 309–331. https://doi.org/10.1080/19361653.2011.607623

McLeroy, K. R., Bibeau, D., Steckler, A., & Glanz, K. (1988). An ecological perspective on health promotion programs. *Health Education Quarterly, 15*(4), 351–377.

Reichers, A. E., Wanous, J. P., & Austin, J. T. (1997). Understanding and managing cynicism about organizational change. *The Academy of Management Executive, 11*(1), 48–59.

San Martín I. (2015). *Pope Francis says Catholics must be open to change*. https://cruxnow.com/church/2015/11/10/pope-francis-says-catholics-must-be-open-to-change/

Chapter 9

The Future of Sexuality in Catholic Higher Education

What might be next for Catholic colleges and universities?

This was an important study for understanding a bit more bout organizational change in Catholic higher education around matters of sexuality. While previous studies examined only a handful of institutions, I examined 17 different institutions in the United States—the largest study of its kind to date. Throughout this book, we have considered some of the supports and barriers, communication strategies and mindsets that helped effect change, and the meaning-making of changemakers' experiences. While there is always more to discover, there is also a great deal we know about the landscape for change. The general consensus from changemakers who have worked at both secular and Catholic colleges and universities is that many Catholic institutions are about 15–20 years behind secular institutions on matters of sexuality—queer student orgs, sexuality resource centers, etc. This does not mean that all Catholic intuitions are behind on all aspects of sexuality. Indeed, some Catholic institutions have been leaders on matters of sexuality, like USF's sexual assault training initiative or fostering scholars on sexual ethics. While some people may be concerned about setbacks or delays in positive change around matters of human sexuality, there have also been great strides. In this concluding chapter, let's take a look at some dialogue affecting the landscape for change, the ways changemaking around sexual orientation and gender identity are synonymous with LGBTQ ministry, guidelines for Catholic institutions, some specific suggestions based on those guidelines with case examples to illustrate their operation, and where the research may go in the future.

Landscape for Change

I have said earlier in this book that sexuality encompasses more than sexual orientation and gender identity. There are matters of sexual

DOI: 10.4324/9781003218159-9

assault, sexual trauma, comprehensive sexuality education, sexualization, intimacy and healthy relationships, contraceptive access, sexual behavior, and so much more. There is, however, a very common focus on gender identity and sexual orientation in Catholic higher education. I would be remiss if I did not bring into the limelight some of the biggest questions that administrators have to deal with today regarding gender identity and sexual orientation.

I mentioned in Chapter 2 that some Catholic institutions are seeking exemptions for including fair or equal treatment of non-heterosexual and non-cisgender people at their institutions. The Religious Exemption Accountability Project (REAP, 2021) is an organization that does advocacy and disseminates information about the discrimination of people on the basis of sexual orientation and gender identity/expression at taxpayer-funded religious colleges and universities. While many Catholic institutions of higher education in the United States are not necessarily taxpayer funded in terms of tuition (as of the writing of this text), they do often receive federal Title IX funding and sometimes seek exemptions that result in discrimination. We see some Catholic institutions digging their heels in about matters of gender identity and sexual orientation. There are bishops claiming institutions can no longer call themselves Catholic if they refuse to fire a gay employee (Burke, 2019) or because they fly a Pride or Black Lives Matter flag (Jones, 2022). There is resistance to using affirming pronouns in many Catholic spaces, exemplified by the Archdiocese of Milwaukee's (2022) document *Catechesis and Policy on Questions Concerning Gender Theory*, where they note "no person may designate a 'preferred pronoun' in speech or in writing" (p. 3).

It is true that not everyone will be on board. There is fear in many Catholic institutional leaders; fear, we know, can come from a lack of understanding. However, we also see great strides in the affirmation of diverse sexual and gender identities. Amidst the fear and exclusive language of some Catholics, we see other Catholic voices like Fr. Daniel Horan (2021) describing why Catholics *should* be using pronouns, and the voices of those who work tirelessly to create dialogue and connect people at conference events for affirmation like Dignity USA, New Ways Ministry, and Outreach. There are voices like Sr. Jeannine Gramick (Outreach, 2022b) who has worked for over 50 years on the affirmation of LGBTQ+ Catholics, Sr. Luisa Derouen (2022) who has ministered to transgender Catholics for decades, activists and authors like Yunuen Trujillo, Fr. Jim Martin, Fr. James Alison, John Boswell, and so many more who have given a voice to the discrimination faced by those with non-heterosexual and non-cisgender identities in the church, but also offer loving, accepting, and affirming language and frameworks.

Finding hope in the future of higher education can also entail looking at current secondary school practices with youth ministry. Initiatives like the Marianist Social Justice Collaborative's (2015) guide on creating a safe welcoming school for youth and Without Exception (2021), a grassroots network of Catholic secondary school educators for LGBTQ+ ministry, indicate a growing desire to communicate love, acceptance, and welcome to gender and sexually diverse people.

While this has been a book about a study regarding organizational change and changemakers' experiences in Catholic higher education, the material contained within these pages is also directly related to LGBTQ ministry. When we change discriminatory institutional practices or offer a place to be heard, understood, or cared for, we are doing ministry. At the Outreach (2022a) conference in New York, Fr. Bryan Massingale said of LGBTQ ministry:

> So often when we gather to discuss LGBTQ ministry, we focus on our relationship to the institutional church, we talk about bishops' statements and formulation of church doctrine—and that's really important work—but it's also limited. LGBTQ ministry must also attend to the social context in which we live. Because that social context impacts our lives—indeed our very survival.
>
> (1:01:47)

Discussions of documents such as the Congregation for the Doctrine of the Faith's (1986, 1975) letters on human sexuality, the US Bishops' (1997) letter *Always Our Children*, or Bishop Mugavero's (1976) letter *Sexuality – God's Gift* are all very important. But in the end, the question to ask is: "Are these documents being used to exclude, condemn, demean, or otherwise brutalize people?" Indeed, Pope Francis (2021) warns against this very thing: attempting to us a "'believers license' to judge and exclude" (para. 3). This exclusion can happen at individual and institutional levels. Struggling with understanding or talking about sexuality (in this case, sexual orientation and gender identity) can lead some administrators to rely on exclusive, condemning rhetoric without feeling personally responsible for its harmful effects on the human family. Yunuen Trujillo (2022), author of *LGBTQ Catholics: A Guide to Inclusive Ministry*, wisely notes about this phenomenon "in a world where people are hungry for love, feeding them a penal code is condemning them to starvation" (p. 92). There is great joy to be had in the inclusion of LGBTQ+ people in the life of the university and the global church, and each of us has the power offer the love for which people are hungry.

Many people in the church are unaware that Catholic sexual theology is still evolving. Sexual theology is constantly undergoing critical reexamination that may still take years to more fully articulate. With that in mind, we still have a good basis for an understanding of sexuality in light of the Second Vatican Council. There are theologians and activists engaging in the dialogue of human sexuality within the Catholic Church for a positive, inclusive, and human understanding of these matters. We see theologians and sexual ethicists like Margaret Farley, Todd Salzman, Michael Lawler, Susan Ross, Chris Gudorf, Bryan Massingale, Hoon Choi, Ed Vacek, Elizabeth Vasko, Mary Hunt, Charles Curran, Lisa Sowle Cahill, Craig Ford, Melissa Pagán, Darryl Stephens, Patricia Jung, and so many more engaging in sexual ethics from a standpoint of critical understanding, compassion, and theological rigor that help articulate a truly human experience of sexuality. There is hope for the future of the church to deal with matters of human sexuality in a healthy, responsible, and real way. In line with this, let's look at some guidelines that Catholic colleges and universities can follow to foster an inclusive atmosphere.

Guidelines Regarding Matters of Sexuality in Catholic Higher Education

In the last chapter, I offered a framework for effecting change at university. The change process could be long and involved, but it can also be relatively short. If there are enough supporting factors in an institutional culture, changes—even big ones—can be done at the discretion of institutional leadership. The way to go about these relatively self-evident changes may be veiled by the fear experienced by some employees of Catholic institutions. These aspects may be simple changes, or something an institution already endorses but does not center or advertise as much as they can. Many people may erroneously believe that creating progressive, inclusive change about matters of sexuality is not a theologically sound practice. Let's review some of the key theological themes that make this reality not only in line with Catholic theology, but in fact, our vocation to live out the Gospel of Love:

Chapter 3
- Catholic revisionist sexual anthropology focuses on a relational-centered morality (versus an act-centered morality) that considers historical context, the goodness of the human person, and norms that reflect this reality.
- Human sexuality is a Catholic theological good and authentically human experience.
- The goodness of our bodies and sexual nature can be found in the *Imago Dei*—the teaching that we are made in the image and likeness of God.

- Because our bodies are made good by God, sexual pleasure is also a good of that creation.
- We are embodied spirits—inspirited bodies—a unity of body and spirit, both components of our goodness as humans.
- Viewing sexuality as "bad" is fundamentally at odds with Catholic sexual theology.

Chapter 4:
- Discrimination and violence toward LGBTQ+ people are contrary to Catholic teaching.
- Communal redemption is required of discrimination that has occurred.

Chapter 5:
- We are called to confront our fears around matters of sexuality to take an active part in the historical process, preventing the church from stagnating.
- We are called to be in right relationship with others—a reality that can be cultivated by practicing the Catholic social teaching (CST) principle of solidarity.

Chapter 6:
- CST offers many avenues that allow us to focus on right relationship, toward a common good of humanity, addressing structural sin that exists in our institutions and culture.

Chapter 7:
- Our conscience has a primary role to play and is an authority in our moral decision-making.
- A culture of fear and silence around sexuality is a type of structural sin that facilitates injustice which we must resolve as it is an affront to human dignity and the common good.

Chapter 8:
- As part of one's vocation, we may be drawn to effect inclusive change, answering a call from God through others, for others.

In light of the theological insights throughout this book, combined with the empirical data, let's examine some basic guidelines for leaders of Catholic colleges and universities to keep in mind about matters of human sexuality on campus.

Human Sexuality Is an Authentically Human Matter

Many people have been socialized to view sexuality (and related matters) as "bad," "unnatural," or something that is "corrupting" making people no longer "innocent." All of these ways of viewing sexuality and sexual diversity have a fundamental philosophical problem: they paint a basic human experience as bad. Of course there are ways people use sexuality for violence, coercion, and exploitation. But to say that sexuality is the *cause* of this because of its nature as sexuality is deeply misguided and quite un-Catholic. Viewing sexuality as abject, bad, or harmful by nature is a problematic philosophical basis that perpetuates what I call a Catholic abuse of sexuality or:

> how we as an institution of Catholics foster an atmosphere of ambiguity, indifference, secrecy, ignorance, and harm around sexuality ... the use and misuse of teachings about sexuality that encourage maladaptive sexual development, the perpetuation of Catholic messages that can be harmful to others, and the perpetuated ignorance of sexuality that harms entire groups of people.
> (Levand, 2022, para. 10)

Catholic institutions have the opportunity to honor sexuality as a truly human experience, rather than a part of being human that must be swept under the rug. We can take solace in the fact that all matters of human sexuality are rooted in our human nature and should be addressed with loving attention.

The human experience of sexuality is very intimately connected to our humanity and how God has created us. If we are to be attending to the "whole development of the person" in Catholic education as described in *Ex Corde Ecclesiae* (para. 20), Catholic higher education must consider all aspects of this human experience, addressing the needs of the community for the common good. First and foremost, the institutional position on matters of human sexuality must not be grounded in the fear and avoidance of sexuality. It can be a big, complex, and even scary topic for people to talk about and understand (especially for people who have not received a comprehensive education around sexuality), but to treat it as "bad" is to deny a fundamental aspect of a truly human experience.

Focus on God's Inclusive Love

This is the theological and pastoral basis for much of the change that may be considered "controversial" around human sexuality. Focusing on God's inclusive love is not only an important doctrinal reality, but one that is rooted in our very name—from the Greek *katholikos*—universal or pertaining to the whole, and in this case, the whole of humanity. The radical love of God that Jesus preached and practiced is not something of the distant past, but the theological foundations of Christianity to which we are called by the Holy Spirit throughout the centuries. As we see in the Pauline letters, the greatest of the theological virtues is love (1 Cor. 13:13). As we hear of the Gospel stories of Christ, the greatest commandment is to love God and love our neighbor as ourselves (Mt. 22:36–39). It is this inclusive love that faithfully calls Catholic institutions to address the needs of those harmed by sexual violence, centering their voice; to include LGBTQ+ individuals, honoring their gifts and offering community; to educate all members of a community about sexual health and wellness; to engage in academic research and dialogue about matters of sexuality; uphold the nondiscrimination of people based on sexual orientation and gender identity; to engage in critical analysis of hegemonic gendered messaging that can create hostility, exclusion, or harm; and the list goes on. The fundamental reality of God's inclusive love is that everyone is loved by God and we, as a people, are called to do the same.

Work toward Education about Sexuality Topics

In order to educate for the "whole development of the person," we must be educating on matters of human sexuality. Most Catholic dialogue about sexuality focuses on behaviors (i.e., sexual orientation) and sexual ethics. However, we saw throughout this book that from a Catholic social ethic, it is crucial to educate about sexuality in more ways than an act-centered, behavioral ethic. As Catholics, we are called to educate on matters of sexuality for a developmentally appropriate base of knowledge from which to make sexual decisions. We must educate about diverse sexual orientations and gender identities to best prepare people for interacting with each other in a diverse world. We must educate on matters of sexual trauma, sexual violence prevention, and sexual health to form citizens "ready to undertake the weighty responsibilities in society" (*Gravissimum Educationis*, para. 10). At Catholic institutions, we must educate our employees on matters of sexuality in ways that recognizes our national failure to supply adequate sexuality education to its citizens—healthy relationship education, diverse sexual and gender identities, the intersection of sexuality and power, sexual goodness, joy, and sexual health—are all part of a deeply human experience. Having this information available to everyone at every level of an institution is one way Catholic colleges and universities can act as resources for knowledge. This education is important because, as the magisterium tells us, we have "an inalienable right to an education" (*Gravissimum Educationis*, para. 1). Education is not only a right as described by the church, but with regard to sexuality, education is also a preventative measure against child sexual abuse (Goldfarb & Lieberman, 2021)—an important step in creating a sexually healthy church. With the assumption that most US Americans have not had adequate sexuality education, offering educational opportunities can be seen as not only helpful to the community culture, but also a moral good. With access to sexuality information, we are given a freedom to make informed decisions. Indeed, in order to make good moral choices, we must be well informed of the topic and our choices at hand (Levand & Ross, 2021).

Commit to a Sexually Safe Atmosphere

Education is an important step to cultivating and fostering a sexually safe atmosphere. Ideally, this should be true of any Catholic institution, but this is not always (nor often) the case. Institutional Catholic erotophobia cultivates a culture of sexual shame and ignorance that create hostile environments on the institutional, interpersonal, and at times, personal levels. Cultivating a sexually safe institution means people should be protected from bias, discrimination, sexual violence, predation, sexual exploitation, perpetuation of sexual shame, and abuses of power related to sexuality. Most often, people think a sexually safe institution means that all employees are trained on sexual harassment in the workplace—which is an important part of this to be sure! So much work has been done to identify and address sexual harassment in the workplace. But a sexually safe atmosphere does not stop there. As institutions, we must ask ourselves: who else remains vulnerable in matters of sexuality on campus? Is our institution a safe place to attend or work at for people of diverse sexual and gender identities— not only being free from discrimination, but are these identities protected and celebrated? Is the sexual assault reporting process safe for survivors and trauma-informed, centering their voices? If the process is not because of unjust laws that remove autonomy from survivors, what are we doing to address those injustices on systemic levels? Is our institution a safe place to ask questions and learn about sexuality in all its forms? Do we have a culture that addresses sexual shame or encourages it? Is it a safe place for rigorous academic discussion on matters of sexuality that is respectful of all people? Is there the protection of academic freedom for scholars who engage with topics of sexuality and is it communicated effectively (i.e., endorsed publicly)? Are matters of sexuality addressed in our institutional policy, and who might be disadvantaged by these policies? A good guideline to follow to ensure a sexually safe atmosphere is to ask the people who are most affected by an institutional rule, policy, or operation how they feel about it, if they feel cared for and supported by the institution, and respond accordingly.

Practice Institutional Accountability around Matters of Sexuality

In Chapter 5, we discussed Gerald Beyer's look at solidarity as moving from recognition to a response, and institutionalizing solidarity into policy. We also saw in Chapter 4 how Rosemary Radford Ruether discusses reconciliation for social harms requiring a communal redemption. Catholic colleges and universities can begin a practice of institutional accountability, apologizing for social harms in the recent or distant past. This demonstrates a respect and an institutional caring for those who have been harmed by institutionalized wrongs. It is great to have sexually safe environments, but the cultivation of those environments is an ongoing process. When systems for safety fail, what is there to offer support? How does the institution respond to the public and to the harmed individual? How can we commit to change in actionable steps? Practicing accountability when safety fails is an important aspect of healing and forming relationship. After this model is formed and an institution practices accountability, how can you take it further? How can you model for others how your institution is cultivating accountability? Presenting at conferences, offering resources to surrounding Catholic institutions, and otherwise disseminating this information is a public service well within the scope of institutions of higher education.

Suggestions for University Administrators

One of the perils of offering guidelines for Catholic higher education is that they must be broad enough to address a wide array of institutions, but doing so will lack the specificity needed to accommodate for the variety of institutional cultures that exist in Catholic higher education. Because institutions vary, I cannot offer specific feedback without a better look at the institution's unique culture—one made up of varying degrees of the many factors we discussed throughout this book. However, I can do my best to illustrate these matters in hypothetical examples under each recommendation, possibly offering some insight into their usefulness. With the above guidelines in mind, there are some areas that Catholic colleges and universities can start examining fairly immediately with little institutional upheaval. Below are some specific suggestions of common areas that may be overlooked and often ready to be changed at Catholic institutions followed by some practical hypothetical situations for a clearer picture on how these suggestions might be applied.

- *Examine the Environment around Sexual and Gender Diversity*
  Consider how the institution perceives and treats sexual and gender diversity. How is your college or university communicating welcome to people of non-heterosexual and non-cisgender identities? When students apply, can they see diverse representation and protection/celebration of diverse identities at your institution? How does your university listen to current student concerns on matters of identity diversity? What do bias and microaggression incidents look like on campus? How has your institution responded to them in the past? Is it adequate according to those who were harmed? Is there an ombudsperson to whom people can report incidences and who can advocate at an institutional level? Are HR employees adequately trained to observe gaps in policy that leave sexually and gender diverse peoples vulnerable to interpersonal and institutional harm? Are students, faculty, and staff properly trained on matters of sexual identity diversity? If not, what can be implemented to make such a change?

Case Example #1:

A Catholic university learned through a climate assessment that many of the current LGBTQ+ students did not feel welcome in their application process or at orientation. The university then puts something on the website to communicate openness and acceptance of sexually and gender diverse people. Upon coming to the campus visit, prospective students notice that the affirming environment is not there. The administration with the help of the director of the Sexuality Resource Center commissions a series of initiatives across campus to institute support for LGBTQ+ students.

In this example, the university showed initiative by conducting a climate assessment of how LGBTQ+ students experienced life on campus. This likely gave the university insights into the unespoused cultural attitudes toward LGBTQ+ people on campus. The university showed commitment and good intention to try and change the admission and marketing material to include sexually and gender diverse people. The university overlooked the fact that "welcoming" means more than just public-facing material but is connected to an entire culture within the university. When alerted to this, the university was able to begin instituting supportive initiatives. Combining the results from the climate assessment (learning there the largest gaps of support exist in the university culture) with the needs of current LGBTQ+ students and employees, the university was able to identify concrete ways to implement supportive components—inviting LGBTQ+ speakers to campus to discuss career matters, naming and celebrating famous LGBTQ+ people in the history of the university, uplifting queer voices on matters pertinent to student success, etc. It is important for this university not to rely solely on queer students for much of this work, as it can foster a sense of tokenism and burnout. Expecting a small group of LGBTQ+ students to change the unwelcoming culture of a university with little support can be an overwhelming and defeating task. This university began a campus-wide initiative throughout several offices to begin working together to change the culture from unwelcoming (or a "don't-ask-don't-tell" culture) into a culture of support and celebration. It is in this wide-spread collaboration that culture change can best take place.

- ***Public Endorsement of Inclusivity of Sexual and Gender Diversity***
  How does the university communicate the value of diverse sexual and gender identities? Where is the visibility on campus? Does your institution have speaker series on events and LGBTQ+ history? Are these identities celebrated in the religious and spiritual life of the institution? If not, consider the ways prayer services, Masses, or vigils can be held. For example, various visibility days or Transgender Day of Remembrance can be observed with minimal administrative effort. Statements of support and appreciation can go a long way. Does your campus allow programing related to sexual diversity? Does your institution have public messaging or discrimination clauses related to sexual identity? Is there inclusive language in public addresses (i.e., "siblings, family") or other gender-natural language in prayer. Does your institution actively support events like Pride? However it is done at your university, remember that visibility and honoring sexual and gender diversity in the community help create a welcoming and safe atmosphere for people of diverse sexual identities.

Case Example #2:

After a local murder of a transgender woman, a Catholic college president is approached by the LGBTQ+ student organization about holding a prayer service on Transgender Day of Remembrance (TDOR) for transgender individuals whose lives were lost due to anti-transgender violence. The president consults with the VP of Mission and Ministry to begin holding an annual prayer service for the vigil. The Office of Mission and Ministry takes steps to publicize the event in advance every year and are sure to make it part of the institutional culture. At the inaugural vigil, the president names why the vigil is being held and commits to holding the vigil every year in a statement that is later disseminated to the college community.

In this example, the president and VP of Mission and Ministry were quick to act in advancing a request that fed the spiritual needs of their campus community. We see the institutionalization of this prayer service versus having a single priest offering the vigil. In other instances, if a single priest or minister offers to hold prayer services, Masses, or vigils like this, the practice may cease when that person leaves the community. A commitment from the university to hold these services is an example of committing to this at an institutional level greater than a single well-meaning faith leader. The statement the president offered could also have been used as an opportunity for accountability as a basis for commitment—recognizing that while TDOR started in 1999, the university is just now instituting a recognition as a long over-due honoring of human life and further committing to these services every year. These statements can go a long way for communal redemption and an important step in communicating public acceptance of diverse gender identities in addition to the denouncing of anti-transgender violence.

- ***Examine Sexual Coercion on Campus***
Check the sources for sexual assault prevention and reporting on your campus. Are the sexual assault policies clearly marked, accessible, and inclusive? These policies may be hidden away/difficult to access and discuss sexual assault as something that implicitly only happens with a man as a perpetrator and a woman as a victim. This perpetuates harmful ideas that men cannot be victims of sexual assault (and are therefore not empowered to report) or that same-sex relationships

do not experience sexual assault or intimate partner violence. Are these policies observed from the centering of voices of survivors? Is your institution taking precautions not to re-traumatize people in this process? While there may be a temptation for institutions to minimize, misrepresent, or avoid conversations about sexual assault on campus (as evidenced by universities under investigation by the Department of Education's Title IX non-compliance), this type of examination is an important step in fostering a sexually safe campus. If the institution has already succumbed to the temptation to avoid or misrepresent sexual assault information and processes, accountability will be a necessary and ongoing step in this examination.

Case Example #3:

After a seminar on inclusivity and trauma sensitivity in the sexual assault reporting process, a Catholic university's Title IX office examined their material and noticed that all of the language frames women as victims and men as perpetrators. The Title IX team carefully addresses the language to include men as victims and diverse gender relationships in the material. At orientation the following year, a university representative presents the material to first-year students. The representative offers a list of resources and clearly identifies the process. When naming that men can experience assault, a student makes a remark about how "if men can get an erection, then they can't be raped." The university representative does not know how to respond.

The university also learns that most people do not report sexual assault because the administrative staff in the Title IX office would often be overheard blaming victims for their assault with "how they dress" or "how much they drank." This was often reinforced by public awareness signs in the wellness office that insinuate drinking causes rape.

This example has a couple of layers. First, the employees and administrators are attempting to make an important inclusive change regarding sexual violence—that all people in all types of relationships can be victims of sexual violence. The language change on the website and Title IX material is a crucial step in this process. However, as evidenced by the student's remark, there is still much education that needs to happen to change the culture of sexual ignorance on campus. Many people may believe that if someone can get an erection or experience vaginal lubrication or even experience orgasm, that means a sexual encounter was consensual. This misinformation is not unique to Catholic institutions but is often a common belief in US culture due to poor sexuality education. Along with the language change in the Title IX material, the university community should be offered educational information on how bodies work and that even during non-consensual sexual activity, physiological sexual arousal may occur (Dr. Emily Nagoski has a good TED talk about this). The change in language on Title IX material is a big step at the beginning of a culture change.

Second, often tied to matters of sexual assault on Catholic campuses are concerns of sexual shame. Even people who are vehemently against sexual violence are not immune to the temptation of shaming others about sexual behaviors. Sexual shame may be imparted by overhearing employees or classmates talk disparagingly about victims of sexual assault, or someone may experience implicit shame because of assumptions about the Catholic environment—if there are no outward signs that victims are protected and honored, there is often the implicit message that "you shouldn't have been having sex in the first place" and "you would get in trouble for reporting." And indeed, this is some people's experience at religious institutions. As an organization, it is important to address the messages that perpetuate blame and shame onto victims of sexual assault whether they come through people in the community (e.g., medical staff, administrators, office staff, classmates) or passive messaging (e.g., wellness center signage that insinuate alcohol is to blame for assault rather than perpetrators, other institutional cultural lore).

- *Academic Freedom for Sexuality Research*

How does your institution support sexuality research? Is there undue policing of grants or IRB applications for matters related to sexuality? Is it clear to junior scholars that sexuality can be studied without negative repercussions for tenure or promotion? If not, public statements about this can help employees feel at ease and trust in the protection they are afforded by academic freedom.

> **Case Example #4:**
>
> *An assistant professor at a small Catholic university is interested in researching sexual development and decision-making in adolescence. They have never been told directly that studying sexual behavior is frowned upon at the institution, but they notice no other scholars at the institution research sexual behavior. They noticed that their colleagues make sex-negative comments, and there is no evidence that sex research is protected at the university. Because of the silence around sexuality research combined with the surrounding community's use of abstinence only curricula, the faculty member has concerns that their research agenda will prevent them from getting tenure in two years. As a result, they hold off on their study until receiving tenure. After they are granted tenure, the Institutional Review Board (that reviews research proposals for ethics issues) is insisting that asking teens about their sexual behaviors is harmful to human participants and will not approve the study.*

This is not an uncommon experience when it comes to researching sexuality at a Catholic institution. Academic freedom and security is often overlooked at institutions of higher education because it is often assumed—"of course you can study what you want, that's what a university is for!" one might say. While this is generally true of secular institutions, it is not uncommon for religious institutions have an un-espoused culture of silence and avoidance of sexuality topics. As such, it is important for Catholic institutions to name this explicitly. In the absence of support and affirmation for sexuality research, the default assumption often falls within the "unspoken rules" scholars observe at the institution. While this particular institution may not have fired (or not promoted) scholars due to their research, the reality that this happens at other Catholic institutions can imply that *this* Catholic environment is also not a safe place for the study of sexuality.

Relatedly, if an Institutional Review Board (IRB) is not familiar with sexuality research, it is not uncommon for its members to be over scrupulous about research proposals pertaining to sexuality (Harger & Quintela, 2017; Irvine, 2014). This type of IRB over-reach is detrimental to sexuality research and professional advancement of scholars at an institution, and it also contributes to sending messages of fear and avoidance of sexuality. It would behoove an institution to ensure their IRB members are trained in reviewing studies related to sexuality, specifically examining their own bias toward sexuality research. Professional organizations like the Society for the Scientific Study of Sexuality (SSSS), the American Psychological Association's Div. 44 (Society for the Psychology of Sexual Orientation and Gender Diversity), and the American Sociological Association's Sociology of Sexualities section may be good places to research and consult about trainings for IRB education on sexuality research.

- *The Catholic Mission and Sexuality*
  Consider how your institution applies its mission and heritage to matters of sexuality. Does it view sexuality as a human experience worthy of attention, or is there a culture of silence and avoidance of this intersection? Often, matters of sexuality are ignored, erroneously labeled as "incompatible with the Catholic faith" either as official statements or un-espoused cultural messages. Consider the way public messages about this intersection can positively impact the culture of the university. The Office of Mission and Ministry can take initiative on emphasizing the holiness of sexuality and the human experience on campus in ways that reduce fear and stigma about the concept, encouraging (combined with education) healthy, authentic dialogue around sexuality. This can happen during various prayer services, Masses, or vigils identified above, or in tandem with other university change efforts around matters of sexuality.

Case Example #5:

After learning about the benefits of comprehensive sexuality education, a small Catholic college is instituting a sexuality education specialization for education students. In so doing, a local group of Catholics unaffiliated with the college hear about the change and begin protesting outside campus. Because of this attention, the bishop would like to hold a meeting with the college president. In the meeting, the president reassures the bishop that the new specialization is in line with the Catholic values of the institution. After the meeting, the president and theology faculty work together to write a public statement about how the new specialization upholds the college's history and tradition of serving the poor through solidarity and upholding the rigor of the Catholic intellectual tradition.

In this example, both external Catholic protesters and the bishop got involved in the process. This will not necessarily be the case for changes at similar institutions. But because it was here, it is worth pointing out that the president exercised great listening skills with the bishop in ways that affirmed episcopal intervention while upholding academic integrity for the common good. Having a president who will support these initiatives publicly is an important catalyst for change around sexuality.

The president then considered who at the institution can help with the writing of a public statement drawing from the college's heritage as a foundation for their commitment to having a sexuality education specialization. In this particular case, solidarity and preferential option for the poor and vulnerable were hallmarks of the college's mission, offering an historical support for meeting the poor and vulnerable where they are. The statement could then include aspects of the Catholic intellectual tradition for the advancement of the common good or the affirmation of human sexual nature as a divine gift. The operative aspects of this example are that the president (1) offered public support rather than abandoning the employees and this initiative and (2) sought input from those educated on matters of theology and ministry to support the change that had a goal of upholding the common good.

- **Work toward education**
    Rooted in the above guideline about education, one relatively easy and basic change is to begin various types of education. Does your school have a sexuality resource center or space dedicated to learning about sexuality? Remember, many of your staff may not have started employment with a history of good sexuality education. Education should be made available to all members of the institution. Whether this is accomplished by a sexuality resource center, weekly or monthly educational sessions, routine speaker series, and/or some other educational opportunities, all members of the institutional community should be allowed to learn about matters related to sexuality. Consider running educational

sessions on various sexual identities to increase understanding across campus. Find areas of discrimination or misunderstanding related to sexuality in your campus culture and allow continued access to resources for learning to help educate and de-stigmatize misunderstood concepts. Training campus counselors to handle matters of sexuality, trauma, orientation, gender identity can also be an important place to focus energy.

Case Example #6:

Administrators at a Catholic university were surprised to hear that their university was featured in an op ed about how poorly people were treated around matters of sexuality— sexual assault, sexual orientation, gender identity, messages about gender and relationships—containing personal accounts identifying problems within the university. The administrators feel overwhelmed and are tempted to treat the story as a public relations issue without addressing any systemic change on campus. However, one administrator found methods of grant funding to encourage a multifaceted educational approach to these issues across campus. Administration chose to respond by surveying the current student body and employees of the university to identify the areas in which people feel most de-valued. Through this climate survey, it became apparent that on campus toxic messages existed about gender role and relationship expectations, anti-gay and anti-transgender attitudes, and misinformation about sexuality information. As a result, the university began educational campaigns about healthy relationships out of the wellness office, they instituted a sexuality resource center that began offering programing and information about sexual health and sexual diversity, and the university encouraged public engagement with local queer organizations while at the same time publicizing the bias reporting procedure for sexual identity bias incidences.

This example is a fairly massive change for what seems like such a little institutional concern (an op ed about the university). However, this example gives us many layers to examine. First, the administration had a choice to ignore the attention from the op ed and continue business as usual despite the many accounts of pain, shame, and isolation, or to address it head on. Educational efforts can be small, grassroots efforts across campus, or they can be instituted as part of an administration's initiative. In this case, the administration decided to do something about the harm many current and former students had experienced in their institution.

The grant-funding aspect of this example is important for this type of change. With changes so large, many university leaders are often concerned about where the money will be coming from. Finding grants specific to this internal work or seeking money specifically for this initiative from alumni can help offset the initial cost of such a big project. The climate survey was an opportunity to learn more and possibly contextualize some of the stories in the op ed. Gathering this type of data is important for understanding where to focus such large educational efforts.

The last part of the change—partnering with queer organizations while publicizing the bias reporting procedures—is an importantly intertwined approach. Many institutions may have to deal with double-edged issues like this. If they encouraged the partnering with queer organization in a campus community that is overtly anti-gay/anti-trans, this could create a hostile environment with university members falling back on epithets or violent behaviors to express their distaste for such a partnership. This university made sure to publicize the bias reporting procedure to (1) deter people from committing bias incidences, educating them about what they are and that they are not acceptable modes of behavior and (2) offer a clear path to reporting for incidences that may occur during this process. The university community may also benefit from affective education across the community to help diminish the anti-gay/anti-trans sentiment within the culture.

In each of these examples, while the institutions have been making meaningful changes in the way they operate, there was still work to be done. The change process is not often a single-layer change, but an intricate and ongoing process. This is why the guidelines of a fostering a safe atmosphere and practicing accountability are so important—they are an ongoing process that support each other. We do not currently have a template for the ideal institution that handles all matters of sexuality well. But when we commit as a church and society to this change, it is through our theology of hope that we believe such a place can exist one day.

Research Yet to Be

While this study spanned 17 different institutions, there is still much research to be done. Future research can benefit from several factors identified in this study: a clearer picture of the fear that exists within the change process; a larger sample size to identify patterns in what helps facilitate change, what does not help, and what acts as a barrier to change; an understanding of why some Catholic institutions refused to be part of this study and what that means for broader change. We can benefit from further study about the outcome of these changes or the longitudinal effects on the campus culture. There is still much to be researched about how bishops feel about these changes, what they do about those feelings, and how it influences their behaviors around these matters.

Beyond the scope of this study, it would be good to know how Catholic institutions in other parts of the world navigate such change. Much of the communication and beliefs about sexuality are culturally bound. While there may be some similarities, cultures differ in deference to power, saving face, social taboos and embarrassment, understandings of sexuality, and cultural theological anthropologies. Similar studies across global institutions can help identify some transcultural themes and possibly how culture interacts more specifically with which changes. The world of research is vast and as noted earlier in the book, can yield empirical data that can play an important part in the advancement of our theological dialogue.

Conclusion

This book was a look at sexuality in Catholic higher education from the broad framework of Dailey's *Circles of Sexuality*. Examining sexuality from frameworks like this is one way we can begin to expand our understanding of what it means to be truly human in our sexuality and how it exists in Catholic higher education. An historical viewpoint inspires me to think that much of the research about sexuality in Catholic higher education has yet to be done. There is a great deal that already exists from various disciplines, but so much more can be explored. It is my hope that the information in this book is one step in working toward the common good for the betterment of the entire human family. I hope we, as a community, continue addressing matters of inequity around sexuality in our institutions with the gospel love for others as our goal. Because indeed, in the words of John Paul II, "we are all really responsible for all" (John Paul II, 1987, para. 38).

References

Archdiocese of Milwaukee. (2022). *Catechesis and policy on questions concerning gender theory.* https://www.archmil.org/ArchMil/attachments/2022GenderTheoryfinal.pdf

Burke, D. (2019, June 21). *An archbishop told a Jesuit school to fire a gay teacher. They said no.* https://www.cnn.com/2019/06/20/us/jesuit-school-indiana-gay-teacher/index.html

Congregation for the Doctrine of the Faith. (1986). *Letter to the bishops of the Catholic church on the pastoral care of homosexual persons.* http://www.vatican.va/roman_curia/congregations/cfaith/documents/rc_con_cfaith_doc_19861001_homosexual-persons_en.html

Derouen, L. (2022, July 28). *Four things Catholics need to know about transgender people.* https://outreach.faith/2022/07/four-things-catholics-need-to-know-about-transgender-people/

Francis I. (2021, September 26). *Angelus.* https://www.vatican.va/content/francesco/en/angelus/2021/documents/papa-francesco_angelus_20210926.html

Goldfarb, E. S., & Lieberman, L. D. (2021). Three decades of research: The case for comprehensive sex education. *Journal of Adolescent Health, 68*(1), 13–27. https://doi.org/10.1016/j.jadohealth.2020.07.036

Harger, B., & Quintela, M. (2017). The IRB as gatekeeper: Effects on research with children and youth. *Sociological Studies of Children and Youth, 22,* 11–33. https://doi.org/10.1108/S1537-466120180000022002

Horan, D. P. (2021, October 13). Wwhy Catholics should use preferred gender pronouns and names. *National Catholic Reporter.* https://www.ncronline.org/news/opinion/why-catholics-should-use-preferred-gender-pronouns-and-names

Irvine, J. M. (2014). Is sexuality research 'dirty work'? Institutionalized stigma in the production of sexual knowledge. *Sexualities, 17*(5–6), 632–656. https://doi.org/10.1177/1363460713516338

John Paul II. (1987). *Sollicitudo rei socialis.* http://www.vatican.va/content/john-paul-ii/en/encyclicals/documents/hf_jp-ii_enc_30121987_sollicitudo-rei-socialis.html

Jones, K. J. (2022, June 17). *Bishop revokes Catholic status of Jesuit school flying LGBT, Black Lives Matter flags.* https://www.catholicnewsagency.com/news/251572/bishop-jesuit-school-lgbt-black-lives-matter-flags

Levand, M. A. (2022, May 23). Fordham conference on abuse highlights ways the church can foster healthier culture of sexuality. *National Catholic Reporter.* https://www.ncronline.org/news/accountability/fordham-conference-abuse-highlights-ways-church-can-foster-healthier-culture

Levand, M. A., & Ross, K. (2021). Sexuality education as a moral good: Catholic support for accurate, holistic sexuality information. *Theology & Sexuality, 27*(2–3), 169–187. https://doi.org/10.1080/13558358.2021.1872827

Marianist Social Justice Collaborative. (2015). *Addressing LGBT issues with youth: A resource for educators.* https://static.showit.co/file/A8pNyctRTwWCVHAoY0YLpg/99684/marianist_lgbt_final_-_2-15.pdf

Mugavero, F. J. (1976). *Sexuality – god's gift*. https://mysticalrose.tripod.com/mugavero.html

Outreach. (2022a, June 25). *Reverend Bryan Massingale - 2022 outreach conference keynote address*. [Video]. Youtube. https://www.youtube.com/watch?v=Q1aSiKW-21w&t=2935s

Outreach. (2022b, July 1). *Sister Jeannine Gramick - 2022 outreach conference keynote address*. [Video]. Youtube. https://www.youtube.com/watch?v=XXS08pjT04E

Religious Exemption Accountability Project (REAP). (2021). *About us*. https://www.thereap.org/about-reap

Sacred Congregation for the Doctrine of the Faith. (1975). *Persona humana: Declaration on certain questions concerning sexual ethics*. http://www.vatican.va/roman_curia/congregations/cfaith/documents/rc_con_cfaith_doc_19751229_persona-humana_en.html

Trujillo, Y. (2022). *LGBTQ Catholics: A guide to inclusive ministry*. Paulist Press.

Unites States Bishops' Committee on Marriage and Family. (1997). *Always our children: A pastoral message to parents of homosexual children and suggestions for pastoral ministers*. https://www.usccb.org/resources/Always%20Our%20Children.pdf

Without Exception. (2021). *A network for LGBTQ+ ministry in Catholic high schools*. https://www.withoutexception.faith/home

Appendix

Study Methods

In this section, I describe the research methods used in the study on which this book was based. This qualitative research yielded data for a composite case-study, or the examination of a number of cases at various institutions. In this study, I looked at 17 different Catholic colleges and universities to see how employees recounted the change they helped create (effect) at their institution. Below, I will clearly identify the purpose of the study along with its guiding research questions. I will then explain the research design, sampling and participants, data collection and analysis, and a note on research ethics.

Purpose of the Study

The purpose of this research study was to identify and describe the experience of employees attempting to introduce a systemic change around sexuality in Catholic colleges and universities. This study was intended to yield data that can identify themes and patterns associated with effecting change specific to meeting the sexuality needs of students in Catholic higher education.

Research Questions

The questions guiding this research study were:

1. What do Catholic higher education faculty/staff/administrators identify as key areas needing change?
2. How do Catholic higher education faculty/staff/administrators contextualize their efforts to create change around sexuality issues within their institutions?
3. Is there a pattern that an inductive thematic analysis reveals in successful efforts?
4. Is there a pattern that an inductive thematic analysis reveals in unsuccessful efforts?

Research Design

To approach the experience of employees attempting to effect change around sexuality in Catholic higher education, I used a qualitative approach with semi structured, in-depth interviews. The *Qualitative Research Methods* book by Hennink et al. (2011) began, before the table of contents, with a simple quote: "qualitative research humanizes society." With human dignity as a main component of Catholic theology and church documents (Paul VI, 1965), a qualitative approach seemed appropriate to humanize an often political issue in Catholic higher education. For Creswell (2013), qualitative research is sensitive to the collecting of data in natural settings while also being sensitive to the people and places under study with a data analysis that establishes patterns or themes. Qualitative research is also necessary when researchers need a complex, detailed understanding of the issue (Creswell, 2013). For Patton (2002), qualitative data tell a story—a detailed, contextualized account of a specific case. For the current study, as described in the theory and research in Chapter 2, a detailed understanding in the case of change around sexuality in Catholic higher education is not readily available. A detailed analysis of the experiences of these changemakers yielded the information in this book that can be a useful tool for guidance of those in similar situations.

Case Studies

This study was a series of cases or instances of people effecting change around sexuality. Creswell (2013) described case studies as an exploration of real-life, contemporary bounded systems (cases) through detailed, in-depth data collection. Case studies can be useful when how or why questions are being posed, the investigator has little control over events, and/or when the focus is on a contemporary phenomenon within a real-life context (Yin, 2009). In this study, each case of change (or attempted change) served as one case that can compare to others. Examining the experiences of effecting change as case studies yielded a composite multi-case study, also called a collective or comparative multi-case study (Rule & John, 2015). In any single instance of change, the boundaries between the "how it went down" (the characteristics of the phenomenon) and the context may be blurred without another case to which it can be compared. The compilation of every case collected and reported together allows for the clarity of boundaries between context and phenomenon characteristic of case studies (Yin, 2009). This approach allows for the cross-case analysis of the experience of individuals in similar contexts (i.e., cases) to identify themes across cases.

Theoretical Grounding

This case study approach was informed by an ecological psychological theoretical model. Weis (1998) claimed the function of theoretical models is to act as a guide to focus the inquiry. Ecological Psychology guided the focus of the interview questions as well as the data analysis portion of this research.

The ecological psychological approach focuses on the relationship between the individual and their environment, seeing them as interconnected in determining an individual's perception and behavior (Jacob, 1987). With employees at institutions of Catholic higher education, the Catholic environment is an important context for this case analysis. Schoggen (1978) described the ecological focus of this approach as studying naturally occurring human behavior and the relationships between human behavior and its environment. In this study, I examined individual behaviors in the context of the institutional steps that must be taken for change as well as the Catholic mission (communication strategies in Chapter 6).

Ecological Psychology was developed in the 1950s by psychologists Robert Barker and Herbert Wright. The goal of this approach is to produce detailed, objective descriptions of naturally occurring behavior (Jacob, 1987). One focus in the work of Barker and Wright (1955) was the behavior setting. A behavior setting is a behavioral pattern in the context of an environment, including part of the milieu to which the behavior is attached—a synomorphic relationship (Barker & Wright, 1955). To better understand a behavior setting, Barker (1978) described the examination of a class setting as including human components (class members, teachers), physical properties (location, duration, equipment), the program (teaching methods, topics to be covered), and institutional influences that create the study milieu. Behaviors and behavior patterns take place in an environment that is influenced by many factors. These tenants of ecological psychology guided the interview questions to ascertain the behavioral aspects in relation to the specific Catholic environment—components of the institution's mission, traditional heritage, academic history, political atmosphere, and personal and departmental dynamics are examples of such influencing components in Catholic higher education.

Sampling and Participants

Because the experience of attempting to effect change specifically around sexuality is unique, I used a convenience sampling procedure known as snowball or chain referral sampling. Wiederman and Whitley (2002) describe three reasons for the use of convenience sampling: a primary focus on the study of diversity; access populations that a researcher has some personal contact with will be more likely to participate (due to the sensitive nature of sexuality); and not all sexuality-specific criteria can be obtained from a general population. The current research suggested that there are both successes and challenges in effecting change, and a diversity of viewpoints with respect to sexuality in Catholic higher education. This diversity is a focus of the study that is not a common experience in the general higher education population in that it includes Catholic theological foundations. Due to my previous work in theological studies, I have encountered many people who know of individuals attempting to effect change around sexuality at Catholic colleges and universities. Personal connection is one way to being the chain referral or snowball process (Noy, 2008).

Chain referral and snowball are defined by some as two different sampling methods identifying specific procedural differences (e.g., Penrod et al., 2003; Qun et al., 2008). It is also true that researchers have used the terms interchangeably with little to no difference in procedure (e.g., Abdul-Quader et al., 2006; Biernacki & Waldorf, 1981; Noy, 2008). Due to this discrepancy in the research literature, I will be using the terms interchangeably (related to the source I'm citing) while identifying my procedural methods.

Snowball sampling begins with an initial set of contacts (often called seeds) that will then refer me to other individuals with similar experiences (Wiederman & Whitley, 2002). Also called chain-referral sampling, this method has some potential problems as well. Biernacki and Waldorf (1981) describe social visibility as a potential challenge in this sampling technique—if the topic of study is sensitive (illegal, immoral, or will possibly get someone in trouble), a researcher may have difficulty in contacting seed members. In the current study, I had what the authors call fortuitous contacts, or contacts gained from an increased sensitivity to the intricacies of the research area.

Another challenge proposed by Biernacki and Waldorf (1981) is controlling the types of chains—the ongoing analysis of participants and possibility of creating more selective criteria as the study progresses. In other words, you may find data in the interviews that tell you how you should narrow or be more selective of the types of people you interview next. As the analysis of data influences the direction of future interviews and participant selection, I had to prepare for the possibility that I may have had to focus on a particular group of people not previously foreseen at the outset of this study. This particular issue is possibly more problematic in less foundational studies than the present. With populations on which much data has already been collected, chain-type control can lead to data not useful for transferability. In the present study, however, so little is known about the experience of this population that any data gathered is likely useful in a foundational sense for future studies.

Snowball or chain referral sampling does come with distinct advantages as well. When trying to sample populations in sexuality research, confidentiality can be a sensitive topic (Meyer & Wilson, 2009; Wiederman & Whitley, 2002). For example, when examining sampling techniques in Lesbian, Gay and Bisexual (LGB) populations, Meyer and Wilson (2009) described the stigma and possible persecution associated with being identified as members of such populations. Snowball sampling, however, gives potential participants a sense of trust with the researcher due to social network familiarity—put simply, the feeling of trust with the researcher on such a sensitive topic because someone in their social network referred them (Penrod et al., 2003). Noy (2008) echoes this sentiment when applied to the concept of social capital. Social capital is seen as social assets gained from membership in a group—a productive credential when speaking to members of a group about possibly sensitive topics (Noy, 2008).

Sampling in positivist quantitative research is concerned with generalizability. Due to the unique nature of the desired environment of participants in this study, researchers suggest transferability as a component to consider (Shenton, 2004). Shenton (2004) discussed transferability as a matter of the results of a qualitative study being understood within the context of the particular characteristics of the organization or organizations from where the data was collected. In gathering data through the interview guide, I was able to have enough information about the institutional context to be useful for individuals and organizations in similar contexts.

For the current study, I identified participants by contacting colleagues and connections at various Catholic institutions of higher education in the Unites States known to have attempted to effect change around sexuality at their institution and/or seek from them the contact information for individuals that they know have attempted to effect change. I invited them to participate through a phone call request or e-mail invitation. At the conclusion of the interviews, I asked study participants if they were aware of anyone else doing similar work either at the same or another institution and request their contact information.

Of all of the interviews, two interviews were lost due to recording malfunction. Of the two interviews that were lost, one participant agreed to a second interview in which I used notes from the first interview as a guide. The second interview was lost with no chance of recovery—the only data that remained were handwritten research notes. As a result, that data was not used in analysis because the analysis protocol required coding transcribed interviews.

The 31 participants represented 17 universities. These universities varied in heritage (e.g., part of the Catholic diocese, Catholic but independent of the diocese, or part of a religious order like Franciscans, Dominicans, Jesuits, Benedictines, etc.). Participants consisted of 10 faculty members; 6 residence life staff; 15 administrators, including directors, deans, and vice presidents of various offices (i.e., student affairs, student life, various diversity offices, etc.); and 3 other staff positions such as campus ministry, health promotion, and Title IX coordination. Some participants held dual roles as administrators. One interview included two participants at once, bringing the total number of participants and participant roles to 31, while the total number of interviews remained at 30.

Table A.1 Participant position

Participant Position	n
Faculty	10
Residence Life	6
Student Life	6
University Life	4
Dean of Students	1
Campus Ministry	1
Health Services	2
Title IX	1

The 17 universities represented various traditions that will not be further divided for anonymity. The general university categories consisted of one diocesan institution, one independent Catholic institution, and 15 ordered institutions. The 15 ordered institutions were made up of 9 different religious orders. Nine of the ordered schools had religious heritages based on priest or friars, while six were founded by sisters or nuns:

Table A.2 University characteristics

University Type	n = 17
Diocesan	1
Independent	1
Ordered	15
Priests/Friars	9
Sisters/Nuns	6

Measures

Qualitative research has a rich tradition of gathering data through interviews (Braun & Clarke, 2013; Hennink et al., 2011; Patton, 2002). As with qualitative research in general, in-depth interviews are fundamentally concerned with an interest in understanding the experience of individuals and the meaning they make of it (Seidman, 1998). In such interviews, open-ended questions are asked that can be broad and general or highly specific (Cottrell & McKenzie, 2011).

Prior to the interviews, I gathered data on their institution available to the general public such as their institutional mission and heritage (i.e., founded by a religious order, set up by the diocese, etc.) on an Institutional Data Points Sheet. These data were used in the thematic analysis to give context to participant responses. This information was a clear way of grouping participants to identify similarities in the change process based on institutional heritage, geographic location, or mission statement. I then gathered data from employees at institutions of Catholic higher education through in-depth, semi-structured interviews using an interview guide. In-depth interviews are used when identifying personal experiences, useful for sensitive issues, and to identify the context of participants' lives (Hennink et al., 2011). These types of interviews are appropriate when the topic is complex, respondents are knowledgeable, and understanding of individual experience is needed (Cottrell & McKenzie, 2011). In the case of employees in Catholic higher education, the experiences may be localized if an attempt to effect change is never fully realized or institutionalized. This results in an experience that can be found in no other place than the individual involved in this change. In times of successful change, the changemaker had a particular experience that played a key role in the efficacy of that change. The goal of this study was understanding this complex process from individuals who have experience in the context of their respective universities and the broader Catholic mission.

Dependent upon the exploratory nature of a study, the interview guide will be more or less structured (Hennink et al., 2011). Interviews were semi-structured to allow for the evolution of natural conversation and data that the participant may find important to include (Creswell, 2013). The open-ended questions encouraged the participants to expand on their experiences, including information that they found important to share. The interview guide consisted of 5–7 open-ended questions. The semi-structured nature allowed me to ask important probing questions as the conversation evolved. These questions about their role in effecting change, the target context of sexuality at the institution for change, strategies used to effect change, and perceived successes and barriers assisted in gaining a better understanding of the environmental factors present in this process. During the interview process, however, I found that questions four and five were quite similar. I deleted question four, and simply asked about future desired changes.

The interviews, guided by the environmental/behavioral synomorphic relationship described in the ecological psychological framework as well as the data described in Chapter 2, was designed to better understand the experience of the individuals attempting to effect change in Catholic higher education. I gathered information about the type of change around sexuality they had effected or were intending on effecting, what steps they had taken in the process, and what did or did not work well for them.

Data Collection Procedures

Consistent with the ecological psychological framework, participant institutions had differing components that affected this process. The publicly available data points were recorded on an Institutional Data Points Sheet prior to the interview. This data was relatively straightforward as the school will be associated with a religious order (priests, brothers, nuns, etc.) or a diocesan affiliation. This information gave context to the environmental factors (e.g., order and mission) of the institution in which an employee is attempting change.

For a clearer understanding of the environmental factors influencing the change process, data was then collected from in-depth, semi-structured interviews. Following the interview guide described above, I asked participants about their experience of effecting or attempting to effect change around issues of sexuality in Catholic higher education. Beginning with connections I had in the Catholic theological academic tradition, I inquired about their experience with change around issues of sexuality at their universities. After informal discussions, I asked about others they may know at various Catholic colleges and universities in the United States doing similar work.

Participants may have been engaging in the change process or have attempted to effect change within the past 15 years. According to Kezar (2014), change in the higher education setting may have been in the works for as long as 10–15 years. Individuals who have recently had experiences of effecting change that ended several years prior to the interview had useful knowledge about the process that may yield time-saving strategy tips for future endeavors. The interviews were audio-recorded. Participants were sent a consent statement prior to the interview and verbal consent was recorded. Upon initial contact over the phone, I read from a phone script designed to highlight important parts of the consent form.

During the interviews, I asked about the types of change with which they have experience. I guided the conversation through open-ended questions about the type of change, why they felt it was important, and areas in the process where progress was found easy or difficult.

The interviews were then transcribed by a professional transcription service. Recorded data as well as the transcribed documents were kept in a locked, secured location when not being analyzed. Along with notes taken during the interview, transcribed data was analyzed for themes. The process of data analysis is detailed in the next section.

Data Analysis

Braun and Clarke (2013) observed that the point of descriptive analysis aims to give voice to a topic or group of people. In the present study, data analysis gave a "voice" to the experience of those attempting to effect change. In data analysis, the environmental factors influencing change (or lack thereof) identified in the interviews took form as various themes arose. This process focused primarily on inductive analysis which involved discovering patterns, themes, and categories within the data (Patton, 2002). I examined this data through thematic analysis (Braun & Clarke, 2006) to identify similarities and differences in the processes of navigating issues of sexuality on these campuses as well as patterns of successful or failed change. These similarities or differences obtained through the interviews were compared along with the institutional data points to identify environmental themes that may correlate to various attempts or outcomes for change.

Creswell (2013) recommended that case study data be analyzed using four forms: categorical aggregation, direct interpretation, cross-case synthesis, and naturalistic generalizations. Categorical aggregation involves seeking a collection of instances and establishing themes or patterns, while direct interpretation focuses on meaning in a single case. After observing what had happened in a given university, I considered the themes or patterns that emerged when compared with other institutions. With emerging patterns, Yin (2009) utilized cross-case synthesis as a way of examining cases to create a uniform framework, for example, in the form of a word table. Once data was collected from numerous institutions, it was compared to give a broader understanding of how this change occurs in the Catholic context. Naturalistic generalizations refers to making the information generalizable to people in similar cases. This type of analysis can be useful for phenomena that require simple explanation. The data was also considered with the thoroughness of thematic analysis to observe any more detailed nuances.

For Braun and Clarke (2006) thematic analysis should be seen as a foundational method for qualitative analysis. The authors also identified thematic analysis as a useful method when the goal is not to create an entire theory based on the data. Braun and Clarke (2006) identify six phases of thematic analysis: familiarizing self with the data, generating initial codes, searching for themes, reviewing themes, defining and naming themes, and producing the report. These six phases also involve the understanding of the data while generating categories, observing how the themes relate with constant review, and synthesizing all of the relations while writing up the data. This process identified general themes and meaning to the patterns and possible outcomes of the attempted change.

Thematic analysis lends itself to flexibility—as opposed to a rigid review of the data based on previous theories (Braun & Clarke, 2006). The authors also encouraged researchers to use thematic analysis for qualitative data for which the derivation of a theory is not the necessary goal. While Braun and Clarke (2006) mentioned similarities to grounded theory analysis, they stressed the uniqueness of thematic analysis for broad uses in qualitative analysis rather than just theory development.

An inductive thematic analysis is helpful for building themes up from the data rather than starting with a theoretical framework (Braun & Clarke, 2013). Building on themes from the data allows for a less restrictive analysis than using a guiding theoretical concept (Braun & Clarke, 2013). In the current study, the collected data was the source of the themes present in how change involving sexuality was handled in Catholic higher education. Building up from the data gave me an understanding of participants' experiences free from a theoretical understanding derived from the minimal existing data.

As I took notes during the interview, I was identifying common themes that arose throughout the interview stage of data collection. I then read through the transcriptions noting general themes. I digested the data a third time to code for major themes using a coding software. Two participants seemed to be unclear about identifying a change they effected around sexuality. Because of this difficulty, I had included a pre-interview point of "What kind of change around sexuality have you been involved in at your university?" on the interview guide. While compiling the results section, I let participants review their excerpts to ensure a comfortable level of anonymity in each quote.

Considering generalizability or transferability, Braun and Clarke (2006), urged that the information yielded from the analysis should be considered within the conditions of the core phenomenon. In the present study, through the ecological psychological lens, the "conditions" of the core phenomenon is what I collectively refer to as the context of these experiences. Based on the transferability considered in the above sampling section (Shenton, 2004), as well as the abstraction of the categories to be labeled which lends to more generalizable results (Braun & Clarke, 2006), this data may be considered applicable to individuals attempting to effect change in other Catholic colleges and universities in the United States so long as they have similar conditions.

Quality

Because of the nature of qualitative research, the quantitative constructs of reliability, validity, and generalizability cannot be applied directly to qualitative data. Shenton (2004) discussed quality of qualitative research in terms of credibility, dependability, and confirmability. The subjective experience of the researcher should also be considered.

Credibility is the trustworthiness that what is being presented in the data represents the reality of the phenomenon (Shenton, 2004). Shenton (2004) provides a long list of provisions for researchers culminating around authenticity of the data from respondents, close examination of negative cases, and checking data from different sources including the present data and previous research. Much of the data review and restructuring through thematic analysis helps keep the information from becoming unrepresentative of reality. I reached a general code saturation at interview number 22.

If the work were repeated with the same context and participants, the likelihood of data being similar to what will be obtained is called the dependability of the research (Shenton, 2004). The repeated measures taken to state my positionality and subjectivity as a researcher speaks to the aspect of confirmability—making one's intentions and biases clear along with the triangulation of the data to ensure the data is from the informants and not reflecting the preferences of the researcher (Shenton, 2004). I intend to control these variables by clear identification of my position along with clear definition of my research design and methods to allow for replication.

Researcher Positionality

Qualitative research has been critiqued for being ungeneralizable and based on the personal opinion or interpretation of the researcher (Cottrell & McKenzie, 2011). This concern of subjective interpretation is not unfounded as researchers identified this subjectivity as an integral part of the qualitative process (Braun & Clarke, 2013; Hennink et al., 2011). In order to mitigate what Ash and Burn (2003) identified as a technical weakness, I make my researcher bias known. This process of reflexivity has been proposed as a way to legitimize, validate, and question the research process (Pillow, 2003). Addressing what Creswell (2013) called the axiological assumption (or researcher subjectivity), I included my researcher positionality in this appendix. This process of making my position and values known in the study is a crucial part of qualitative research.

To address this researcher bias (Creswell, 2013), I will identify generally my own biases in relation to this topic that may impact the study, and more specifically the factors relating to specific components in my design. I am a Catholic, white, male US citizen of Irish, Polish, and Italian heritage. I have attended Catholic institutions of higher education for all of my undergraduate and part of my graduate studies. During those years, I encountered many institutional regulations that not only prevented the development of sexual knowledge but also caused significant harm to individuals of diverse sexual identities. As a product of Catholic sexuality education (or lack thereof), I was left with many questions during my college years with very few resources at my disposal. In college, there was not much direction that gave clarity to many of the issues college students often encounter. As I grew in my knowledge of both theology and sexuality, I became curious about the inner workings of university life around sexual issues. As I witnessed people struggle within the Catholic higher education environment, I watched their questions and pleas for help frequently go unanswered.

In regard to sampling procedures, I mentioned the importance of social network familiarity (Penrod et al., 2003) and social capital (Noy, 2008). Because of my previous work in Catholic higher education as both a student and an employee, the criteria for a viable participant are evident to me. Making the contacts for this study has been a process of several years of networking in Catholic higher education.

My previous education in Catholic theology at the undergraduate and graduate levels has given me an intimate glimpse at the historical as well as contemporary role of church doctrine and how it works in peoples' lives. I have also been witness to the process of negotiating these church teachings with lived experience in the lives of people who attend Catholic colleges and universities. The knowledge about theological groundings combined with current biopsychosocial information about human sexuality in the United States today drove me to understand more thoroughly how Catholic institutions are working to address issues around sexuality in the lives of their community members.

My values of right relationships and love for one another stem from my years of living the Catholic faith. Through studying scripture and church teachings, I find great value in the function of the Catholic Church today in bringing about the love of God in the world. These core values of love have driven me to understand more about the dialogue around sexuality especially for those who have minimal support in their navigation around this dialogue. It is from these values that

I believe change should happen when injustices are present within these systems—when people are being hurt by institutional or environmental factors, change should take place. I am operating under the assumption that if some Catholic institutions can effect change around sexuality issues that give people the tools they need to navigate this dialogue, others may want to follow their lead for the benefit of their community.

Most of my educational career has been spent in Catholic educational institutions. The opportunity to learn and grow developmentally and intellectually in an environment that valued the role of faith in education has been important to me. I value my Catholic education and the values of care for others which it has instilled in me. It is because of my love for the Catholic Church that I desire to use research to better Catholic institutional practice.

As a result of all of this, I recognize that my positionality may influence how other people perceive and interpret me and affect how I interpret the data. Some of the steps I took to prevent myself from reading values into the data involved identifying key words used by participants—such as "fear," "afraid," or "resistant"—as code groups, rather than creating codes based on assumptions before analyzing the data.

I recognized the way I may have been perceived by participants as mysterious since they were not able to see me due to the phone interview format. I also may have been interpreted as more open to listening to their stories because of my previous Catholic educational background. Participants may have been concerned or comforted in the fact that I conducted interviews over the phone.

Ethics

The Belmont report (1979) identifies the basic ethical principles of respect for persons, benefice, and justice. The protection of research participants and their information is of utmost importance to me as a researcher. Through informed consent clauses, my participants were made aware of the types of data that were collected, the analytical intentions of this information, as well as the confidential nature of the reporting of this information. Because of the possible threat to one's career in Catholic higher education (McCarty, 2014), I took care in reporting geographic information with minimal location markers and as anonymized as possible, reported by area of the United States (mid-Atlantic, mid-West, etc.) only when necessary. My participants were not intentionally deceived and were made aware of their ability to drop out of the study at any time. All participants were consulted when direct quotes were used to ensure confidentiality.

References

Abdul-Quader, A. S., Heckathorn, D. D., Sabin, K., & Saidel, T. (2006). Implementation and analysis of respondent driven sampling: Lessons learned from the field. *Journal of Urban Health: Bulletin of the New York Academy of Medicine, 83*(6 Suppl), i1–i5.

Ash, C., & Burn, J. M. (2003). *Composite case study method to build e-business transformation theory 14th Australasian Conference on Information Systems Perth*, Western Australia. http://aisel.aisnet.org/cgi/viewcontent.cgi?article=1326&context=acis2003

Barker, R. G. (1978). Return trip, 1977. In R. G. Barker (Ed.), *Habitats, environments, and human behavior* (pp. 285–296). Jossey-Bass.

Barker, R. G., & Wright, H. F. (1955). *Midwest and its children*. Harper & Row.

Biernacki, P., & Waldorf, D. (1981). Snowball sampling: Problems and techniques of chain referral sampling. *Sociological Methods & Research, 10*(2), 141–163. https://doi.org/10.1177/004912418101000205

Braun, V., & Clarke, V. (2006). Using thematic analysis in psychology. *Qualitative Research in Psychology, 3*(2), 77–101.

Braun, V., & Clarke, V. (2013). *Successful qualitative research: A practical guide for beginners*. Sage.

Cottrell, R. R., & McKenzie, J. F. (2011). *Health promotion and education research methods* (2nd ed.). Jones and Bartlett Publishers.

Creswell, J. W. (2013). *Qualitative inquiry and research design: Choosing among five approaches* (3rd ed.). Sage.

Hennink, M., Hutter, I., & Bailey, A. (2011). *Qualitative research methods*. Sage.

Jacob, E. (1987). Qualitative research traditions: A review. *Review of Educational Research, 57*(1), 1–50. https://doi.org/10.3102/00346543057001001

Kezar, A. J. (2014). *How colleges change: Understanding, leading, and enacting change*. Routledge.

McCarty, R. W. (2014). Objects of the inquisition, or the trials of religion scholars at Catholic institutions who engage with sexuality studies. *Academe, 100*(1), 24–29. www.aaup.org

Meyer, I. H., & Wilson, P. A. (2009). Sampling lesbian, gay, and bisexual populations. *Journal of Counseling Psychology, 56*(1), 23–31. https://doi.org/10.1037/a0014587

Noy, C. (2008). Sampling knowledge: The hermeneutics of snowball sampling in qualitative research. *International Journal of Social Research Methodology, 11*(4), 327–344. https://doi.org/10.1080/13645570701401305

Patton, M. Q. (2002). *Qualitative research & evaluation methods* (3rd ed.). Sage.

Paul VI. (1965). *Gaudium et spes: Pastoral constitution on the church in the modern world*. http://www.vatican.va/archive/hist_councils/ii_vatican_council/documents/vat-ii_const_19651207_gaudium-et-spes_en.html

Penrod, J., Preston, D. B., Cain, R. E., & Starks, M. T. (2003). A discussion of chain referral as a method of sampling hard-to-reach populations. *Journal of Transcultural Nursing, 14*(2), 100–107.

Pillow, W. (2003). Confession, catharsis, or cure? Rethinking the uses of reflexivity as methodological power in qualitative research. *International Journal of Qualitative Studies in Education, 16*(2), 175–196. https://doi.org/10.1080/0951839032000060635

Qun, H., Ye, W., Yan, L., Yurun, Z., Peng, L., Fang, Y., Xiaobing, F., Jie, L., Raymond, H., Li, L., & McFarland, W. (2008). Accessing men who have sex with men through long-chain referral recruitment, guangzhou, China. *AIDS & Behavior, 12,* 93–96. https://doi.org/10.1007/s10461-008-9388-y

Rule, P., & John, V. M. (2015). A necessary dialogue: Theory in case study research. *International Journal of Qualitative Methods, 14*(4), 1–11. https://doi.org/10.1177/1609406915611575

Schoggen, P. (1978). Ecological psychology and mental retardation. In G. Sackett (Ed.), *Observing behavior: Theory and applications in mental retardation* (Vol. 1, pp. 33–62). University Park Press.

Seidman, I. (1998). *Interviewing as qualitative research: A guide for researchers in education and the social sciences* (2nd ed.). Teachers College, Columbia University.

Shenton, A. K. (2004). Strategies for ensuring trustworthiness in qualitative research projects. *Education for Information, 22*(2), 63–75.

The National Commission for the Protection of Human Subjects of Biomedical and Behavioral Research. (1979). *The Belmont report: Ethical principles and guidelines for the protection of human subjects of research.* http://www.hhs.gov/ohrp/humansubjects/guidance/belmont.html#xbasic

Weis, D. L. (1998). The use of theory in sexuality research. *Journal of Sex Research, 35*(1), 1–9. https://doi.org/10.1080/00224499809551912

Wiederman, M. W., & Whitley, B. E. (Eds.). (2002). *Handbook for conducting research on human sexuality.* Lawerence Erlbaum Associates.

Yin, R. K. (2009). *Case study research: Design and methods* (4th ed.). Sage.

Index

Note: page numbers in *italic* type refer to figures, those in **bold** type refer to tables.

academic freedom 4, 30, 41–43, 50, 91, 107, 161, 168, 199, 205–206
accountability 200, 203–204, 210
act-centered morality 83, 86, 195, 198
active education as a change strategy 149–150, 153, 159, 160–161, 182
Alison, James 193
alumni 43, 54, 55, **119**, 123, 133, 134, 139, 140, 210
American Council on Education 30, 56
Aquinas, Thomas 2, 36
Arnett, J. J. 19, 22, 27, 56, 168, 179
assessment of your change strategies 187
Association of Catholic Colleges and Universities 26, 48, 56
Astin, A. W. 22, 25, 56
Augustine of Hippo 2, 8, 35–36, 56

barriers or challenges: assessing *185*, 187, 189; being brought to light 175; cultural 28; in creating change 5–6, 117–137, 139–142; in Love 28, 54–55; in Maher & Sever 52–53; in McEntarfer 54; language sensitivity and 162; requiring trust 76; to sexuality education 52
be a resource 170, **171**, 174, 178
be not afraid 170, **171**, 175
Benedict XVI 37
Benedictine University 47
birth control *see* contraception
Bishop Mitchell Rozanski 49–50
bishops: as external/peripheral constituents **141**; as resistant to change 183, *185*, 193; condemnation of books 42; feelings about changes 211; in participant interviews 81; in proximity to the change process 71, **72**, 74–75; involvement in the change process 81, 107, 110 *see also* church hierarchy involvement; involvement in the sexual abuse scandal 37; *see also* US Bishops
board of trustee 45; as a barrier to change 54, 55, 140; as supportive in the change process **119**, 132–133, 134
Boswell, John 193
bullying, student experience of 17, 91, 100, 189; *see also* discrimination

Cahill, Lisa Sowle 195
calls for change 13, 14, 47, 49
campus ministry: as an entity of controlling behavior 110; as a support to change 55, 109, **119**, 130, 131, 132, 138; as participant staff position 219
Cardinal Newman Society 43, 46
case studies 215–216, 222; *see also* Hughes, Bryce; Coley, Jonathan
Catechism of the Catholic Church 84, 105, 112, 143, 175
Catholic abuse of sexuality 197

Catholic erotophobia 6, 112, 174, 189, 199
Catholic history 5, 35, 47
Catholic identity: self-reflection and 172; as a barrier 53; as a reason for resistance to change 102, 104–105; as support 53, 135; individual 109, 112, 182; institutional 38, 52, 131, 155, 172; navigation/negotiation 5, 71, **74**, 80, 177, 178
Catholic orthodoxy, self-appointed public defenders of 117, **118**, 121, 124, 140
Catholic sexual theology 39, 82, 84, 87, 194, 196
Catholic social teaching 6, 49, 145, 157, 175, 176, 196
Catholic social thought 7
Catholic Theological Society of America 42
CDF *see* Congregation for the Doctrine of the Faith, Sacred Congregation for the Doctrine of the Faith
chain referral sampling 216, 217, 218
Chickering, A. W. 22, 24; and Reisser, L. 1, 22–24, 167
Choi, Hoon 195
church hierarchy involvement, in the change process 55, 101, **103**, 106, 107, 110
closeness to student experience 71, **72**, 75, 144
Coley, Jonathan 7, 54, 139, 148
collaborative, as a method of navigation 53, 148, 158
common good 6, 7, 42, 87, 143, 162–165, 175–176, 189, 196, 197, 208, 211
communal reconciliation 144
communal redemption 111, 113, 196, 200, 203
communal repentance 5
communication strategies 6, 54, 77, 81, 111, 149, **150**, 160, 162, 163, 164, 165, 181, *185*, 192, 216; *see also* methods of communication
communication tactics *see* methods of communication
Confessions 36, 83
Congregation for Catholic Education 177

Congregation for the Doctrine of the Faith 41, 194; *see also* Sacred Congregation for the Doctrine of the Faith
conscience 6, 114, 174, 175, 178, 196
conservative constituents 102, 110, 117, **118**, 121–124, 140; donors 117, **118**, 121, 123, 140 faculty/administrators 117, **118**, 121–122, 140; parents 117, **118**, 123–124, 140; self-appointed public defenders of Catholic orthodoxy 117, **118**, 121, 124, 140; student groups 105, 117, **118**, 121, 122–123, 140, 157
continue dialogue/study 170, **171**, 172–174, 175, 177
contraceptives 3, 16, 38–39, 40, 46, 50, 153, 168, 193
Copeland, M. Shawn 85
Cornelius Jansen *see* Jansenism
counseling center **119**, 130, 131, 132
CST *see* Catholic social teaching
culturally Catholic avoidance of sexuality discussion 168
curiosity about other schools 71, **74**, 81
Curran, Charles 40, 42, 195
curriculum: as a proposed area of change 91, 94, 101, 120, 132, 133; in the change process 48, 97, 148; inclusion of sexuality in 3–4, 31, 41–42, 55, 149, 162

Dailey, Dennis 2, 15–17, *18*, 20, 211
Dale, B. 86
data analysis 222–224
data collection procedures 221
De La Torre, M. 85
Declaration on Certain Questions Concerning Sexual Ethics see *Persona Humana*
Dei Verbum 38
Derouen, Luisa 193
Dignitatis Humanae 175
Dignity USA 193
discreet methods of communication **151**, 156–158, 161–162
discrimination: as an area of change 90, 91, 96–97, 99, 100; as stemming from Catholic teaching

39; in Hughes 138; prohibition of 3, 31–32, 45, 202 *see also* non-discrimination; student safety and 79, 163, 198, 199, 209; theological insights on 111–113; toward sexual minorities 4, 28, 33, 78–79, 91, 193
domestic partner benefits 102; *see also* same-sex partner benefits
domicile adults 126; *see also* domestic partner benefits
donors: as influencing factor in Catholic higher education 1; in the change process 53, 55, 110, 124; in the change process, as a barrier 117, **118**, 121, 123, 139, 140 *see also* conservative constituents; in the change process, as a support **119**, 132, 133
"do not be afraid" 143; *see also* be not afraid
dormitory and sexual activity 32, 91, 97–98
drag **72**, **150**, 154; show **73**, **103**, 104, 154
DSM 39
dysfunctional leadership **118**, 125

ecological psychological as a grounding theory 14, 216, 221, 223
Eisenberg, M. 3, 31, 34, 46, 52
Elizabeth Antus 85
emerging adulthood 19, 22; *see also* Arnett, J. J.
employee resource group 183
engaging the institutional tradition 156–157, 161; *see also* methods of communication
episcopal intervention 107, 208; *see also* church hierarchy involvement
epistemological stages 22, 24
erasure 44, 94, 142, 186
Erikson, Erik H. 1, 19, 20, 21, 22, 167
espoused culture 110
Estanek, S. 48
Evangelii Gaudium 50, 144, 163
Ex Corde Ecclesiae 41, 43, 144, 169, 175, 197
External Atmosphere 71, **73**, 77; *see also* geographic environment; geo-political environment
external protesters 124, 183, 208

Farley, Margaret 2, 13, 36, 42, 50, 84, 168, 175, 195
fear: around sexuality 36, 37, 44, 84, 104, 125, 163, 195, 206; as a barrier in the change process 52, 53, 55, 117, **118**, 139, 140–142, 211; as a reason for resistance to change 101, 102, **103**; of alumni 54, 55; of being targeted 140; of discrimination 97; of community reaction 28, 140; of conservative constituents *see* conservative constituents; of creating scandal 105; of job termination 117, **118**, 124, 129, 140; of negative media attention **73**, 124; of parents 54, 55; of priests 54; of parishes 54; of potential funding sources 54, 110; of protesters 140; of the board of trustees 54, 55; of the administration 48, 117, **118**, 120; of the local bishop 55, 71, 124, 126, 107, 117, **118**, 121; as a theological theme 143–144, 145, 174; as an obstacle to overcome *see* be not afraid; in Chickering's vectors 23; of sexuality in Catholic culture 47, 82, 87, 112, 168, 174–175, 193, 197 *see also* Catholic erotophobia; related to sexual victimization 78
flying under the radar 137, **151**, 162
Ford, Craig 195
forums *see* methods of communication, forums
Francis I 2, 3, 50, 87, 112, 143–144, 162–163, 188, 194
Franciscan University of Steubenville 44
Fratelli Tutti 143
Freitas, Donna 13, 27, 43
Freud, Sigmund 19, 20
friars **119**, 132, 133, 186, 219

gathering data in effecting change 6, 149, **150**, 152, 159, 160, 184, 186, 218
Gaudium et Spes 83, 112, 163, 176
gender diversity: in participant experience 76, 130; as a key area of change 91, 92, 94–96, 138, 152; to be examined by administrators 201–202

gender identity: college student development and 22, 25, 169; discrimination and 111, 164; pastoral care and 192–194, 198; religious exemptions and 43; as a sensitive topic 190; as an area of change 95–96, 107, 192, 209; as related to non-discrimination policies 3, 32, 96, 153, 156; in the circles of sexuality 16, *18*, 20; participant understanding of 95, 96, 107
gender-inclusive housing: as an area of change 3, 32, 80, 91, 95, 152; in Catholic higher education 44, 110, 130, 158
gender-neutral: bathrooms 3, 95, 96 *see also* gender-neutral, restrooms; housing 44 *see also* gender-inclusive housing; living arrangements 4, 96 *see also* gender-inclusive housing; restrooms 95, 126, **151** *see also* gender-neutral, bathrooms
gendered: bathrooms 3, 30, 32, 35, 44, 55; restroom *see* gendered, bathrooms
geographic environment 77, 135, 139, 160; *see also* geo-political environment
geo-political environment **73**, 117, **119**, 135, 159, 160
Getz, C. 4, 7, 51, 52, 53, 108, 137, 138, 160, 161, 162, 184, 187
God's inclusive love 112, **151**, 189, 197–198
good organization in affecting change **119**, 135, 136–137, 139, 186
Gramick, Jeannine 193
grant funding: as a means to effect change 94, **150**, 155, *185*, 209–210; as related to Title IX 43
Gravissimum Educationis 144, 169, 177, 198; *see also* Paul VI
Greenberg, J. S. 2, 15, 17
Greytak, E. A. 3, 30, 32, 44, 108
GSA 17, 51, 53, 54; *see also* student groups
Gudorf, Christine 84, 195
guidelines for Catholic institutions 192, 195–200

Hahnenberg, Edward 188–189
health centers 34, 168
Hedgepeth, E., & Helmich, J. 2, 15, 52
hegemonic: gendered messaging 198; masculinity 43
higher administration buy-in **119**, 131, 133
higher education, purpose of 29–30
homophobia: addressing in higher education 33, 55; and church norms 43, 55; reduction of 31; student experience of 28
hope for the future of Catholic higher education 6, 167–174, 178
hostile environment/safety as a theme in the change process 71, **73**, 78–79
Hughes, Bryce 7, 54, 108, 110, 111, 137–140, 142, 159–162, 186–187
human dignity 7, 100, 109, 112, 114, **151**, 157, 164, 175, 176, 188, 215; as a tenant of Catholic teaching 112, 157, 164, 175, 176, 215; in Catholic social thought 7; in the change process 100, 114, **151**, 188; LGB Catholics and 109
human sexuality 2; as a Catholic theological good 5, 83–86, 195; as a topic to continue studying/discussing 172–174, 178; as broad and complex 15–16; as human nature 75, 83–86, 196–197; as part of Catholic higher education 174; Augustine and 36; bishop letters on 194; programs about 48
Humanae Vitae 38–39
Hunt, Mary 85, 195

Imago Dei 84, 195
inclusive language 126, 202; *see also* language sensitivity
inclusive love *see* God's inclusive love
inclusivity, administrator endorsement of 202
increasing visibility of LGBTQ persons: as a theme in the change process 152; as a strategy to effect change **150**, 159, 160
inductive thematic analysis 222–224
institutional accountability 200

Index 233

institutionalization: of a change 71, **74**, 80, **119**, **151**, 161–162, 187, 203; of an ethic of care 113; related to social sin 164; related to solidarity 145, 200
intimacy: as a part of sexuality 15, 31, 190, 193; in the circles of sexuality 15, 16, 17, *18*, 20, 22, 24, 25, 26; and healthy relationships 23, 31
intimate partner violence 204
Irish culture, Jansenism and 36–37

Jansenism 36–37
job security 128, 168, 178
John Paul II 2, 30, 39–40, 41, 42, 74, 144, 163, 164, 169, 175, 177, 211
John XXIII 177
Jordan, Mark 85, 86
Jung, Patricia Beattie 85, 195
Just Love see Farley, Margaret

katholikos 113, 197
Keenan, James 45, 51
key areas of change in Catholic higher education 90–100
Kezar, Adrianna 3, 159, 182–183, 186, 221
Kirkley, E. A. 4, 7, 51, 52, 53, 108, 137, 138, 160, 161, 162, 184, 187
Kosnik, A. 2, 35, 36, 84, 86
Kramer, Fred 176

lack of resources 55, 71, **73**, 79
language issues, as a barrier to change 117, **118**, 126–127; *see also* language sensitivity
language sensitivity 95, 142, **151**, *185*; as a method to effect change 156–157, 161–162, 184, 186, 187
late adolescent development 19, 20, 55
Laudato Si' 87, 163
Lawler, Michael 13, 35, 42, 50, 82, 83, 85, 168, 195
legality as a theme around change in Catholic higher education 71, **73**, 78, 93
letters: as a form of public conversation 153; used to harass institutions over change 124
Levinson, Daniel 19, 21, 22, 167

Levinson, Judy 19, 21, 22, 167
LGBTQ+: acceptance 54, 108, 163, 201; Catholic higher education conference and 81, 120, **141**, **150**, 153; culture at institutions 54, 91, 111, 160, 202; educational initiatives **151**, 153; events 123, 136, 154, 157; experience of harassment/discrimination 33, 78–79, 106, 111, **118**, 121, 168, 196; facing cultural barriers 28, 55, 122; marginalization 172; ministry 6, 47, 112, 133, 192–194, 203; programing and 53, 81, 98, 105, 108, 153; resources and 45, **74**, 79, 92–93, 155, **171**; sexual health information and 34; support of 108–109, 113, 120, 136, 138, 139, **151**, 157, 198; student groups 4, 17, 53–54, 55, 91, 95, **103**, 104, 110, **119**, 125, 132, 138, 142, 149, 157, 183; topics in the curriculum 94, 202; visibility on campus 75, 91, 152, 160, 202
listening: in relation to gender 177; to Catholic sexual theology 85; to those marginalized 189
living arrangements: coed 32, 44; gender-neutral *see* gender-neutral, living arrangements; of students 3, 30, 32–33, 39, 44, 55
Love, P. 4, 7, 13, 19, 26, 28, 51, 54, 55, 108, 109, 110, 138, 139, 140, 142, 160, 177

Maher, M. J. 13, 37, 49, 52, 53, 138, 139, 140
Marquette University 43, 46, 47
Martin, James 108–109, 112, 193
Masses 133, 202, 203, 207
Massingale, Bryan 176, 194, 195
McCabe, Megan 176
McCarty, Rich 4, 13, 27, 41, 42, 46, 47, 50, 51, 53, 55, 168, 175, 226
McEntarfer, H. K. 4, 7, 51, 53, 54, 108, 137, 138, 139, 140, 142, 148, 149, 157, 158, 160, 161, 162, 187
McLeroy, K. R. 182
mega sources 90
methods of communication **150–151**, 152–162, *185*; active educational **150**, 153, 159, 160,

161, 182; assertive 53, 148, 158; collaborative 53, 148, 158; conciliatory 53, 148, 149, 158; data gathering *see* gathering data in effecting change; direct confrontational 148; discreet methods **151**, 157–158, 161–162; forums 153, 154, 160, 187; extra institutional 148 *see also* methods of communication, institutional; increased visibility *see* increasing visibility of LGBTQ persons; institutional 148 *see also* methods of communication, extra institutional; one-to-one education **150**, 153, 155, *185*, 187; outside resources **150**, 154–155, 160, 187; preemptive 149, **150**, 159, 160, 182, 184; protests 6, 45, 96, **151**, 156, 161, 187; public conversation **150**, 153–154, 160, 187; pushing the envelope/persistence 71, **73**, 79–80; student protest 96–97, **151**, 153, 156, 161, 187; student-focus **150**, 152–153, 160, *185*; trainings **150**, 154–155, 160–161, *185*, 186–187; underground/subversive 53, 148, 157, 158, 162
mindsets for change 149, 152, 160, 182, 184–186, 192
minority sexual identities 30, 33, 45, 55; *see also* sexual minorities
mission and ministry, office of **119**, 130, 131, 186, 203, 207; in participant interviews 122, 131
mission of the institution 3, 101, 131, 146, **151**, 188; as an organizational characteristic *see* mission/history/heritage; engaging for change 6, 100, 135, 138, **151**, 157, 184–187, 207, 208 *see also* engaging the institutional tradition; in Hughes 160; perceived incongruence, as a reason for resistance 101, 102, **103**, 104–105, 111, 121; perceived incongruence, fear of **141**; perceived incongruence, reflection on 173
mission/history/heritage 121, 135, 139, *185*
morality clauses 3, 31, 34–35, 46–47, 53, 55

Morey, M. M., & Piderit, J. J. 1, 3, 4, 13, 28, 30, 37, 41, 45, 51, 52, 107, 110, 139, 140, 160

natural family planning 38, 50
NCCB Committee on Marriage and Family 2, 41
nebulous culture 110
negative public or media attention 71, **73**, 77–78, **118**, 124, **141**
Nelson, James 85, 87
New Ways Ministry 47, 193
non-discrimination: clauses 91, 96, **151**, 153; federal government and 43; policy on sexual orientation and gender identity 3, 5, 45, 156
nuns **119**, 132, 133, 186, **219**, 221; *see also* sisters

Office for Civil Rights 30, 31, 32, 43, 93
ongoing dialogue *see* continue dialogue/study
organizational barriers 117, **118**, 125, 126–127
organizational change: literature 159, 184; models/components of 160, 182, 186–187, 190; theories 159, 161
organizational characteristics, as supports in change efforts **119**, 128, 135, 139
organizational miscommunication, as a barrier to change **118**, 127
Ott, K. M. 3, 30, 31, 43, 85
out faculty/staff 71, **72**, 75–76, 81; *see also* increasing visibility of LGBTQ persons
Outreach 193, 194
outside speakers 161, *185*; *see also* active education as a change strategy; methods of communication, active educational

Pacem in Terris 182; *see also* John XXIII
Pagán, Melissa 195
paradox, as a theme in the change process 54, 55, 109, 138, 142
parents: as educators 41; in the change process 52, 104, 117, **118**, 140, 155 *see also* conservative constituents; fear of 52, 54, 55, 139; in relation to student development 1, 29, 78, 86

Paul VI 2, 38, 112, 144, 163, 169, 176, 177, 215; *see also Dignitatis Humanae*; *Humanae Vitae*; *Gaudium et Spes*; *Gravissimum Educationis*; *Populorum Progressio*
perceived limitation 45, 142
Perry, W. G. 1, 22, 24–25
Persona Humana 2, 39, 176; *see also* Sacred Congregation for the Doctrine of the Faith
petition 53, **150**, 153; *see also* methods of communication, active educational; methods of communication, assertive
Piaget, Jean 19, 20
pleasure: from imagination 16; sensual 22; sexual 36, 84, 85, 196
politeness, as a theme in the change process 71, **72**, 76–77
political environment *see* geographic environment, geo-political environment
Pontifical Council for the Family 2, 41
poor organization, as a barrier in the change process 117, **118**, 126, 127, 137, 142
Pope Benedict XVI *see* Benedict XVI
Pope Francis *see* Francis I
Pope John Paul II *see* John Paul II
Pope Paul VI *see* Paul VI
Populorum Progressio 176, 177
prayer service: as an active educational strategy 153; as an institutional change **74**, **150**, 202, 203, 207
preemptive mindsets *see* methods of communication, preemptive
president: as a barrier in the change process **103**, **118**; as a support in the change process **72**, 101, 132, 133, 156, 203, 207–208; fear and 102, **103**, 123; on relation to the local bishop 74–75, **103**, 107, 111, **119**
preventing unjust harm 84, 177, 178; *see also* Farley, Margaret
priests: clerical faculties 42, 83; in the change process, as barriers 54; in the change process, as supports **119**, 132–134, 186, 203; related to sexual abuse 37

principal changemakers **119**, 128–130, 137–138
protests: as an assertive technique 53; as ineffective 164–165; as resistance to change 123, 124, 139, 183–184, 207–208; *see also* methods of communication, protests
providing resources 160, 188; *see also* methods of communication, active educational
provosts 132–133
proximity: of the bishop to the change process 71, **72**, 75; to student experience 138; *see also* closeness to student experience
public conversation *see* methods of communication, public conversation
public endorsement of inclusivity *see* inclusivity, administrator endorsement of
public forum *see* methods of communication, forums
purpose of the study 7, 214
pushing the envelope/persistence *see* methods of communication, pushing the envelope/persistence

Rainbow Educators 53, 184
rape culture 176
rape prevention education 34; *see also* sexual assault, prevention training
reactions to change 101–107, 109–111, 140, 149, 182–183, *185*
Reisser, L. *see* Chickering, A. W., Reisser, L.
relational-centered morality 83, 86, 195; *see also* act-centered morality
relationship *see* right relationship
religious identity: of college students 26; sexual identity and 71, **74**, 81, 177
Religious Exemption Accountability Project (REAP) 193
representation/visibility as a theme 71, **72**, 75, 94; *see also* increasing visibility of LGBTQ persons
research questions 90, 214

residence life: as close to the student experience *see* closeness to student experience; as supportive of change 101, 105, **119**, 120, 130, 138; staff as principal change makers 125, 129–130, 153, 154, 156, 219
resistance: as a response to change 101, 110–111, 117, **118**, 121–123, 124–125, 134, 140, 144; language sensitivity and 157; managing 161, 184, *185*, 187; reasons for 102–107; to using affirming pronouns 193
respect/trust, as a theme in the change process 71, 76
responses to change *see* reactions to change
restricted words *see* language issues
restrooms: as a place for condoms 198; *see also* gender-neutral, restrooms
revisionist sexual anthropology 82–83, 85, 88, 195; *see also* Catholic sexual theology
right relationship 6; at an institutional level 112–113, 200; fear as undermining 143; theological insights of 144–146, 162, 164
Robinson, B. 2, 15, 17
Ross, Karen 144, 176, 199
Ross, Susan 195
Ruether, Rosemary Radford 2, 43, 113, 200

Sacred Congregation for the Doctrine of the Faith 2, 39, 176; *see also* Congregation for the Doctrine of the Faith
Sachs, John R 85
safe atmosphere 199, 202, 210
Salzman, Todd 13, 35, 42, 50, 82, 83, 85, 168, 195
same-sex partner benefits **73**, 93–94, 102, 104, 126, 148, 157, 189; *see also* domestic partner benefits
sampling, snowball 216–218
scandal: assumptions about 111; Cardinal Newman Society and 46; Catechism definition 105; perceived 101, 102, **103**, 105; sexual abuse *see* sex abuse scandal; sexual assault as 45; universities and *see* negative public or media attention
Schlossberg, N. K. 22, 25
Second Vatican Council 83, 163, 188, 195; *see also* Vatican II
semi-structured interviews 220, 221
sensuality, circle of 15–16, 17, *18*, 20, 21, 24, 25, 26
sex abuse scandal 37
sexiled 33
sexual activity: higher education and 30, 31, 33, 55; *Humanae Vitae* and 38; marriage and 40; sexual health and 97, 205; part of sexuality 3
sexual anthropology: revisionist 82–83, 85, 88, 195; traditionalist 82–83, 85; *see also* Catholic sexual theology
sexual assault 30, 32, 33–34, 176; as addressed on campus 3, 55, **73**, 148, **150**; as addressed in Catholic higher education 45–46; by priests 37; calls for change around 48–50; change around 162, 163; in the circles of sexuality *18 see also* sexualization, circle of; presence on campus 4, 17, 35; prevention training 3, 100, 138, 152, 173, 192; reporting and policies 91, 93, 101, 113, 169, 203; mishandling cases 78, 154, 168; process 199, 204; response 187; survivors 49, 189; shaming of 78, 99; victimization and 78, 99, 189, 203–205
sexual behavior 107, 172, 193; avoiding conversation of 170; circles of sexuality and 16, *18*, 20, 22, 28, 39; ethical development and 25; on campus 98; shaming of 205; study of 94, 206; *see also* sexual activity
sexual decision-making 19, 206; in the change process 162; in the curriculum 94; student sexual health and 97, 98, 169
sexual harassment 3, 32, 93; in the circles of sexuality 16–17, *18 see also* sexualization, circle of; trainings on 4, 31–32, 199; *see also* Title IX
sexual health: as a topic for change 90, 91, 148; behavior

Index 237

and 15; education about 100, 198; *Humanae Vitae* and 39; in the curriculum 52, 113, **119**; information/resources access 3–4, 31, 34–35, 46, 50, **73**, 79, 172–173, 178, 189, 209; negative public media attention and 77, 105; sexual shame and 78, 163; students and 97–98, 106, **150**, 153
sexual health and reproduction, circle of 15–17, *18*, 21, 22, 25, 39
sexual identity: as part of sexuality 15, 28; circle of 16, 17, *18*, 20–22, 24–26; discrimination and 96, 111, 156, 202, 209, 225 *see also* discrimination; in Catholic higher education 105; minority *see* minority sexual identities; organizational safety and 169 *see also* safe atmosphere; pride in 176; religious identity and *see* religious identity, sexual identity and; student groups and 93 *see also* student groups; training on 201, 209 *see also* methods of communication, trainings; visibility and 152 *see also* increasing visibility of LGBTQ persons
sexual minorities: discrimination and *see* discrimination, toward sexual minorities; faith and 27–29, 81; visibility and 75–76 *see also* increasing visibility of LGBTQ persons; *see also* sexual minority
sexual minority: as a term 28; discrimination and *see* discrimination, toward sexual minorities; experience of 52; identity *see* minority sexual identities; students 27, 28, 138
sexual norms 84; *see also* Farley, Margaret
sexual orientation: as a component of one's sexuality 2, 14–15, 158, 190; Catholic higher education and 45, 148, 193, 194, 198; circles of sexuality and 16, *18*; college student development and 17, 24, 27, 31, 33; discrimination and 111 *see also* discrimination, toward sexual minorities; fear and **141**; honoring of **118**; in the curriculum 52, 169, 198;

institutional culture and 54, 92, 99, 120, 209; ministry and 6, 192; non-discrimination and *see* non-discrimination; trainings and 92 *see also* methods of communication, trainings; visibility and 75 *see also* increasing visibility of LGBTQ persons
sexual pleasure *see* pleasure, sexual
sexual shame: as a theme 71, **73**, 78; Augustine and 36; Catholic culture and 49, 168, 175, 199, 205, 209; sexual assault and 99, 205; silence and 177; student development and 169; theological insights of 82, 84, 86–87
sexual trauma 50, 169, 190, 193, 198
sexual violence 84, 176, 198, 199; prevention and 31, 49, 204 *see also* sexual assault, prevention training; victimization and 163, 198, 204
sexual/religious identity 71, **74**, 81; *see also* religious identity, sexual identity and
sexuality: as a theological good 82–88; definition of 2, 14–19; Catholicism and 35–41; circles of 14–19, *18*; fear of *see* Catholic erotophobia; four-dimensional model 2 *see also* Greenberg, J. S.; in Catholic higher education 4–5, 41–51, 169–179, 181–188, 192–211; in higher education 2–4, 30–35; student development and 19–26, 167–169; ten-pointed star 2, 15 *see also* Robinson, B.
sexuality education 198, 199, 205, 208; barriers to 52; developmental appropriacy and 167–168; in Catholic institutions 144, 164, **171**, 207, 225
Sexuality Information and Education Council of the United States 47
sexuality resource center 92, 93, 106, **118–119**, 126, 192, 201, 208, 209
sexualization 193; circle of 15–17, *18*, 20, 21, 26
sexually healthy church 199
sexually safe atmosphere *see* safe atmosphere; sexually safe campus 204
shadow culture 110, 140; *see also* un-espoused culture

238 Index

SIECUS *see* Sexuality Information and Education Council of the United States
silence: around sexuality 111, 144, 145, 175, 182; culture of 175–177, 196, 206, 207; silence/avoidance as a reaction to change 76, 101, **103**, 106, 110, 127; silence-inducing culture of fear 47, 168, 175
sin: cultural/culture of 176–177; doctrine of original 35; in the *penitentials* 83; institutional 113; of discrimination 111, 113; social 114, 164, 165, 177; structural 162, 165, 176, 177, 196
sisters 134, 135, **219**; *see also* nuns
social sin *see* sin, social
social/political environment 159, 160, 186; *see also* geo-political environment
solidarity: as a principle of CST 6, 7, 196; as a theological theme in change **74**, 200, 208; theological insights of 143, 144–146, 162–165; vocation and 188
Sollicitudo Rei Socialis 163, 177, 211; *see also* John Paul II
speaker: as an active educational strategy *see* methods of communication, active educational; as an outside resource *see* methods of communication, outside resource; as controversial on campus 123; as helpful for change **171**, *185*, 202, 208; dis-invitation of 77, **103**, 107, 110
spiritual: development 19, 26, 48; health **150**; identity 13, 177 *see also* religious identity; life of the institution 202; needs of the campus community 203
spirituality 15, 17, 26; sexuality and 27, 85
St Mary's college 46
Stayton, W. R. 85
Stephens, Darryl W. 3, 30, 31, 43, 195
structural sin *see* sin, structural
student affairs 48, 130, 131, 138, 186, 219; office of **73**, 131; vice president of 122, 127, 133, 156

student development 48, 167–168; faith and 27; late adolescent and young adult 19–29; personnel 130; theories 22, 24
student groups: conservative constituents and 105, 117, **118**, 121, 122–123, 140, 157; GSAs 17, 51, 53, 54; LGBTQ+ 17, 53–54, 91, 95, **103**, 104, 110, 142; *see also* sexual identity, student groups
student life 75, 91, 93, 125, 131, 144; office of **119**, 130, 138, **219**; *see also* student affairs; staff 101; vice president of 133
student protests *see* methods of communication, student protest
student-focus 149, **150**, 152–153, 160, *185*
students: as changemakers **119**, 128, 137–138; as unequipped to address sexuality 169; living arrangements *see* living arrangements, of students
study methods 214–226
subversive *see* methods of communication, underground/subversive
support: for sexuality education 144, 167–168; in change efforts **72**, 75, 105, **119**, 120, 127–139, 184, *185*, 186–187, 190, 195, 199, 201–202, 205, 208
survivors of sexual assault *see* sexual assault, survivors

task forces 134, 136, **151**, 153, 155–156, 161, 187
Terry, K. J. 37
tenured faculty as change makers *see* principal changemakers
thematic analysis *see* data analysis
theological anthropology 38, 40, 82, 211; *see also* Catholic sexual theology
theology and religious studies departments: as resistant to change 94; as supportive in change efforts 109, **119**, 130–132, 138 *see also* support, in change efforts; sexuality in the curriculum 3, 31, 48

Theology of the Body (TOB) 39–40; *see also* John Paul II
Thomas Aquinas *see* Aquinas, Thomas
Title IX 173, 204–205, **219**; exemptions 3, 45, 183, 193; in Catholic higher education 43; in higher education 30–32; investigations 204; gendered bathrooms and *see* gendered, bathrooms; sexual assault and 46, 91, 93
Torrell, J. P. 2
Tracy, D. 83
traditionalist sexual anthropology *see* sexual anthropology, traditionalist
transgender: bathrooms 95, 102, 126 *see also* gender-neutral, bathrooms; healthcare 156; housing 158, 163 *see also* gender-neutral, housing; identity 17, 44, **72**, 95, 96, 108, 203; living accommodations 14 *see also* gender-neutral, living arrangements; ministry and 193; students 14, 32, 33, 91, 95, 102, **103**, 106, 108, 110, 163
Transgender Day of Remembrance **150**, 202, 203
Transgender Day of Visibility **74**
Trujillo, Yunuen 193, 194

Ullerstam, Lars 28
United States Catholic Conference 2, 86; *see also* NCCB Committee on Marriage and Family

United States Conference of Catholic Bishops 40–41; *see also* Terry, K. J.
US bishops 42, 194
US Catholic bishops 86, 163; *see also* United States Conference of Catholic Bishops
un-espoused culture 110, 201, 206, 207; *see also* shadow culture
under the radar *see* flying under the radar
underground/subversive *see* methods of communication, underground/subversive
University of Notre Dame 46
University of San Francisco 4, 44, 49, 50
unspoken: culture 140; messages 189; rules 206; *see also* un-espoused culture

Vacek, Ed 195
Vasko, Elizabeth 195
Vatican II 83, 169, 176; *see also* Second Vatican Council
vectors of development 22–24; *see also* Chickering, A. W.
vocation 51, 195, 196; theological insights of 188–190; *see also* Hahnenberg, Edward
voices of change 167–174

WHO 48
whole person: development 14, 26, 30, 48, 144, 169, 175; education of 2, 41

Taylor & Francis eBooks

www.taylorfrancis.com

A single destination for eBooks from Taylor & Francis with increased functionality and an improved user experience to meet the needs of our customers.

90,000+ eBooks of award-winning academic content in Humanities, Social Science, Science, Technology, Engineering, and Medical written by a global network of editors and authors.

TAYLOR & FRANCIS EBOOKS OFFERS:

- A streamlined experience for our library customers
- A single point of discovery for all of our eBook content
- Improved search and discovery of content at both book and chapter level

REQUEST A FREE TRIAL
support@taylorfrancis.com